PROSPECTS FOR GROWTH

TURNING POINT Christian Worldview Series
Marvin Olasky, General Editor

PROSPECTS FOR GROWTH

*A Biblical View of Population,
Resources, and the Future*

E. Calvin Beisner

CROSSWAY BOOKS • WESTCHESTER, ILLINOIS
A DIVISION OF GOOD NEWS PUBLISHERS

Prospects for Growth.

Copyright © 1990 by E. Calvin Beisner.

Published by Crossway Books, a division of
Good News Publishers, Westchester, Illinois 60154.

Published in association with the
Fieldstead Institute
P.O. Box 19061,
Irvine, California 92713

First printing, 1990

Printed in the United States of America

Library of Congress Catalog Card Number 89-81260

ISBN 0-89107-554-2

Unless otherwise noted, all Bible quotations are from *New American Standard Bible*, copyright © 1977 by the Lockman Foundation.

To Kilby

And what does the LORD require of you
But to do justice, to love kindness,
And to walk humbly with your God?

Micah 6:8

TABLE OF

CONTENTS

LIST OF TABLES

LIST OF TABLES IN APPENDIX 2

ACKNOWLEDGMENTS

*T*his book was a long time in the making. I could not have committed the necessary time to research and writing without the generous support of the Fieldstead Institute, for which I am grateful. I am thankful, too, to Howard Ahmanson, president of the Fieldstead Institute, for stimulating my thoughts in this direction, and to Larry Arrn and Steven Hayward of The Claremont Institute for introducing me to some of the philosophical and practical intricacies of the growth-limitation movement. They gave generously of their time and printed materials during a very pleasant visit with them near the beginning of this project. My editor, Marvin Olasky, has provided invaluable suggestions for every chapter. Not only I, but readers also, owe him great thanks for his part in making this book easy to digest. I have drawn heavily on the thought of a wide variety of writers. Particular thanks need to go to Julian Simon, author of *The Economics of Population Growth*, for his ground-breaking work in this field. Lots of mysteries were resolved for me as I worked my way carefully through that book. Of course, I alone am responsible for the positions endorsed here, including whatever errors there might be.

As always, my wife Deborah provided a sounding board for initial ideas and read chapters in draft, suggesting improvements throughout. She and my children, David, Susan, Kilby, and one on the way, encourage and inspire me to do my best.

This poor world. It's overpopulated. Exploited. Polluted. Unorganized. Nothing short of radical and stringent new measures will prevent catastrophes. Left to themselves, people do silly things. They breed mindlessly, multiplying geometrically to their own destruction. They rape the earth, stripping it of its resources, leaving nothing for future generations. They poison air, water, and land, heedless of their own safety. They crowd together in nasty, smelly, dangerous cities. They brazenly gobble up all the wide open spaces that offer respite from the rat race.

This, anyway, is the assessment of unfettered human activity one hears constantly in the popular media and from bureaucratic agencies charged (often by themselves) with the task of bringing some method to the madness of people's choices about questions like these: How many children should we have? What resources, and how much of them, should we use for all our purposes? What, in fact, are our purposes? Where should we live? How should we go from place to place? To hear the enlightened tell it, ordinary people just can't make rational decisions about these issues. Somebody's got to plan things. Who better than the guys at the top? After all, they have a bird's-eye view. They can see farther into the future than the rest of us, more broadly around the world. They have pierced the dark mysteries of the interdependencies of nature and human civilization. Nothing could be wiser than for all of us to give them free rein to steer us wherever they think best.

But is it really so? Do the media, bureaucrats, and agency officials who want to control our lives really understand the dynamic interrelationships of population, economics, resources, environment, and civil government? Do they really know the future? Do they even know the present? Are their central plans any better than the diverse and localized plans of the world's billions of individuals, families, communities, and corporations?

Is the world really overpopulated? Or fast approaching it? Are the teeming millions in cities and suburbs approaching critical mass, ready to explode in bursts of violence and disease? Are living conditions deteriorating or improving? Do sprawling megalopolises threaten to gobble up all our best agricultural land? Are we really running out of resources? Is the environment getting cleaner and safer, or dirtier and riskier? (And what, after all, is the environment?)

This book looks at these and related questions. But it doesn't look at them just from the standpoint of empirical observation, although it includes plenty of that. Instead, it applies Biblical principles of theology, anthropology, and ethics to them. What does the Bible say about human population? About resources and the environment? About human freedom and civil government? What rights, privileges, and responsibilities do people have in decisions about procreation, resource management, pollution, stewardship of the environment, and the constitution and powers of the state? Where do the doctrines of creation, providence, and divine omniscience fit into all these concerns? What is man's proper relationship to the earth? Is he servant, master, or steward? What are the proper principles of human relationships in reproduction, economics, resource use, and the environment?

Chapter 1 paints a picture of the problems and opportunities we face. Chapters 2 and 3 develop Biblical principles of theology, anthropology, ethics, civil government, and economics that supply the foundation for all the rest of our discussion. Chapter 4 develops Biblical notions of population and reproduction and evaluates warnings of overpopulation and crowding. Chapter 5 looks at the effects of population growth on housing, transportation and communication, and recreational space, and Chapter 6 at interrelationships of population growth and the economy. Chapter 7 explains relationships among population growth, economic growth, and resource use, while Chapter 8 examines the effects of these on the quality of the environment. Chapter 9 outlines basic principles of resource management, and Chapter 10 sets forth principles of planning for population and economic growth.

Will the world of tomorrow be richer, safer, and healthier than the world today, or poorer, riskier, and sicker? Will people live in more- or less-crowded conditions? Will they enjoy more and cheaper resources, or scrounge for fewer and more expensive ones? Will the environment be cleaner or dirtier? How much will population grow, and how fast? Will there be enough food, water, energy, and space for everyone? Will people be free to direct their own lives, or will they be ordered about by powerful committees, commissions, and agencies with little accountability to the public they ostensibly serve? Will civil government be servant or master?

No one can make infallible predictions about the future (aside from divine revelation). But we can try to understand the cultural, economic, and technological forces that shape it. By understanding them, we can help make the choices that will lead to a better world for our children and grandchildren.

Edmund Burke, a great Christian statesman who always took the long view of things, taught that the civil social order is "a partnership not only between those who are living, but between those who are living, those who are dead, and those who are to be born." He saw that each generation owes much to its ancestors and much to its posterity. Without this "great primeval contract of eternal society, linking the lower with the higher natures, connecting the visible and invisible world, according to a fixed compact sanctioned by the inviolable oath which holds all physical and all moral natures, each in their appointed place," the "whole chain and continuity of the commonwealth would be broken; no one generation could link with the other; men would become little better than the flies of a summer."[1]

Burke's understanding of human society was rooted in Christian doctrine. Scripture, too, urges us to look to the interests of posterity. "A good man leaves an inheritance to his children's children," wrote Solomon thousands of years ago (Proverbs 13:22). What kind of inheritance will the generations now living leave to the generations yet to be born?

ONE

CHALLENGES AND OPPORTUNITIES OF GROWTH

Nobu Hara, a friend of mine, moved his family several years ago to Covina, California, to escape the skyrocketing housing prices of Long Beach and be within a reasonable commute from his office in Culver City. Until recently, he tried to be on the freeway by 5 A.M. each day to beat rush-hour traffic. That put him at his office, thirty-five miles away, by about 5:45. (Nobu is lucky; lots of Los Angeles-area commuters travel from fifty to 100 miles each way to work.) He used the company's exercise facilities, showered, and was ready for work by 7 A.M. Braving the evening rush hour, he left at 5 P.M., arriving home at about 6:15 or 6:30. By the time dinner, baths for his four children, and family devotions were finished, he and Jane Marie had little time to themselves before they got to sleep around 11:30 or midnight.

The long hours took their toll. Lately Nobu doesn't leave for work until 6:30. The once forty-five-minute drive now takes an hour and a half, putting him in his office at 8 A.M. He still leaves at 5, though, meaning he spends an hour less each day working than he used to. But he's gone from home about twelve hours a day (which is better than things were before), and time with the family in the evenings isn't any more than it used to be. He spends forty-five minutes longer on the freeway now than he used to, doesn't get the exercise he used to, but does get more sleep. Still, his life style isn't very satisfying.

Why doesn't he just move closer to his office? Covina, after all, is on the east side of Los Angeles, and Culver City, where Nobu works as human resources manager for VSI, the aerospace fasteners division of Fairchild Industries, is on the west side. Why does he put up with the commute from one suburb to another, right through downtown?

Because even on his salary, over $50,000 per year, he can't begin to afford a home anywhere near Culver City. He bought his two-bedroom home in Covina, an old community with low housing prices relative to surrounding towns, in 1986 for $115,000; by early 1989 it was valued at $180,000. But a similar house in Culver City would cost him $300,000 to $350,000. "My income can't support that, even with the equity I have in my own home," Nobu says. "In fact, I couldn't even buy my own home now."

The Haras' story could be repeated, with slight variations, millions of times for families in the Los Angeles metropolitan area, with its nearly 13 million people. And it could be repeated millions of times more for the millions of Americans who live in metropolitan areas. Metropolitan living has its pluses and minuses. Success can breed its own failure as high incomes and good living conditions attract crowds that raise real estate prices and lower living conditions.

Nobu Hara's struggle to balance his own needs for sleep, family time, and exercise costs his company an hour of work a day. That doesn't sound like much till you multiply it by the millions of other workers whom burgeoning traffic has forced to cut back their work time. As of January 1988, for instance, it was estimated that Los Angeles workers wasted a cumulative 100,000 hours per day in traffic jams on the area's 740 miles of freeways, some 300 miles of which are jammed with cars moving under fifteen miles per hour each morning.[1] That's the equivalent of 12,500 full-time workers' labor burned up on the freeways. At median income of $30,000 per year, that's a loss of $375,000,000 of annual personal income or $44,250,000 per year in state and local taxes.[2]

The lost production, income, and taxes on the one hand, and the heightened personal tension and family stress on the other caused by traffic congestion in Southern California's metropolitan areas are only the tip of the iceberg. They are but symptoms of the problems that accompany rapid regional growth, growth that sometimes—as it does there—outpaces the development of transportation, communication, waste disposal, and other government-provided services.

Other symptoms include skyrocketing housing prices (nice if you already own a home, dreadful if you don't); crowded living, working, and recreational conditions; polluted air, water, and land; and, in low-income neighborhoods that suffer from family breakdown, crime rates that impose a burden of fear on all but the hardiest souls.

THE FLIP SIDE

But problems aren't all that comes with rapid economic and population growth. There are opportunities too. In the eyes of millions of people who live in fast-growing regions of the United States, the opportunities outweigh the problems.

People who live in major metropolitan areas enjoy ready access to a wider variety of stores, health and medical services, transportation services, and cultural and recreational opportunities than can be found in small towns and rural areas. Economies of scale involved in wholesaling and retailing to millions of people instead of thousands make many consumer prices lower in high-density areas than they are in low-density areas (although housing is almost always more expensive). Often they can choose among several good junior colleges, four-year colleges, and universities within commuting distances of their homes, while rural residents may have to go hundreds of miles to find the equivalent. And while city dwellers' roads might be crowded, they are rarely unpaved, as are many in rural areas.

Furthermore, cities offer more opportunities for employment, and almost always at higher wages, than do small towns and rural areas. The concentration of people creates a demand for goods and services that can be met only by workers, whether executives, managers, secretaries, or common laborers. The variety of jobs in cities far exceeds that outside them as well.

ATTITUDES TOWARD GROWTH

In short, there are advantages and disadvantages to living anywhere, whether in cities and suburbs or in small towns and rural areas. What they all have in common, despite their differences, is that they are all tied together in a worldwide interactive web of cause-and-effect relationships. Central to that web are population growth and economic growth occurring around the globe. While some communities and regions here and there are shrinking in population and economic activity, the global trend is upward. Growth affects everyone

one way or another, and attitudes toward it range from euphoria to resentment.

Our goal is to try to understand some of the basic problems and opportunities connected with economic and population growth and to apply Biblical ethics to them to help us shape our attitudes toward growth and our views of appropriate public policy. Should we champion all growth, oppose all growth, or take some moderating view? What policies related to population growth, resource use and conservation, the environment, and economic growth meet the tests of morality and practicality? What ought Christians to think of growing pressure for civil government to control growth through planning?

Millions of people believe that only strict limits to population growth—or even population reduction—and strict limits to resource use will protect future generations from catastrophes like overcrowding, famine, exhaustion of energy sources, energy-production-related disasters, and deadly pollution of air, land, and water. The effects of this belief include the rapid adoption of municipal, county, regional, and statewide policies to limit and plan growth; voluntary and mandatory birth control policies that strain the ability of new generations to care for aging forebears; frequently counterproductive environmental policies; calls for a "simple life style" as the only conscientious choice; and a generally pessimistic attitude toward the future that may be a self-fulfilling prophecy.

Believers in the omnipotent and providential Creator have reason for hope in the face of such problems. While we do not deny their reality, we question the accuracy of many assessments of them and the wisdom of many prescriptions for their solution. Biblical ethics and sound thinking persuade us that attitudes different from those that prevail in much of the secular world are not only more hopeful but also more realistic. Opportunities abound for faithful people to apply God's moral and physical principles to solve the problems we face.

We can't pretend in a single book to provide comprehensive understandings of and strategies for dealing with the many problems and opportunities that come with economic and population growth. What we can do is to search for sound Biblical principles and prudent applications of them that will give us a basis for continued thought and discussion. This book doesn't offer quick fixes; it does offer a consistent, Biblical basis from which Christians can develop wise policy positions.

GOD, MAN, AND MORALS

" *T*he economic problem," wrote political philosopher Russell Kirk some thirty-five years ago, "blends into the political problem, and the political problem into the ethical problem, and the ethical problem into the religious problem. There exists a hierarchy of difficulties, as well as a hierarchy of values."[1]

This comprehension, once common, is rare in the age of the technobureaucrat. Rarely are economic and political problems seen as rooted in ethical problems. Instead they are seen merely as technical difficulties to be surmounted—surmounted by the scientific know-how of governmental agents equipped with the full coercive and parasitic powers of the state, agents who use whatever means seem most direct and efficient. Rarely, too, are ethical problems seen as rooted in religious problems, in theology. More often, they are seen as mere disagreements among ethically equal human beings over ethically equal options favored or rejected solely because they promote or fail to promote various persons' amoral happiness.

But that old notion that underlies classical Western political philosophy remains true. Theology, in all its departments, supplies the guiding principles by which to answer all the pragmatic problems of political economy. It tells us where true authority is to be found, and likewise what expressions of authority are usurpations. It tells us the nature of man, and hence of the chief subject and object of our political and economic deliberations and actions. It tells us right from wrong, not only in ends but also in means. And in so doing it tells us the proper reaches and bounds not only of coercion but also, by implication, of human liberty—i.e., of choice. And choice is what economics and economic growth are all about.[2]

In this chapter we will survey three groups of principles—theological, anthropological, and ethical—that underlie any proper consideration of population growth, economic growth, resource use, the environment, and planning.[3] In the next we will consider governmental and economic principles.

1. THEOLOGICAL FOUNDATIONS

Fundamental to our conception of God the Creator is that He is omnipotent and omniscient: "Great is our Lord, and abundant in strength; His understanding is infinite" (Psalm 147:5); "Ah, Lord God! Behold, Thou hast made the heavens and the earth by Thy great power and by Thine outstretched arm! Nothing is too difficult for Thee . . ." (Jeremiah 32:17); "Who has directed the Spirit of the LORD, or as His counselor has informed Him? With whom did He consult and who gave Him understanding? And who taught Him the path of justice and taught Him knowledge, and informed Him of the way of understanding?" (Isaiah 40:13, 14); "Woe to those who deeply hide their plans from the LORD, and whose deeds are done in a dark place, and they say, 'Who sees us?' or 'Who knows us?' . . . Shall . . . what is formed say to him who formed it, 'He has no understanding'?" (Isaiah 29:15, 16).

From God's omnipotence and omniscience we may infer several principles important to our understanding of man's economic activity and use of resources:

(a) Nothing we ever do will frustrate God's purposes. He is not a god who stands helplessly by waiting to see what his creatures will do, hoping that they will acquiesce in his wishes. Quite the contrary; "He does according to His will in the host of heaven and among the inhabitants of earth; and no one can ward off His hand or say to Him, 'What hast Thou done?'" (Daniel 4:35). He "works all things after the counsel of His will" (Ephesians 1:11).[4] Hence some seemingly profound ideas, like one theologically liberal denomination's protest that nuclear arms threaten all of creation, turn out to be mere imbecility.[5]

(b) While we can recognize the reality of injustice and oppression, we can never say that God is not in control even of the present order of things: "I have made the earth, the men and the beasts which are on the face of the earth by My great power and by My outstretched arm, and I will give it to the one who is pleasing in My sight" (Jeremiah 27:5).

(c) Nothing man ever does will surprise God or find Him unprepared to handle the resulting situation: "I am God, and there is no one like Me, declaring the end from the beginning and from ancient times things which have not been done, saying, 'My purpose will be established, and I will accomplish all My good pleasure'" (Isaiah 46:9, 10).

(d) While we may hide injustice from our fellowmen, we will never hide it from God.

Closely related to God's omnipotence and omniscience is His sovereignty: "Behold, to the LORD your God belong heaven and the highest heavens, the earth and all that is in it. . . . For the LORD your God is the God of gods and the Lord of lords, the great, the mighty, and the awesome God who does not show partiality, nor take a bribe" (Deuteronomy 10:14, 17); "the kingdom is the LORD's, and He rules over the nations" (Psalm 22:28); "The earth is the LORD's, and all it contains, the world, and those who dwell in it. . . . Who is the King of glory? The LORD strong and mighty, the LORD mighty in battle" (Psalm 24:1, 8). God is "the blessed and only Sovereign, the King of kings and Lord of lords. . . . To Him be honor and eternal dominion! Amen" (1 Timothy 6:15, 16).

Because God is the sovereign Lord of all the earth, part of the Christian task is to declare His Lordship and call rebellious sinners to submit to Him in humble obedience in every aspect of their lives. "All authority," said Jesus, "has been given to Me in heaven and on earth. Go therefore and make disciples of all the nations, baptizing them in the name of the Father and the Son and the Holy Spirit, teaching them to observe all that I commanded you . . ." (Matthew 28:18-20). We are soldiers of the King. But His is a spiritual, not a fleshly, Kingdom, and so "the weapons of our warfare are not of the flesh, but divinely powerful for the destruction of fortresses. We are destroying speculations and every lofty thing raised up against the knowledge of God, and we are taking every thought captive to the obedience of Christ . . ." (2 Corinthians 10:4, 5).

Also closely related to God's omnipotence and omniscience is His providence. This all-wise and all-powerful Creator condescends to serve His subjects—even the rebels among them—in a multitude of ways, for their well-being. In His providence God gave mankind fruits and vegetables (Genesis 1:29) and animals (Genesis 9:3). He has made special promises of providential care to those who love and serve Him: "If you walk in My statutes and keep My commandments so as to carry them out, then I shall give you rains in their season, so that the land will yield its produce and the trees of the field will bear their fruit . . ." (Leviticus 26:3, 4; cf. vv. 5-13). And these promises apply not only to ethnic Israel, but also to the chosen people of the New Covenant: "And we know that God causes all things to work together for good to those who love God, to those who are called according to His purpose" (Romans 8:28). Thus His children can rest fearlessly whenever they walk according to their calling in Christ Jesus, knowing that as they seek first righteousness and the Kingdom of God, He will provide all that they need, physical and spiritual (Matthew 6:19-34; Proverbs 10:3).

As we discuss, in coming chapters, various aspects of the management[6] of the resources God has providentially put at our disposal, we must remember constantly that God is the ultimate Owner of all things, the Master to whom all men, as stewards of His riches, are accountable. But He is not a silent partner in a business venture. He is ever active in managing the affairs of His creation. Our efforts at management will prosper to the extent that they harmonize with His.

2. ANTHROPOLOGICAL FOUNDATIONS

Not only the nature of God, but also the nature of man must inform a Christian understanding of stewardship and the various problems and opportunities that accompany it. Let us look here at four aspects of Biblical anthropology that influence our understanding of economic relationships: (a) man as bearer of the image of God; (b) man's relationship with the rest of creation in light of the cultural mandate; (c) the corruption of the image of God through the fall, and the consequences of the fall on dominion and the cultural mandate; (d) God's provision for man's redemption and restoration, and its consequences for dominion and the cultural mandate.

Imago Dei and Dominion

What did God mean when He said, "Let Us make man in Our image, according to Our likeness . . ." (Genesis 1:26)? There are three chief elements of the image of God in man: (1) rational spirituality and morality; (2) righteousness and holiness; (3) dominion.[7] The first tells us that man, as originally created, had intellectual, moral, and volitional capacities: he could think, he was aware of right and wrong, and he could choose; the second, that he was originally created morally upright and pure; and the third, that because of his spiritual nature (the first two elements), he shared in God's rule over the creation.[8]

After God had formed Adam's body from the dust of the ground, He "breathed into his nostrils the breath of life; and man became a living [soul]" (Genesis 2:7, NASB margin). Man is not only matter but also spirit.[9] "The essential attributes of a spirit are reason, conscience, and will. A spirit is a rational, moral, and therefore also, a free agent."[10] Logical thought, awareness of right and wrong, and the ability to choose were, therefore, essential attributes of man as originally created.

When God finished His creative work, He "saw all that He had made, and behold, it was very good" (Genesis 1:31). Nothing as originally created, including mankind, bore any stain of evil. Everything about Adam, including the whole of his spiritual nature—his rationality, his conscience, and his volition—was unmixedly good. As Hodge puts it, Adam's "reason was subject to God; his will was subject to his reason; his affections and appetites to his will; the body was the obedient organ of the soul."[11] In his rationality he had true knowledge—not only the objective knowledge of true facts, but also the subjective knowledge of personal acquaintance with God; in his conscience, he had the testimony of righteousness, of complete and perfect congruity with the moral character of the Creator in whose image he was made; in his volition, he was perfectly submitted to God.

When God created Adam and Eve, He said, ". . . let them rule over the fish of the sea and over the birds of the sky and over the cattle and over all the earth, and over every creeping thing that creeps on the earth" (Genesis 1:26; cf. v. 28). Indeed, God made man "a little lower than God," and "crown[ed] him with glory and majesty!" He made him "to rule over the works of [His] hands," putting "all things under his feet" (Psalm 8:5, 6). His intention was to share dominion over all the rest of creation with mankind.[12]

The Cultural Mandate

After God created Adam, He put him into a garden, instructing him "to *cultivate* it and *keep* it" (Genesis 2:15). There were, then, two aspects of Adam's dominion: guiding, aiding, and increasing the earth's productivity (cultivating), and guarding it against natural degradation that might result from neglect (keeping). Clearly the purpose of the cultivation was to enable it to meet man's needs more fully than it naturally would.

The cultural mandate found in Genesis 2:15, when viewed in light of the dominion mandate in Genesis 1:26-30, clearly means that the earth, with everything in it—though it all belongs to God (Psalm 24:1)—was intended by God to serve man's needs: "The heavens are the heavens of the LORD; but the earth He has given to the sons of men" (Psalm 115:16). As man was not made for the sabbath, but the sabbath for man (Mark 2:27), so also man was not made for the earth, but the earth for man. It is man, not the earth or anything else in it, that was created in the image of God. To make man subservient to the earth is to turn the purpose of God in creation on its head.[13]

The Fall

It doesn't take a genius to see that all of the attributes of man—spirituality, righteousness, and dominion—have been sorely corrupted. Consequently, man has often botched both aspects of the cultural mandate: he has neither cultivated nor guarded the earth effectively. Why? What happened?

Man misused his volition, rebelling against God's dominion over him. On his submission to God had depended all the glories of his nature and position: his sound thinking, his clear conscience, his moral freedom; his knowledge of truth, and of the One who is the Truth, his righteousness, his purity; his rule over the creation. When his volition was misused, each of these was corrupted. What had been a sound mind full of the light of truth, full of the God who is the Truth, became unsound and darkened by falsehood (Romans 1:21). What had been a clear conscience became fouled with the stench of guilt and fear (Titus 1:15). What had been a free will became enslaved to sin (Romans 6:17), so that, in the words of the Lutheran *Formula of Concord*, ". . . the understanding and reason of man in spiritual things are wholly blind, and can understand nothing by their proper powers . . . and . . . the yet unregenerate will of man is not only averse from God, but has become even hostile to God, so that it only wishes and desires those things, and is delighted with them, which are evil and opposite to the divine will."[14] The once living soul (Genesis 2:7) died (Genesis 2:17), becoming mere dust again (Genesis 3:19). The one who had been alive in righteousness and holiness became "dead in . . . trespasses and sins" (Ephesians 2:1).

Not only man's inward nature, but also his relationship with creation, was corrupted by the fall. Since man refused to submit to God, he was no longer worthy of the creation's unreserved submission. Hence God said, "Because you have . . . eaten from the tree about which I commanded you, saying, 'You shall not eat from it'; *cursed is the ground* because of you; in toil you shall eat of it all the days of your life. Both thorns and thistles it shall grow for you; and you shall eat the plants of the field; by the sweat of your face you shall eat bread, till you return to the ground, because from it you were taken; for you are dust,[15] and to dust you shall return" (Genesis 3:17-19). The glorious reign of man over the earth was shattered. Who can tell what joys were foregone, what sorrows became inevitable?

Thank God (literally!), this is not the end of the story. God did not leave us to sink by ourselves.

Redemption and Restoration

Adam—the first Adam—was created with the knowledge of God, with righteousness and holiness, and with dominion. By his disobedience, in which he represented all his posterity, he lost all these, not only for himself, but for the whole human race after him (Romans 5:12, 15-19). But God in His grace provided a new Adam—the "last Adam" (1 Corinthians 15:45)—Jesus Christ, who by perfect obedience, in which He represented all *His* posterity, restored all these, not only for Himself, but also for all who trust in Him (Romans 5:15-19). Thus, all those who are in Christ are "being renewed to a true knowledge according to the image of the One who created" them (Colossians 3:10) and are given a "new self, which in the likeness of God has been created in righteousness and holiness of the truth" (Ephesians 4:24). Not only that but also, when this last Adam rose in victory over sin and death, "He put all things in subjection under His feet" (Ephesians 1:22), renewing in Himself the dominion intended for the first Adam and his posterity, and "He led captive a host of captives, and He gave gifts to men" (Ephesians 4:8). In other words, He liberated them from their slavery to sin and made them slaves of righteousness instead, seating them "with Him in the heavenly places," "far above all rule and authority and power and dominion, and every name that is named, not only in this age, but also in the one to come" (Ephesians 2:6; 1:21).[16]

In Christians, then, God is about the work of restoring not only the inward *imago Dei* in man (Romans 8:29), but also the outward dominion over creation that belongs to man because of that image (1 Peter 2:9). Jesus, the "ruler of the kings of the earth . . . [has] released us from our sins by His blood, and He has made us to be a kingdom, priests to His God and Father" (Revelation 1:5, 6), to share His reign over the earth (Revelation 20:6), as surely as Adam shared it before the fall.

Those, then, in whom the image of God has been restored and is being perfected by His gracious, sanctifying work (Philippians 1:6), are called to exercise the same rule that Adam was called to exercise. The cultural mandate is our mandate. Like Adam, we are to "cultivate . . . and keep" the garden. Of course, our task is, in an important way, more difficult than was his. Because of sin, "the whole creation groans and suffers the pains of childbirth until now," for it "was subjected to futility." Yet even the curse was placed on creation "in hope that the creation itself also will be set free from its slavery to corruption into the freedom of the glory of the children of God," so that just as believers eagerly await "the redemption of our body," so creation awaits its own restoration to wholeness and fullness (Romans 8:19-23). To what extent will it be possible for the sons of God to restore creation before the bodily return of Christ? We don't know. But we ought to be working toward that end.[17]

Fine. We're supposed to go about cultivating and keeping (or, in modern parlance, developing and conserving) the earth and everything in it, exercising the dominion mandate and the cultural mandate. But how are we supposed to do it?

We're supposed to do it by applying principles from the three remaining foundational areas: ethics, government, and economics.

3. ETHICAL FOUNDATIONS

Biblical ethics deals with four chief elements: rules, motives, acts, and ends. In what follows, we'll consider these under the headings of justice, love, prudence, and seeking the Kingdom of God.

Justice

While *justice* is an oft-mistreated word, bandied about with little respect for its real meaning, careful analysis of the concept as presented in Scripture reveals that it has definite content. In the Bible, *justice* means rendering impartially to everyone his due according to the right standard of God's moral Law.[18] Among others, passages that insist on just weights and measures (Leviticus 19:35, 36; Isaiah 28:17; Micah 6:11) emphasize the dependence of justice on a right standard. Others instruct us to render to everyone his due, as God does (Job 34:10b-12; Romans 13:7). And God also sets the example of impartiality (Romans 2:11; Colossians 3:25; Psalm 82:1-4), an example He requires all His people to follow (Deuteronomy 1:17; Leviticus 19:15; Exodus 23:3, 6).

Justice requires conformity with a standard in two domains, the personal and the social; in two forms of interaction, commutative and distributive; and in the pursuit of two special goals, remediation and retribution. Personal justice entails governing oneself, in thought and word and deed, in conformity with God's moral Law, while social justice entails a whole society's governing itself in conformity with that Law. Commutative justice requires honesty in exchanges, while distributive justice describes the condition of a society in which all exchanges are characterized by commutative justice. Finally, remedial justice requires reparation for injury, while retributive justice requires punishment (which differs from and goes beyond simple restitution) when injuries are intentional or result from culpable negligence.[19]

The standard to which justice points is God's moral Law, summarized in the Ten Commandments (Exodus 20) and their various applications in Biblical case law. Framed negatively, these form the minimum standard of conduct in our relationships with both God and man. As such, violating them is the sole proper ground for *punishment*, one of two chief sorts of external incentive. (The other is *reward*, which should be applied only for behavior above and beyond the minimum standard of justice.) That is, punishment (by whatever jurisdictional authority, whether state, church, family, or even self) may properly be used only as a response to violations of justice. No one may properly punish someone for failing to give charitably, for failing to choose a given career, and so on.[20] Aside from activities prohibited in God's moral Law, however, Biblical ethics grants complete personal liberty, at least so far as any risk of human punishment is concerned (Romans 14).[21]

Love

Parallel to justice is the Biblical ethic of love. Love differs from justice, however, in that while justice sets the minimum standard, love describes the high goal toward which we ought all to strive. Never contradicting the Law (Romans 13:8-10),[22] and hence never countenancing injustice, love rises above the minimum standard of conduct to self-sacrificial service. While justice refrains from taking what belongs to another, love sees a need and graciously extends to another a gift.

This gracious character of love is revealed supremely in God's own gift of His Son, Jesus Christ, to die for sinners despite the claim of justice that they should be punished (John 3:16). Indeed, "We know love by this, that He laid down His life for us; and we ought to lay down our lives for the brethren" (1 John 3:16). Love, not justice, calls us to charitable works. Thus John adds immediately, "But whoever has the world's goods, and beholds his brother in need and closes his heart against him, how does the love of God abide in him?" (1 John 3:17). Hence charitable works are worthy of reward (2 Corinthians 9:6, 7, 11), but their lack is never the basis of punishment (Acts 5:1-4). Indeed, the word *charitable* is derived from the Greek *charis*, "grace." Whatever is of grace is so far from being *due* (as justice requires that we render to everyone his due) that Paul could write, "Now to the one who works, his wage is not reckoned as a favor [*charis*, grace], but as what is due" (Romans 4:4).

Properly understood, love, together with all good works expressive of it, arises out of gratitude to God for His grace showered on His people. *The Heidelberg Catechism* (1563) asks, in Question 86: "Since, then, we are redeemed from our misery by grace through Christ, without any merit of ours, why must we do good works?" "Because," it answers, "Christ, having redeemed us by his blood, renews us also by his Holy Spirit after his own image, that with our whole life we may *show ourselves thankful* to God for his blessing, and that he may be glorified through us; then, also, that we ourselves may be assured of our faith by the fruits thereof, and by our godly walk may win our neighbors also to Christ."[23] Love is not a primary—i.e., underived—motive in the human heart, but a responsive motive: "We love, because He first loved us" (1 John 4:19).

The good works by which love expresses itself are those of service to God and our fellowmen. Love mimics the grace that excites the gratitude from which it springs (2 Corinthians 9:6-10; cf. 8:8), and so replicates itself in its beneficiaries, in whom it engenders a new generation of love-producing gratitude to God (2 Corinthians 9:11-15). Thus grateful love inspires gracious service by which the

Kingdom of God grows as more and more people experience the King's love and respond in grateful, loving service.[24]

Prudence

As justice sets the minimum standards of conduct and love the high goal of sanctified service to God and men, prudence selects, from among just alternatives, the most efficient means of achieving the high ends sought by love. Many principles of economics, from personal choices to economic systems that encompass whole civilizations, are matters of prudence.

Prudence differs from justice and love in that it has ends, rather than standards and motives, in mind. It is teleological, while justice and love are deontological, in nature.[25] Prudence is utilitarian, but it is not unrestrictedly utilitarian. It selects *from among just alternatives* the most efficient means of achieving the ends of justice and love.[26] Thus efficiency is never an excuse for violating the right standard of God's moral Law to which justice appeals. Indeed, because moral and physical reality are consistent, no unjust act (i.e., an act contrary to God's moral Law), contrary appearances notwithstanding, is ever ultimately efficient toward good ends.[27] It is not the end that justifies the means, but the conformity of the means with justice; it is the end, however, that measures the degree to which a just choice is also a prudent choice.

Seeking First the Kingdom

The highest goal in Christian ethics is the glory of God.[28] One means of that is bringing more people and things under submission to His rule—the building of the Kingdom of God by "taking every thought captive to the obedience of Christ" (2 Corinthians 10:5). Jesus urges His followers, ". . . seek first [God's] kingdom, and His righteousness; and all these things [the supply of ordinary human needs] shall be added to you" (Matthew 6:33). Thus the growth of the Kingdom takes precedence over any personal needs; indeed, commitment to it ensures believers that their personal needs will be met by God's providential care. Their greatest concern, therefore, is that God's Kingdom should come, that His will should be done on earth as it is in Heaven (Matthew 6:10).

Two facets of Christians' identity and of their relationship with God are particularly important in shaping our understanding of what it means to seek the Kingdom of God: sonship and priesthood.[29] It can be helpful to see these as related, respectively, to dominion and the cultural mandate. As sons of God, believers enjoy royal privileges to rule over creation within the boundaries of God's rule. As priests, we bring the redeeming work of God to bear in creation, lifting it out of unfruitful bondage and into productive liberty. All of our acquisitive activities should be undertaken with the purpose of extending godly rule, or dominion. Our priesthood, on the other hand, obliges us to serve others, even at our own expense, also for the sake of the Kingdom. Thus the Christian must "labor, performing with his own hands what is good, in order that he may have something [dominion] to share with him who has need [priesthood]" (Ephesians 4:28).

Justice, love, prudence, and Kingdom-seeking, then, are chief ethical principles that underlie the Christian's economic conduct. But all such conduct takes place in the context of the civil social order. The shape of that order has important implications for the degree to which people are encouraged to act consistently with those principles. We will consider foundational principles of civil government and economics in the following chapter.

THREE

STATE AND ECONOMY

*T*he shape of the culture in which we live necessarily affects the shape of our lives. Rare are the people whose ethical judgment transcends all cultural givens. More commonly, we accept most of our culture unquestioningly, dissenting from it only here and there, on issues of particular poignancy or peculiar personal interest.

Two of the most significant cultural factors shaping human behavior relative to economic growth, use of resources, and economic planning are civil government and the economic system.

1. GOVERNMENTAL FOUNDATIONS

In the Stone Lectures of 1898, delivered at Princeton Theological Seminary, Dutch theologian and later prime minister Abraham Kuyper outlined what has since become known as the idea of *sphere sovereignty* in the Christian understanding of government.[1] In those lectures, Kuyper argued that a Biblical notion of government recognizes three spheres, or jurisdictions, of governmental authority: the individual, the church, and the state, each of which is accountable to God and should be shaped according to God's revelation in Scripture. Kuyper's insights have been tremendously important in shaping the philosophy of government among Reformed Christians. The discussion that follows rests upon them, with the exception that I suggest a fourth sphere: the family.

Scripture gives authority over some matters to individuals, over others to families, over others to churches, and over still others to states. When those entities respect each other's jurisdictions, there is social harmony. When they ignore or scorn those jurisdictions, social conflict arises as the entities vie for authority. Much of the present conflict in American society stems from our failure to understand and respect these distinct jurisdictions.

When the state, for instance, attempts to take over some of the duties of the family, like education, it finds itself involved in inevitable contradictions. The statist educational system, which uses coercive taxation to fund itself, would seem bound to neutrality regarding the various religious and moral opinions of its students. But in practice there can be no neutrality. Carefully avoiding the topics of morality and religion is not neutrality—it is antimoralism and antireligionism. Attempting to present all religious and moral values as equally valid is not neutral to those religions and systems of morality that claim to be valid to the exclusion of others. Ultimately, the state finds itself coercively proselytizing for one religious and moral system instead of others, and doing so at the expense of those whose systems it opposes.

Similarly, if the church attempts to take on the authority of the state, it inevitably falls into injustice. God has ordained the state, not the church, to bear the sword. He has given the church authority to enforce orthodoxy *within the church* through teaching and church discipline, up to and including excommunication. But He has not ordained it to enforce orthodoxy outside the church.

In the last century or so, the state has exerted ever wider claims of authority, at the expense of individual, family, and church. As a result, personal, familial, and religious liberties are at stake. The freedom of individual contract once held sacred among Americans has been severely curtailed through minimum wage laws, price controls, zoning laws, import/export quotas and restrictions, and a mountain of other state legislation. The freedom of families to train children according to religious beliefs has been curtailed by the state's taxing them even if their children don't attend the state's schools, thus forcing them to pay for education twice. The freedom of churches to preach the gospel and gather in worship has been curtailed by zoning laws that prohibit the location of churches in some areas, by regulations outlawing religious organizations on state elementary and secondary school campuses, and by employment regulations that often prohibit churches' using volunteer or low-wage laborers.

Why this discussion in a book on population growth, economic growth, resources, and the environment? Because blurring these jurisdictions often has serious consequences for those topics. Zoning laws frequently prohibit people from living where they could otherwise afford to live, forcing them to live in urban slums instead.[2] They often make it economically impossible for some businesses to start or locate in particular places where they otherwise could, and so contribute to local or regional unemployment. "Slow growth" and "no growth" initiatives often restrict the supply of housing and so drive up its price, or curtail the growth of businesses and so depress employment.

Often in the following chapters, we will see that problems related to growth and resources arise because jurisdictional boundaries have been ignored, especially by an ever-expanding state. Often it will be necessary to recommend shrinking the state's claims to authority as part of the cure to those problems.[3] Of special importance to our subject is the state's respect for property rights derived from the Eighth Commandment ("You shall not steal," Exodus 20:15) and acknowledged in the United States Constitution ("No person shall . . . be deprived of . . . property, without due process of law; nor shall private property be taken for public use without just compensation," Fifth Amendment). Frequently, state regulations violate property rights as Biblically understood, and in so doing cause serious harm not only to individuals, but also to whole societies.

2. ECONOMIC FOUNDATIONS

A wide range of economic principles necessarily colors the way in which anyone thinks of economic growth and its related problems and opportunities. While others will come into play occasionally in later chapters, the four below are of especially broad application.

The Meaning of Scarcity

The word *scarcity* conjures up radically different images for economists from those it conjures up for laymen.[4] When laymen hear that oil is scarce, they tend to think there's very little of it around; when economists hear that oil is scarce, they tend to think there's less of it around than people would use if they could get it for free or if the maximum legal price for it were below a market price, or simply that its price is going up because its supply in the market (not necessarily in the physical world) isn't keeping up with demand. Unfortunately, since it's usually economists (or journalists who pass on their thoughts) who make the statements, and laymen who hear them, communication is bound to fail.

Unfortunately for clarity, laymen in economics often are professionals in fields closely related to it, particularly resource development and distribution. As a result, experts in resource supply—petroleum geologists, for instance—might tell us that something is scarce, meaning by it what laymen mean, while economists, who advise civil governments on resource policies, hear the news and translate it into their own notions of scarcity. As a result, price trend forecasts and even resource production forecasts often are badly skewed.

The usual idea following news that some resource is scarce is that soon it will be practically nonexistent. We will, we fear, run out of it. But this ignores the important definition of scarcity for economists, and the distinction is not just academic. For the economic notion of scarcity, which tells us that there isn't enough of something to go around if everyone is permitted to have as much of it as he wants at zero price, allows us to predict what will happen in the real world. As the gap between the amount of oil available and the amount people would use at zero price grows, the price of oil rises. The rising price suppresses *demand*—not the amount of oil people want at zero price, but the amount they're willing to pay for—and as a result the amount of oil brought to market necessarily equals the amount demanded. The higher the price, the lower the demand. Eventually, if the price gets high enough, there will be no effective demand, and the resource no longer will be employed. There will be a surplus.[5]

But some people forget this simple truth. Unfortunately, those who forget often shape public resource policy. And in their forgetfulness, they enact policies designed to slow the use of the resource artificially: they set minimum prices above current market levels, or maximum production levels below current market demand, or some combination of these measures. The result is an artificial appearance of shortage and the shifting of capital investments into producing more of it or more of its substitutes in order to profit from the artificially high prices. This capital shift deprives other segments of the economy of capital investments, resulting in an economy that does not meet the needs of consumers as well as if the policymakers never stepped in in the first place.

Repeatedly in the following chapters we will see how keeping a clear idea of the real nature of scarcity can help us solve problems related to economic growth, planning, and resource development and conservation.

Marginal Utility Theory of Value

Like *scarcity*, the word *value* also evokes different notions among different people and in different contexts.[6] Particularly because of Christians' concern to maintain and rebuild respect for absolute moral values, Christians in particular are likely to misunderstand the economic concept of value.

Economic value is always subjective, not objective; i.e., it is attributed to the thing valued by someone who wants it (or doesn't want to lose it without some form of reimbursement). Marginal utility theory tells us that the subjective value a potential buyer assigns to anything is always a measurement of the added satisfaction he expects if he acquires one more unit of the item, and the subjective value a potential seller assigns to anything is always a measurement of the loss of satisfaction he expects if he gives up one unit. Ordinarily this means that the more units of a given item someone has, the less he will value one more unit, while the fewer he has, the more he will value one more. Thus the value of an item may differ not only from one person to another, but even for the same person from one time to another depending on circumstances.

The constantly changing marginal utility judgments of buyers and sellers in the marketplace have important effects on scarcity. The more buyers already have of something, the less they're going to value more of it, and hence the less they're going to be willing to pay; the less they have of it, the more they're going to value more of it, and hence the more they're going to be willing to pay. Conversely, the more sellers already have of something, the less they're going to value it, and hence the less they're going to demand in payment for it; the less they have of it, the more they're going to value it, and hence the more they're going to demand in payment for it.

As the supply of an item drops relative to demand for it, its price will rise. As the price rises, buyers "at the margin"—those whose marginal utility valuation of the item barely justified their buying it at the old price, but won't justify it at the new price—will stop buying it, or will reduce their purchases. Similarly, as the supply rises, its price will fall. As it falls, buyers once "off the margin"—those whose valuation of the item barely missed justifying it at the old price, but does justify it at the new price—will begin buying it, or will increase their purchases. In this manner, the interaction of marginal utility valuations by buyers and sellers and of supply in the marketplace—a complex interaction with constant signals back and forth—will always balance supply with demand. Always, that is, unless the market is artificially affected by a non-economic factor, like price controls, production quotas, and so on.[7] Such non-economic factors can have severe adverse effects on the availability of goods and services in the marketplace. More to the point in this book, they can adversely affect our ability to foresee trends and plan accordingly.

Imagine for a moment that a county that has, until now, had no restrictions on land development suddenly adopts severe restrictive zoning laws and even sets aside a large portion of the remaining undeveloped land as "open space." One day land, housing, and commercial, industrial, and agricultural property prices will have been judged by buyers and sellers based on expectations of continued free land use. The next day, they will have to be judged based on expectations of strictly curtailed choice of land use. Prices of certain kinds of land will rise, while prices of certain other kinds of land will fall, both dependent on the effect of the zoning and open space set-asides on the availability of those types of land. Instantly potential buyers and sellers of all kinds of real property in the county will have to make drastic changes in their plans. Some potential buyers might be permanently excluded because of resulting price increases; other people might become potential buyers because of resulting price decreases. The central point is that people will change their plans. The changes will mean that future buying, selling, and use of the land in the county will no longer conform to the expectations that led planners to devise the zoning and set-asides. Consequently, the zoning and set-asides will eventually—and probably inevitably—make themselves obsolete. They will need to be revised in light of people's new choices. But the revisions will set off a new round of changes in private persons' plans, which will make the revisions obsolete.[8]

All of this will happen because of people's changing marginal utility valuations. What this means is that trend forecasts and planning other than on economic bases are necessarily self-defeating. In future chapters we will observe practical implications of this insight.

Economic Efficiency vs. Technical Efficiency

When economists think of efficiency, they have in mind the extent to which a given activity or object produces a desired end at minimum cost. But technicians tend to think of efficiency more as the degree to which a given activity or product uses state-of-the-art technology to achieve the highest possible degree or amount of the desired end.

Sometimes the two concepts have nearly identical practical implications. Sometimes they don't.

An example of the divergence of the two ideas of efficiency is a frequent quandary over environmental pollution. Technicians concerned about the environment often can tell us ways to reduce the pollution generated in the pursuit of some particular end to next to nothing. Then they use the media to alert the public to this more "efficient" alternative to the prevalent ways of pursuing the desired end. As a result, people think those who resist the alternative technology don't care about the environment. It might be, however, that they do care about the environment, but that they also care about other factors the technicians, the media, and the general public don't have in mind. Chief among them is cost: What will it cost to use the technically "efficient" process instead of the prevalent process? If the cost is so high that the end result won't justify the use of the technically "efficient" process, then that process is by definition not economically "efficient." (It is important to keep in mind that *cost* here doesn't refer chiefly to amounts of money, but to lost opportunity to do other things. Installing a pollution control device might make a manufacturer unable to install some safety device for his workers, or to pay them higher wages, or to provide more of his product to consumers at lower prices.)

Similar ambiguities regarding efficiency arise in relation to many problems and opportunities connected with economic growth, and we will encounter them repeatedly in this study. Whether economic or technical efficiency is to be preferred in any given case is an important judgment, but it cannot be made until the two different kinds of efficiency are recognized.

Free Market vs. Controlled Economy

One other economic foundation is the difference between a free-market economy and a controlled economy, and how the two measure up to Biblical standards of ethics and to the test of economy productivity.[9]

The two chief distinguishing factors between a free-market and a controlled economy are not the different relationships between capital and labor, despite the fact that the free market often is called *capitalism* and the controlled market *socialism*, but the different conditions under which capital, labor, and resources are brought together and allocated to one or another of various alternative uses.[10] The key questions are, "Who controls capital?" and "To whom are those who control capital answerable?" In the free market, private persons control capital, and they answer chiefly to consumers for their use of it, aside from complying with laws prohibiting such things as fraud, theft, and violence. (Thus the American economy, which limits private control of capital beyond mere prohibition of fraud, theft and violence—e.g., through legal monopolies, licensure, trade route restrictions, tariffs, etc.—is not, technically speaking, a free market, although it is more free than many other economies.) In the controlled economy, agents of the state control capital (regardless whether technical title of ownership remains in private hands or is transferred to the state), and they answer chiefly to the state for their use of it, with little regard to the needs and demands of consumers. As Russell Kirk puts it:

> There is capital in Russia, just as in the United States. And there are capitalists in Russia—that is, persons who control that capital. But the Communist capitalists are a much smaller class than American capitalists, and infinitely more powerful as a class. The Soviet Russian capitalists are the commissars and Communist party officials who control Soviet industry and agriculture. . . . They can . . . force the peoples of Soviet states to work under whatever conditions they prescribe, for as small wages as they like. . . . None of the exaggerated charges of Marx and Engels against nineteenth-century capitalism accuse the private capitalists of such methods as are now employed daily by the Communist capitalists of the Soviet states. The exploitation of the worker which Marx and his followers predicted would be carried out by the private capitalist of the future, now is executed, instead, by the disciples of Marx.[11]

The conditions under which capital, labor, and resources are brought together and allocated in the two different economic systems may be understood under the headings of the two key words *free* and *market*, both of which stand opposed to the one word *controlled*.

Freedom in the Market

In the free market, people choose for themselves how to employ capital, labor, and resources, and toward what ends. Private, uncoerced consumer choices in the market determine prices, which in turn determine profits (rewards), which in turn determine how producers allocate capital, labor, and resources. Thus consumers control the direction of the economy by exerting demand (offer of reward) for desired products, and producers respond by allocating the factors of production to meet the demands.

It is important to understand that *freedom*, in the sense of a free market, does not mean (1) political self-determination (the ability of a national population to determine, through some form of elections, those who rule); (2) ability to do whatever one chooses without regard to natural or economic restraints; (3) that goods and services are available at no cost (something impossible regarding any economic goods and services); or (4) absence of moral restraint (often enforced by civil law). Rather, *freedom* means exemption from arbitrary coercion by others.[12] Particularly, freedom is to be contrasted with slavery. So far is it from implying absence of moral restraint that the Bible describes the free man as one whose slavery to sin has been exchanged for slavery to righteousness (Romans 6). Thus free-market economics is no justification for economic behavior that injures others with impunity.

By a free *market*, we mean an economy in which the market—the vast set of relationships among freely-choosing buyers and sellers of producer goods, consumer goods, labor, information, capital, etc.—guides the direction of economic activity, rather than governmental planners backed up by threat of force. By processing information about people's subjective valuations of goods and services, the market provides essential information about the most efficient allocations of resources—*efficient* here defined as meeting, at lowest practical cost, the demands of consumers.[13] By this means the market enables consumers to guide the economy. Producers know that they must meet consumers' demands if they are to earn profits (rewards). Thus the free market facilitates both high productivity and voluntary service to others.

The Controlled Economy

In stark contrast to the free market stands the controlled economy. In it, planners employed by the state instruct people how to bring capital, resources, and labor together, and toward what ends. Their plans are based on their own assumptions about people's wants and needs and on the goals of the government they represent—goals that often do not coincide with the best interests of the population. Those who refuse to comply with the planners' instructions face sanctions (punishment). Thus the controlled economy seriously curtails freedom.

At the same time, planners set prices of goods and services. They may set them based on their computations of the cost of production or on their predetermined state goals. Regardless, setting prices independently of consumers' choices frustrates the information-processing function of the market. As a result, people's needs are sacrificed to the desires of the bureaucratic apparatus, and capital, labor, and resources are misallocated, resulting in stunted production.

Ethical and Practical Assessment of Free-Market and Controlled Economies

In discussing justice, we saw that punishment is properly used only as a sanction against violations of the minimum standard of right conduct—against injustice. It is never proper to use punishment (or the threat of punishment) to force action not required by justice itself. But that is precisely what a controlled economy does: it threatens punishment by the state (fines, revocation of licenses, and so on) for economic choices permitted by the standards of justice if they don't fit well with the plans of those in power. Thus the controlled economy fails a key test of Biblical ethics. In a free market, however, punishment is meted out only for violations of justice; hence the free market passes this test.

In addition, we noted that reward is properly offered only for actions that exceed the minimum standard of justice. An economic system that rewards such behavior therefore passes this test of Biblical ethics, while one that neglects or prevents reward for such behavior fails this test. Again, the free market passes this test by rewarding people for serving others beyond the minimum requirements of justice, while the controlled economy often prevents someone's being rewarded for extraordinary service (by forcing economic equality, or some degree of it, for instance) and sometimes even rewards people for violating justice (for instance, when it makes someone's upward progress in bureaucracy dependent on his efficiency in enforcing unjust economic controls).

A system that rewards people for going beyond minimum standards provides strong incentive for high productivity, while one that fails to reward such performance provides little incentive for it. We should not be surprised, then, to find that the more free an economy is, the more productive it tends to be, while the more controlled it is, the less productive it tends to be. Certainly the current upheavals in the Eastern European socialist states testifies to this.

Thus the free market excels over the controlled market in regard to both Biblical ethics and productivity.

FOUR

PENULTIMATE RESOURCE OR POPULATION PLAGUE?

On our way into the hospital for the birth of our first child one bright and shiny day in 1985, my wife and I saw a bumper sticker that said, "Beam me up, Scotty. This planet sucks!" We laughed. Little did we know.

"The world has cancer," said a top Rockefeller Foundation official in 1962, "and that cancer cell is man."

No longer are people desirable in themselves. Indeed, they are a curse on the land. They are the "population bomb," a "population explosion," and "people pollution." Or as Kingsley Davis puts it, "In subsequent history the Twentieth Century may be called either the century of world wars or the century of the population plague."[1]

Why such a gloomy view of people? Because there are too many of them, that's why. At least, that's what proponents of population control believe, and they have frighteningly vivid ways of telling us:

The current rate of growth, continued in 600 years, would leave every inhabitant of the world with only 1 square yard to live on. By the year 3500, the weight of human bodies on the earth's surface would equal the weight of the world itself. By the year 6000, the solid mass of humanity would be expanding outward into space at the speed of light.[2]

Or take this cheery picture:

A British scientist recently calculated that with the population of the world now about 3 billion and doubling every 37 years, we will reach the ultimate terrestrial limit of 60 million billion humans in somewhat less than 1,000 years. At that state, people will be jammed together so tightly that the earth itself will glow orange-red from the heat.[3]

(Do these statisticians, calculators in hand, ever consider that people might lose their taste for making love long before these prognostications come true?)

WHAT'S HAPPENING WITH POPULATION?

Statistical games can be fun. They can also be misleading, which I suppose is why someone coined the aphorism, "There are three kinds of lies: lies, damned lies, and statistics." In fanning the flames of the population scare, statistics are more misleading than fun.

Consider, for a moment, applying statistical growth-rate projections to another sort of population: inmates in American state and federal prisons. In 1980, there were 315,974; in 1981, there were 353,674, an increase of 10 percent; and in 1982, there were 396,072, another 11 percent. Suppose this same growth curve continues, so that we add 12 percent the next year, 13 percent the following, and so on. In the year 2012, 415,389,484 Americans will be in state and federal prisons. Now that *is* a frightening prospect, particularly granted that the total U.S. population projected for that year is only about 315 million.[4] Apparently we're going to have to find an extra hundred million people just to fill our prisons; and that doesn't even address the question of who will guard us all. (Juvenal's old enigma, *Sed quis custodiet ipsos Custodes?*—"But who shall guard the guards themselves?"—suddenly takes on new meaning!)

What's wrong with this projection of prison population? The computations are impeccable. The trend sample, the method of defining the trend, and the assumption that the trend will continue forever are wrong. Why assume that the prison population will grow by 1 percent more each year than the last? Why not average the growth rates of the three years and use that as a steady rate? That would have yielded far lower long-term growth. Furthermore, had we looked back a few more years, we would have found that prison population actually fell by about .2 percent per year in 1961 through 1965 and by about 1.4 percent per year in 1966 through 1970; that it grew by only about 4.5 percent per year in 1971 through 1975; that it grew by 6.2 percent per year in 1976 through 1980; and that it grew by about 2.8 percent per year in 1951 through 1960. Overall, from 1950 through 1982, prison population grew an average of only about 4.3 percent per year, and the occasional declines show us that any increase at all is not inexorable.[5] From this longer-term perspective we might have learned that trends can slow, quicken, or even reverse, dependent on outside variables.

Furthermore, while prison population as a proportion of total population continued to rise through 1986,[6] public pressure to reduce prison expenditures began to rise, too, so that today there is growing pressure for alternative sentencing, especially for nonviolent offenders, that could result in substantial reductions in prison populations, both absolutely and as a percentage of population.[7] Statistical trend projections often fail to take into account external variables like this—variables that can quicken, slow, or reverse trends.

Projections and Retrojections

So what's wrong with the population projections cited above? A simple question might cast doubt on their validity: What happens if we figure population *retrojections* instead of *projections* using the same criteria? Take, for instance, the projection based on population's doubling every thirty-seven years (i.e., annual population growth of 1.945 percent). What if we halved the population for every thirty-seven years into the past? The projection was made in 1965, with the population at roughly 3 billion. So in 1928 world population would have been 1.5 billion, in 1891 750 million, and so on, back to when Adam and Eve were created not (*pace* Archbishop Ussher) in 4004 B.C., but in A.D. 818! Poor William the Conqueror might have been surprised to learn that he could have brought not 7,000 men with him to the Battle of Hastings in A.D. 1066, but, at most, 143 men, women, and children—the whole world's population aside from his enemy King Harold and himself.

Okay, let's be generous. Let's assume that population growth has only been half as fast in the past as it is today—doubling every seventy-four years (.973 percent per year) instead of every thirty-seven. Then creation occurred in 267 B.C. How about half as fast as that—doubling every 148 years? Creation in 2623 B.C. Half as fast yet (annual growth .24 percent)? Creation in 7211 B.C. The population scaremongers are in deep trouble unless they're prepared to endorse young-earth (or at least young-mankind) creationism.[8]

What's wrong with population growth projections (and retrojections) like the frightening (and humorous) ones cited above is that they arbitrarily, and stubbornly, assume steady growth rates over long periods of time. But growth has never been steady over long periods. Sometimes it has been fairly rapid, sometimes very slow, sometimes even negative.

Growth and Equilibrium

In fact, reliable estimates put world population as recently as 1650 somewhere between 465 million and 545 million.[9] Assuming the lower figure for a moment, an average population growth rate of roughly .67 percent per year would yield the present population in the intervening 340 years—by and large, the healthiest centuries in humanity's history, and hence probably the centuries of fastest population growth. Earlier growth was surely much slower, viewed as a long-term average; Braudel suggests about .173 percent per year from A.D. 1300 through 1800, which is only about one-tenth the present rate.[10]

Regular growth, in fact, is the exception, not the rule of history. More often, population rises and falls in various regions. For instance, population in the lower Diyala region of Iraq grew from about 10,000 around 4000 B.C. to about 90,000 in 2000 B.C., but fell to about 15,000 in 1000 B.C. It skyrocketed to about 300,000 at the time of Christ and to about 840,000 in A.D. 900. But it plummeted to under 400,000 in the next two hundred years and by about 1800 was only about 50,000. Then it skyrocketed again in the next 150 years, reaching about 750,000 in 1950—still about 90,000 less than it was a thousand years before.[11]

Again, the population of central Mexico plummeted from nearly 26 million in the early sixteenth century to under 2 million in the early seventeenth.[12] The population of Egypt went from about 2.5 million in 700 B.C. to 25 million in 525 B.C., then fell to about 7 million around A.D. 75, rose to nearly 30 million in A.D. 541, fell to about 10 million in A.D. 719, rose to about 25 million in A.D. 1010, then fell in fits and starts to about 2.5 million around 1750, after which it rose to about 30 million by 1966.[13]

Forecasts of stable population growth rates assume that governmental, political, economic, and social organization remain unchanged and that no major wars, epidemics, or natural disasters occur.[14] Yet none of these assumptions has proved true over long periods of time in any part of the world. Indeed, the stable growth forecasts even assume that no minor fluctuations in such naturally unstable things as agricultural harvests occur. Yet historical studies indicate that parents in heavily agricultural societies time births by harvests, having more children when harvests are good and fewer when they are bad.[15] The steady trend forecasts also ignore the complex variety of reasons why birth rates fall as societies progress from less developed to more developed.[16]

The Demographic Transition

Why, then, has there been such sudden—some call it explosive—population growth all over the world[17] in the last century or two? Will such growth continue, or will population level off (or even decline)? The answer to the first question gives us pretty good footing for a tentative answer to the second.

Population specialists refer to this century or so as a period of *demographic transition*, a time when population patterns went through a major change. Before this period, most populations were characterized by high birth rates and high death rates. Average life expectancy was low—in the late-twenties in most countries—and infant and child mortality was high. Hence few people lived to old age, and lots, in some countries and periods as many as half, never made it to childbearing age. With the onset of the Industrial Revolution and the great multiplications of per-capita income that it brought, however, death rates plummeted: fewer people died in childhood, and more people lived to old age. But birth rates, for a while, stayed what they had been. As a result, there were far more people alive at a given time. Soon, however, birth rates began to fall toward equilibrium with death rates. Parents no longer had six or eight children, hoping to see three or four grow to maturity; instead, they bore the same number of children they expected to see mature.

The result of this transition has been a sudden and steep increase in population, followed by a leveling off of population at new, higher equilibrium levels. Population levels historically have not been described by a sweeping, exponential curve, but by a series of wide plateaus, each followed by a sudden upward curve. Indeed, the most accurate long-term picture of population growth rate was probably given by Ronald Freeman and Bernard Berelson, who saw it as holding almost perfectly steady at about .1 percent per year from 8,000 B.C. to A.D. 1800, shooting up to about 2 percent around 1950, and collapsing back to about .1 percent a century or so later, after which it will stay there for many centuries.[18] On a line graph, the result is a long straight line with a narrow upward spike in the middle of it spanning the years 1800 to 2000.

The demographic transition has occurred at different times in different countries, is still in process in some, and is just beginning in a few, but it seems likely that if the pattern of the transition continues, worldwide population will level off around the middle or end of the next century, probably somewhere between 8 and 15 billion, mostly likely around 10 billion—from 60 percent above to double or triple the present population.[19] Population forecasts that fail to take the demographic transition into consideration and therefore warn of incredibly high populations in the foreseeable future are absurd because they assume that a short-term pattern is actually a long-term trend.

Nonetheless, while the long-term forecasts of the doomsayers may be indefensible from the standpoint of legitimate demography and statistics, there is no denying that there are more people in the world today than there have ever been at any one time in the past.[20] That can raise the specter of crowded living conditions; shortages of food, even to the extent of widespread famines; exhaustion of natural resources; and life-threatening pollution. In the face of these perceived threats to human well-being, many influential people, especially in civil government and the media, call for increased planning and control of population and economic growth by the state. Determining what we, as Christians, should think about such matters requires our seeing what the Bible says about population and examining carefully the empirical interrelationships among population growth and various aspects of human well-being.

The remainder of this chapter will outline a Biblical ethic of population and population growth and will address the question whether the United States and the world as a whole are becoming overpopulated. Chapter 5 will examine, in light of our findings here, the effects of population growth on living space, transportation and communication, and recreation. Chapter 6 will survey the interrelationships of population growth and economic growth, focusing especially on food supplies. Chapter 7 will discuss future supplies of natural resources, especially energy, in light of the trends we see in this chapter and the next for population and economic growth.

Chapter 8 will examine pollution as it is related to population and economic growth and will strive for some ethical policy foundations. Chapter 9 will suggest the outlines of a sound policy of resource management. Chapter 10 will discuss the place of planning in dealing with all these problems and opportunities.

Now let's look at two questions: (1) What does the Bible say about population and population growth in general? (2) Is the world, or are various parts of it, full already?

THE BIBLE ON POPULATION

While it nowhere explicitly addresses questions about population growth and its effects on human well-being, the Bible still has a good deal to say about people—particularly about people begetting more people.

We begin at the beginning, even before the creation of man. When God had made the creatures of sea and air and declared them good, He "blessed them, saying, 'Be fruitful and multiply, and fill the waters of the seas, and let birds multiply on the earth'" (Genesis 1:22). From the very first, then, it is apparent that the God of Scripture favored bountiful life. Indeed, the depopulation of the earth at the time of the Flood was the effect of His judgment for sin (Genesis 6—7). Abundance of life, not scarcity, is God's plan for the world. This applies not only to the animal world, but also to mankind. For precisely what He said to the birds and fishes He said also to Adam and Eve after creating them: "Be fruitful and multiply, and fill the earth" (Genesis 1:28).

The piling up of words with similar meanings in these passages indicates the intensity of God's intention. It was not enough that He should say, "Be fruitful;" He added, "and multiply." And it was not enough that He should say, "Be fruitful and multiply;" to make the goal clear, He added, "and *fill* the earth." Three Hebrew words work together to express the strength of this intention: *pârâh*, "blossom, bear fruit"; *râbâh*, "become many or numerous, become great, grow, increase"; and *mâlê*, "fill, overflow."[21]

Fill the Earth

In light of fears of overpopulation, the last word, *mâlê*, is crucial. Moses used the same word in writing that the glory of Yahweh "filled the tabernacle" (Exodus 40:34, 35).[22] Elijah used it when he told men to "[f]ill" pitchers with water (1 Kings 18:33). In the absolute, it is used to describe the Jordan River overflowing its banks (Joshua 3:15). The Greek verb *plēro'ō*, which translates *mâlê* in the Septuagint, precisely expresses its meaning; it means to fill completely so that nothing is left over.[23] Is the earth "filled" to this extent? Certainly not, and it appears unlikely that it will become so in the foreseeable future, particularly with the slowing population growth rates that historically have accompanied industrialization and economic betterment. (We will return later to the empirical, yet value-laden, question of whether the earth is getting crowded.)

This preference for fruitfulness, multiplication, and filling the earth continues after the creation narrative. Following the Flood, God told Noah to release the animals and birds from the ark "that they may breed abundantly [literally, "swarm," NASB margin] on the earth, and be fruitful and multiply on the earth" (Genesis 8:17). Then He gave Noah and his sons the same command He had given Adam and Eve: "Be fruitful and multiply, and fill the earth" (Genesis 9:1). And shortly thereafter, by mandating capital punishment for murder, He made more explicit than ever the preference for life: "Whoever sheds man's blood, by man his blood shall be shed, for in the image of God He made man. And as for you, be fruitful and multiply; populate [literally "swarm in," NASB margin] the earth abundantly and multiply in it" (Genesis 9:6, 7). The Hebrew word translated "swarm" in these two verses is the same verb used to describe the plague of frogs that swarmed over Egypt (Exodus 8:1-15). It conveys the idea of a tremendous number of objects densely populating an area.

Population Growth Is a Blessing

It is important to note that in each of these instances, the command to be fruitful, to multiply, to fill the earth and swarm in it (Genesis 1:22, 28; 8:17; 9:1, 7) comes in the context of God's blessing. "God *blessed* [the fish and birds], saying, 'Be fruitful and multiply, and fill . . .'" (Genesis 1:22); "God *blessed* [the man and woman]; and God said to them, 'Be fruitful and multiply, and fill . . .'" (Genesis 1:28); "God *blessed* Noah and his sons and said to them, 'Be fruitful and multiply, and fill the earth. . . . Swarm in the earth abundantly and multiply in it'" (Genesis 9:1, 7). A teeming population, then, should normally be thought of as a blessing, not a curse.

This is the general principle in regard to all mankind, represented first in Adam and then in Noah. If anything, it is intensified in regard to the elect people of God, as we see in God's promises to Abraham: ". . . I will make you a great nation, and I will bless you . . ." (Genesis 12:2); "Now look toward the heavens, and count the stars, if you are able to count them. . . . So shall your descendants be" (Genesis 15:5); "I am God Almighty; walk before Me, and be blameless. And I will establish My covenant between Me and you, and I will multiply you exceedingly. . . . And you shall be the father of a multitude of nations. . . . And I will make you exceedingly fruitful, and I will make nations of you, and kings shall come forth from you" (Genesis 17:1-6). This promise was renewed to Isaac (Genesis 26:4, 24). So it was a sign of God's blessing on Israel that the nation, by the time of the exodus, had grown to be "as numerous as the stars of heaven" (Deuteronomy 10:22; cf. 1:10; cf. Genesis 47:27).[24]

Growth didn't stop being a blessing after that. Instead, it was promised as a blessing on Israel's obedience: "And He will love you and bless you and multiply you; He will also bless the fruit of your womb and the fruit of your ground, your grain and your new wine and your oil, the increase of your herd and the young of your flock, in the land which He swore to your forefathers to give you. You shall be blessed above all peoples; there shall be no male or female barren among you or among your cattle" (Deuteronomy 7:13, 14; cf. 30:5). In contrast, a decline in population was one form of curse God might send on His people if they rebelled (Deuteronomy 28:62, 63; Leviticus 26:22).[25]

Not only in mankind in the aggregate, but also in individual nations and families, population growth appears in the Bible as a blessing from God. "In a multitude of people is a king's glory, but in the dearth of people is a prince's ruin" (Proverbs 14:28).[26] As with nations, so with families: "Behold, children are a gift of the LORD; the fruit of the womb is a reward. Like arrows in the hand of a warrior, so are the children of one's youth. How blessed is the man whose quiver is full of them . . ." (Psalm 127:3-5). "How blessed is everyone who fears the LORD. . . . Your wife shall be like a fruitful vine, within your house, your children like olive plants around your table" (Psalm 128:1, 3). It is difficult to reconcile the present preference for small families—usually not more than two children per couple—with this Biblical view of children. Ordinarily, Christians should welcome, not try to avoid, additional children.

As we approach New Testament times, the promises of numerical growth to Israel broaden to include a prophesied extension of the people of God, the believing Gentiles who would be grafted into the olive tree (Romans 11:17-21). For "it is not the children of the flesh who are children of God, but the children of the promise are regarded as descendants" (Romans 9:8), and hence rightful heirs of the promises to Abraham (Romans 4:13-16). This is how it comes about that "the number of the sons of Israel will be like the sand of the sea, which cannot be measured or numbered; and . . . that, in the place where it is said to them, 'You are not My people,' it will be said to them, 'You are the sons of the living God'" (Hosea 1:10; cf. Romans 9:26). This new body, including believing Jews and Gentiles alike, will grow so large that, like "the host of heaven" and "the sand of the sea," it will be innumerable (Jeremiah 33:22).

God's original intention, then, was for man to multiply and fill the earth (Genesis 1:28). That intention was renewed in the covenant with Noah (Genesis 9:1, 7), and again with Abraham (Genesis 17:2) and Isaac (Genesis 26:4, 24), then with the nation of Israel (Deuteronomy 7:13). Then it was renewed with all believers (Hosea 1:10; Romans 9:26). And in the New Testament, the Apostle Paul tells us that God "made from one every nation of mankind to live on *all* the face of the earth, having determined their appointed times, and the boundaries of their habitation" (Acts 17:26, emphasis added). Clearly the Bible envisions, as part of God's purpose, a tremendous human population spread over the globe.

IS THE EARTH FULL ALREADY?

Nonetheless, the Bible is not specific about the magnitude of population that corresponds with the idea of filling the earth. After all, we're not frogs, and perhaps what it means for people to swarm is not quite what it means for frogs. Is it possible that mankind is on the verge of filling the earth, or has reached it already, or has surpassed it, so that now we suffer from overpopulation? Anyone who travels extensively, whether by ground or by air, certainly doesn't get that impression.

Are the United States Crowded?

While doing the research for this book, I drove with my family from northwest Arkansas, where we live, to my old home of Southern California to study regional growth. In the nearly 1,800-mile drive, we passed through scores of large and small towns and moderate-sized cities. Yet mostly we drove through almost-uninhabited country or sparsely populated agricultural land. We traveled in six states with population densities ranging from 12 (New Mexico) to 172 (California) persons per square mile. By comparison, the District of Columbia—which, although mostly central city, has many miles of beautiful parks, parkways, nature trails, a large zoo, and landscaped monuments—has a population density of 9,936 persons per square mile. (To match the District's population density, California's population would have to be fifty-eight times what it is, or 1.6 billion!)

Our experience of open spaces wasn't solely because we traveled in the southwestern portion of the country. A month earlier we had traveled east through Missouri, Illinois, Indiana, Kentucky, Ohio, West Virginia, Virginia, North Carolina, Tennessee, and back through Arkansas. Although towns were closer together, still we drove mostly in agricultural or wilderness areas. In one area of eastern Kentucky we were far enough from any towns big enough to be on our state map that we wondered whether we would run out of gas before we came to the next service station—even though we were pretty sure we had about fifty miles' worth of gas left. The most densely populated state we were in was Ohio (262 persons per square mile); the least was Arkansas (46 persons per square mile).[27]

Even had we traveled in the most densely populated region of the United States—the northeast, with an average of 307 persons per square mile—we still would have driven more miles outside of towns than inside them. Indeed, "urban" areas (defined by the Bureau of the Census as "central cities and adjacent urbanized fringe zones of urbanized areas *plus all incorporated and unincorporated places of 2,500 or more inhabitants outside urbanized areas*") made up only 2.1 percent of the total U.S. land area in 1980.[28] For average 1980 urban-area population density to be maintained for the entire U.S. land area, the country's population would have to be thirty-five times its 1980 size, or almost exactly 8 billion (roughly 80 percent more than present world population).

But does this mean that most Americans suffer extreme crowding? After all, 73.7 percent of our population lives in urban areas, on just 2.1 percent of our land.[29] Do these people live in the "standing-room-only" conditions warned of by population-growth foes? No. As Table 4-1 shows, only about one in ten urban Americans lives in a really large city; one in fifteen in a moderately large city; one in fourteen in a moderate-sized city. Most of our "urban" dwellers live in towns under 100,000.[30]

In fact, most Americans probably consider anyplace with population under 25,000 almost rural. And in 1986, places like that contained about 60 percent of our population.[31] In short, the notion that the United States are being overrun rapidly by crowded cities is simply false.[32]

TABLE 4-1

URBAN AND RURAL POPULATION, BY SIZE OF PLACE, 1980

CLASS, SIZE, NUMBER, AND POPULATION	PERCENT OF POPULATION
Urban*	73.7
Places of 1,000,000 or more (6) (17.5 mil.)	7.7
Places of 500,000-1,000,000 (16) (10.9 mil.)	4.8
Places of 250,000-500,000 (33) (11.8 mil.)	5.4
Places of 100,000-250,000 (114) (16.6 mil.)	7.5
Total in moderate- to large-sized cities (169) (56.8 mil.)	25.4
Places of 50,000-100,000 (250) (16.3 mil.)	8.7
Places of 25,000-50,000 (526) (18.4 mil.)	10.3
Places of 10,000-25,000 (1,260) (19.8 mil.)	12.2
Places of 5,000-10,000 (No. and Pop. not avail.)	6.8
Places of 2,500-5,000.(No. and Pop. not avail.)	4.1
Places under 2500 (No. and Pop. not avail.)	6
Total in "small-town America"	7
Other urban	5.6
Rural	26.3
Places of 1,000-2,500	3.1
Places under 1,000	1.7
Other rural	21.4
Total in rural and "small-town" America	69.0

*Urban = incorporated and unincorporated areas of 2,500 or more persons plus surrounding environs.
Source: U.S. Bureau of the Census, *Statistical Abstract of the United States, 1984*, p. 27, Tables 26, 28.

It might be objected that this view fails to consider the massing together of cities with barely discernible boundaries—what we have come to call *suburban sprawl*. While someone might live in a city with a population of only 75,000, that city might be part of a concentration of such cities with total population in the millions. Do those people suffer more crowding?

Quite the contrary. Suburbs are considerably less crowded than inner cities. Indeed, if we look at Metropolitan Statistical Areas (MSA's) in the United States (which better reflect suburban spawl) rather than at "urban" land, we find that such areas comprise some 16.2 percent of U.S. land area (nearly eight times the area defined as "urban"), but have only marginally more of our population: 76.6 percent as opposed to the 73.7 percent "urban."[33] Compared with an "urban" density of 2,260 per square mile in 1980, the MSA density was only 320.[34] Furthermore, many MSA's include large areas that are rural, since "the general concept of a metropolitan area is one of a large population nucleus, together with adjacent communities which have a high degree of economic and social integration with that nucleus."[35] As we should have figured immediately upon seeing that MSA's comprised nearly eight times as much U.S. land as "urban" areas, MSA's must include roughly seven times more rural than "urban" land.[36] Even most MSA's, despite their including not only cities but also their surroundings, don't have terribly large populations. Of the 332 MSA's in 1986, thirty-five had populations under 100,000; 141 had from 100,000 to 249,999; seventy-two had 250,000 to 499,999; forty-three had 500,000 to 999,999; thirty-two had 1 million to 2,499,999; and only nine had 2.5 million or more.[37]

Another way to determine whether the United States are crowded is to look at a proportional breakdown of land use. Table 4-2 shows that the largest proportion of U.S. land is in forest (not including national and state parks and related recreation areas, and national wilderness and primitive areas). Forest, grassland pasture, and active cropland together make up over three-fourths of our land use. If all of our "urban" land were put into the cropland we use only for pasture, over a fourth of the latter would be left over. In fact, we set aside twice as much land to propagate and protect wildlife as we use for the "urban" land on which three-fourths of our population live. These facts are hardly consistent with the idea that we are overcrowded.

Nonetheless, it's easy to think that the three-fourths of Americans who live in "urban" areas suffer crowding. Yet the 1980 density of 2,260 persons per square mile in "urban" America equates to 12,336 square feet of *land* per person (a figure deceptively high, since some land is used for commercial, industrial, and transportation purposes, but deceptively low too since multi-story buildings greatly increase the effective living area available). The median size of the heated area of a single-family home in the United States is about 1,225 square feet.[38] The average individual "urban" dweller in

TABLE 4-2

LAND USE IN THE UNITED STATES, 1982

TYPE OF LAND USE	ACRES (MILLION)	PERCENT OF TOTAL
TOTAL LAND AREA	2,265	100.0
Forest	655	28.9
Grassland pasture	597	26.4
Cropland used for crops	383	16.9
Marshes, open swamps, bare rock area, deserts, tundra, urban area, and miscellaneous other*	226	10.0
Cropland used only for pasture	65	2.9
Recreation areas (includes national and state parks and related areas, national wilderness and primitive areas)	116	5.1
Urban area*	48	2.1
Wildlife protection and propagation areas	95	4.2
Non-urban transportation (rural highways, roads, railroad rights-of-way, plus airports)	27	1.2
Idle cropland	21	.9
National defense	24	1.1
Farmsteads, farm roads, farm lanes	8	.4

*In the source, urban area is subsumed under "Other land" (represented above by the category description "Marshes, open swamps, etc."). It is listed separately here and estimated based on *Statistical Abstract. . .* 1984, p. 26, Table 24. The figures for "Other land" here are adjusted accordingly.
Percentages do not add up to precisely 100 percent because of rounding.
Source: U.S. Bureau of the Census, *Statistical Abstract of the United States, 1988*, p. 185, Table 320.

America, therefore, has over ten times more square feet of land available to him than the average American family has of heated housing, without even taking into consideration the fact that, in cities, total residential square footage is many times more than total land area because housing units are multi-story.

Are we misled because these figures take into account "small-town America" and not just the major cities most of us call to mind when we hear of urban America? Slightly perhaps, but not much. Population density in central cities in 1980 was 3,551 per square mile, or one to every 7,851 square feet, still over six times the square feet *per person* that the average single-family house affords *per family*, again without considering the multiplication effect of multi-story housing. Furthermore, average density of "urban areas" is decreasing: from 5,408 per square mile in 1950 to 3,752 in 1960, to

2,760 in 1970, to 2,260 in 1980.[39] People are living with more space, not less.

Is the World Crowded?

Are teeming cities gobbling up the world's land? Certainly not. One study in 1974 indicated that all human settlements—including everything from tiny tribal encampments to multi-million-person cities—took up only about 1 percent of the land surface of the earth.[40] The percentage isn't likely to have grown much since then, especially since population growth has tended, worldwide, to be more rapid in densely populated than in sparsely populated areas. Even if only one-fourth of the earth's land surface were suitable for human habitation, total human settlements would cover only 4 percent of that area. And as the market value of habitable space rises, new technology will be found to make more land suitable for habitation.

If the United States, with their population density of roughly 68 per square mile, aren't crowded, what about the world, with its density of about 96 per square mile (excluding Antarctica)?[41] On the average, hardly. That density equates with 290,400 square feet per person, or space equivalent to 237 median-sized American single-family homes or 9.68 football fields. Put another way, if all the people on earth were spread evenly over its land area (excluding Antarctica, but including inland waters), each would have a square to himself measuring 539 feet on each side. If each person stood in the middle of his square, his two closest neighbors would be 539 feet away (the length of 1.8 football fields), and his next two closest would be 1,078 feet, or 3.6 football field lengths, away.

We can get another perspective on world population density by asking what would happen if the world's population were packed into a smaller area. If all of the projected 5.32 billion people living in 1990 lived in the United States, population density would be 1,470 per square mile, about 7 percent less than it was in Taiwan and about 24 percent less than it was in Bangladesh in 1987.[42] If everyone were to live at densities equivalent to the 1980 density of America's central cities (3,551 per square mile), they could live in a single city with four equal sides measuring 1,224 miles (i.e., about 41 percent of the U.S. land area). If everyone lived in Texas, population density would be 20,304 per square mile (1,373 square feet of land area per person), slightly under twice the density of Singapore and three-tenths the density of Macau in 1987.[43] In that case, Texas would form

> one giant city with a population density less than that of many existing cities, and leaving the rest of the world empty. Each man, woman, and child in the 1984 world population could be given more than [1,300] square feet of land space in such a city (the average home in the United States ranges between 1,400 and 1,800 square feet). If one-third of the space of this city were devoted to parks and one-third to industry, each family could still occupy a single-story dwelling of average U.S. size.[44]

Or if all 5.32 billion were invited to a giant party in Anchorage, Alaska, each could stand in a ground area of nine square feet (a square with three-foot sides), leaving all the rest of the world empty.[45] (An architect friend, by the way, tells me that this is about the room-occupancy density at which discomfort begins to turn to panic.)

What About Crowding in Cities?

Are living conditions bearable in densely populated cities? They must be, at least for those who choose to live in them (that is, who could choose otherwise if they were so inclined). Despite the higher-than-average rents in such places, millions of people would rather suffer their disadvantages than forego their advantages. Nearly 1.5 million people lived in Manhattan in 1986 at a density of 66,577 persons per square mile (nearly nineteen times average central-city density in the U.S. in 1980).

What makes big-city crowding endurable? High-rise residential buildings multiply the amount of floor space that can be constructed per square mile, services tend to be available within short distances, and economies of scale make many prices lower in the city than elsewhere. The impact of multi-story apartment complexes is particularly important. Table 4-3 compares two imaginary land-use efficiencies: single-family suburban homes and eighteen-story apartment buildings. For the suburbs, the data assume 2,000-square-foot houses (each including a 500-square-foot, two-car garage) on 3,600-square-foot lots in the suburbs with four-lane streets (plus a parallel parking lane on each side) separating double rows of houses, crossed by four-lane streets (parallel parking on both sides) separating blocks twenty-one houses long, the average house renting for $2,000 per month. For the city, the data assume eighteen-story apartment buildings on 32,400-square-foot lots (each building lot equals nine single-family housing lots adjacent to each other), each building with a 22,320-square-foot base, fifteen stories of 1,500-square-foot apartments renting at $1,000 per month, and three stories of parking garages, with four-lane streets (parallel parking on both sides) separating every building lot from every adjacent building lot, and one 21,600-square-foot recreation area for every five buildings. Both cases assume an average of four persons per residential unit.

TABLE 4-3

LAND USE EFFICIENCIES: CITY VS. SUBURB
(Fictional Example)

USE	QTY PER SQ. MILE		QTY PER CAPITA	
	CITY	SUBURB	CITY	SUBURB
Buildings	400	5,040	.0012	.25
Residential units	8 9,200	5,040	.25	.25
Recreation area, square feet	3,686,400	8,064,000*	10.3	400
Grass area	254,975	*	.71	0
Living units, square feet	133,800,000	10,080,000	375	375
Residents	356,800	20,160	NA	NA
Streets	40 mi.	32 mi.	.59 ft.	8.38 ft
Parking spaces in garages	178,400	10,080	.5	.5
Parking spaces on streets	21,120	16,896	.058	.838
Total parking spaces	199,520	26,976	.559	1.338
Gross rents/yr. ($2,000/mo sub, $1,000/mo city)	$1.07 Bil.	$120,000,000	$3,000	$6,000

*"Recreation area" for the suburban single-family homes consists entirely of single yards, not of large areas dedicated solely to recreational uses.

In this case, high-rise residential buildings made possible a population density almost eighteen times what was possible with single-family homes. Yet the high-rise area still included recreational and grass areas equivalent to 131 football fields. The suburban dwellers enjoyed more parking spaces per person, but the high-rise dwellers still had more than two per household, including street parking, and urban dwellers usually don't need as many cars as suburban and rural residents need. There are fewer suburban dwellers to every mile of their streets, but since they will have to drive farther to get to work than city dwellers, they are more likely to have to drive through each other's neighborhoods, increasing the volume of traffic on their streets. By comparison, many city dwellers can walk or use public transportation for their short commutes.

The point is not to argue that city and suburban living are equivalent in every way, but to show that living in downtown high-rises is not necessarily as crowded as many people who have never lived in them think it is. What most people consider most important is that they have ample living space in their own residences, and in the examples compared in Table 4-3, both city and suburban dwellers had 1,500-square-foot living areas in their homes (the suburbanites having an additional 500 square feet for their two-car garages, the city dwellers having two parking spaces per residence in the large parking garages). Open spaces are more readily available to the suburbanites, but shopping, mass transit, financial institutions, hospitals, and work places are all likely to be much closer to the high-rise residents. And this fanciful example assumes a high-rise density of 365,800 persons per square mile, whereas even in Manhattan, one of the most densely populated inner-city areas in the world, actual population density is only about 67,000 persons per square mile, less than a fifth as high.

True, some people would like to get out of cities. The Hara family we met in Chapter 1 is like many families in big cities. They would like to move, but feel they can't, at least not right away. They've bought a home that might be difficult to sell, Nobu has a job that could be hard to replace elsewhere, and so on. Far from disproving the point that people choose cities, however, this simply proves it. They *could* move, if they were willing to make the necessary sacrifices, but they choose, at least for the present, to suffer the disadvantages rather than to forego the advantages. In addition, people who leave big cities don't always move to rural areas; normally they move to other cities. The Haras, for instance, hope to move from Los Angeles to Seattle, i.e., from a Consolidated MSA of 13 million to one of 2.3 million.[46] It's not so much city living, then, as the sort of life that a particular city gives that seems to bother some people.

Certainly there are problems in cities. The larger the city, the higher its crime rate is likely to be.[47] (It is not, however, high population density that leads to higher crime rates. If other factors—educational level, family income level, family stability, employment, and so on—are controlled for, studies indicate that population density has no significant correlation with crime rates, so that upper-class sections of cities tend to have crime rates about equal to the national average, while lower-class sections of the same density have much higher rates. Neither does population density significantly affect other measures of welfare like longevity, mental illness, or access to recreational facilities.)[48] Air pollution is normally worse in large cities than in rural areas, although drinking water tends to be safer. Cities are noisier than rural areas and small towns.

In short, city life—like suburban or "fringe" or rural life—is a trade-off. I, for one, chose against it. After living in metropolitan Los Angeles for fifteen years, I chose rural life, accepting major sacrifices in income, in access to cultural institutions like museums, concert halls, and libraries, in convenience of shopping (the nearest large supermarket is fifteen miles away, the nearest Sears store about forty-five), in availability of medical care (the nearest town, five miles from me, has only one medical office with two doctors, and a part-time dental office; the nearest small hospital is fifteen miles away, the nearest moderate-sized one forty-five miles, and the nearest large one with multiple specialists about 120 miles), and in access to mass transportation (there are no municipal bus lines within seventy-five miles, no major airports within 100). Yet significant proportions of the nation's and the world's people still choose to live in cities and suburbs, indicating that, in their minds, the advantages outweigh the disadvantages. Who am I to insist that they shouldn't make that choice, or that if they do, they should be pitied?

So long as some people prefer the ratio of conveniences to inconveniences in the city over the ratio outside the city, "crowding" in cities will continue. To speak of this as a problem is misleading because such commentary neglects that it is something people would rather live with than without, granted the costs of eliminating it. As Edward Banfield put it:

> The presence of a great many people in one place is a cause of inconvenience, to say the least. But the advantages of having so many people in one place far outweigh these inconveniences, and

we cannot possibly have the advantages without the disadvantages. To "eliminate congestion" in the city must mean eliminating the city's reason for being. Congestion in the city is a "problem" only in the sense that congestion in Times Square on New Year's Eve is one; in fact, of course, people come to the city, just as they do to Times Square, precisely *because* it is congested. If it were not congested, it would not be worth coming to.[49]

Crowding, after all, is in the mind of the beholder. It all depends on what you're there for. Who, after all, seriously complains about overcrowding at a football game? Yet the population density in, say, the Rose Bowl, assuming the whole stadium complex is the size of five football fields (i.e., 150,000 square feet), is roughly 20,460,000 per square mile (307 times the density of Manhattan)!

What About the Future?

In general, then, neither the world nor our nation nor our cities are "overpopulated" in any meaningful sense of the word. Crowding exists in some places—mainly in inner cities—but it is not necessarily bad. For many people its advantages outweigh its disadvantages. Mankind is a long way from filling up the earth (Genesis 1:28; 9:1, 7).

But how long will things stay this way? Are we on the verge of overrunning the earth's capacity to provide all that we demand? Future chapters will examine this question as it relates to housing, transportation and communication, and recreation (Chapter 5), food and economic growth (Chapter 6), energy and non-energy resources (Chapter 7), and environmental quality (Chapter 8). Before we look at the future, though, we need to address one misconception.

It is not the earth that provides what human beings demand. In fact, aside from a marginally adequate biosphere, the earth provides us with very little. Only about 25 percent of the surface of the globe is land, and of that only a small part is suitable for habitation without man's building shelter to protect himself from the elements. Even land itself—for agriculture, industry, transportation, and habitation—is as much a product of man's making as it is a given; most land is unsuitable for most uses without considerable alteration. Mere hunting and gathering would, in those parts of the world where they are rewarding at all, afford sufficient food for only one to two persons per square mile. It is man's mind operating through his body—both gifts of God—that provides most of what man wants and needs as he reshapes, reconstitutes, and recombines what he finds in nature. In an important sense, the earth has no resources; it has only raw materials, materials that man, by applying knowledge and muscle and machine, turns into resources.[50]

This cautionary note taken, what of the future? Will population overrun the supply of land? What, in fact, will population be at various times in the future?

Unfortunately, reliable population forecasting over the long haul is probably impossible, as demonstrated by repeated failures in the past. Consider, for instance, Julian Simon's brief review of authoritative population projections:

> . . . we have seen some astonishing flipflops in world population forecasts. As of 1969, the U.S. *Department of State Bulletin* forecast 7.5 billion people for the year 2000, echoing the original UN source. By 1974, the figure quoted in the media was 7.2 billion. By 1976, Raphael Salas, the executive director of the UN Fund for Population Activities (UNFPA) was forecasting "nearly 7 billion." Soon Salas was all the way down to "at least 5.8 billion." And as early as 1977, Lester Brown and the Worldwatch Institute (which the UN is supporting) dropped it down again, forecasting 5.4 billion people for the year 2000. This change must be astonishing to laymen—to wit, that the forecast for a date then only twenty-three years away, when a majority of the people who will then be living were already living, could be off by 2 billion people, a change of more than a third of the total current forecast. Does this example of forecasting "science" give us any reason to be impressed by population predictions?[51]

Simon then adds, "Nor is there reason to believe that contemporary forecasting methods are better than older ones."[52]

Why? A variety of reasons might be given. Clearly the population-control efforts supported by the United Nations, the United States Agency for International Development, and a coterie of semipublic agencies based mostly in the United States have had some effect in reducing population growth rates.[53] By attaching conditions of government-sponsored birth-control programs to promises of U.N. and U.S. aid, these efforts have reduced birth rates in a large number of developing countries. (Chapter 6 will argue that this is more likely to harm these countries and their people economically than to help them, contrary to the expectations of their "benefactors.")

More important, however, is the simple unpredictability of much human action. People are not machines; they cannot be programmed and expected to behave as ordered. They have imagination, hopes and fears, emotions, volitions, and goals. These and many other determinants of human action change relative to a constantly changing environment. Begetting and bearing babies are human actions, and like all other human actions they are determined by humans' constantly changing hopes, fears, goals, and choices. In a world in which so many things change so rapidly, it is intellectual suicide for anyone to pretend to predict with accuracy and reliability what large numbers of people will do over long periods of time.

What will happen to population after the next century or two? Will it continue in equilibrium, grow slowly or quickly, or fall slowly or quickly? It is impossible for finite, time-bound minds to know. While there are good reasons to believe that population growth rates will diminish considerably from what they have been in the last two centuries, probably dropping to about a tenth of a percent per year,[54] we cannot unfailingly project what will happen by extrapolating recent and present conditions into the distant future, precisely because the recent and present conditions will not obtain at that time. From the Christian perspective of faith in a God of providence, however, we can be confident that human population will never present an insuperable problem.

One thing that should be clear by the end of this book, however, is that if historical trends[55] continue (and there is no reason to think they are reversing themselves), there is no rational basis for believing that population will ever outgrow its ability to provide for itself using the resources it develops—including the resource of space in which to live and work and play (which is what we really mean, after all, by *land*). On the contrary, what we learn from history is that over the long haul and on the average per-capita health, economic well-being, and psychological well-being tend to improve faster than population grows. Contrary to what seems common sense, we get more land, food, and other resources, and less pollution *per person*, as the world's population grows.[56] This view indicates not an idealistic faith in man (something entirely contrary to my belief in original sin and total depravity), but faith in the marvelous providence of God working through His creatures despite their moral corruption.

POPULATION AND LIVING STANDARDS: HOUSING, TRANSPORTATION AND COMMUNICATION, AND RECREATION

*I*n the previous chapter we saw that, contrary to many popular fears about population growth, the world is neither overpopulated nor likely to get that way in the near future. Rather than a curse on the earth, a large and growing human population should be seen as a blessing.

Here we will address three questions: (1) What are the interrelationships of population growth and housing? (2) What effects do population growth, on the one hand, and transportation and communication, on the other, have on each other? (3) What effects does population growth have on the supply and availability of recreational space?

POPULATION GROWTH AND HOUSING

Since in most parts of the world people don't remain healthy without some sort of shelter from the elements, growing populations require growing stocks of housing. How is housing doing at keeping up with population growth, and what appear to be the prospects for the future?

Housing in the United States

In the United States, housing is keeping up very well. If historical trends are any indicator—and they are all we have to go on—it will keep doing well. Let's look at several measures of how well Americans are housed and see what's happened in them over the years.

1. **Number of rooms per housing unit.** The median number of rooms per housing unit in the United States rose steadily from 1960-1983. In 1960 it was 4.9, in 1970 5.0, in 1980 5.1, and in 1983 5.2. That's an increase of roughly 6 percent in the median number of rooms per unit in twenty-three years. More significant, however, as Table 5-1 demonstrates, is the fact that housing with very few rooms has fallen considerably as a percentage of total housing units. The proportion of housing with one to four rooms fell consistently during those years; the proportion with five and six rooms remained fairly steady; and the proportion with seven or more rooms rose dramatically, from slightly under one in six to slightly over one in five. On the average, then, Americans live in more rooms per household today than they did before.

2. **Number of persons per housing unit and room.** The number of persons per housing unit fell significantly from 1960 through 1983. In owner-occupied housing, the median fell from 3.1 to 2.5, a decline of 19 percent. In renter-occupied housing, the median fell from 2.6 to 2.0, a decline of 23 percent. These declines occurred simultaneously with the rise in median number of rooms per unit from 4.9 to 5.1.[1] Thus, in the eleven years from 1970 through 1981, crowding in American homes diminished significantly. The proportion of American homes with an average of one or fewer persons per room grew from 92 percent to 96 percent, while the proportions of homes with 1.51 or more and 1.01-1.5 persons per room both were cut in half.[2]

3. **Percentage of housing units owned by occupants.** In recent years a common complaint has been that rising housing prices have made the goal of home ownership increasingly difficult for people to attain. The complaint, however, is inconsistent with the facts. The proportion of Americans who own the homes in which they live has

TABLE 5-1

ROOMS PER HOUSING UNIT, 1960-1983
as percent of total

ROOMS	1960	1970	1980	1983	CHANGE
1-3	19.5	16.1	15.4	14.7	-24.6
4	21.3	20.6	19.2	18.9	-11.3
5	24.6	24.8	22.6	23.2	- 5.7
6	19.1	19.8	19.2	19.8	+ 3.7
7 or more	15.5	17.4	21.7	21.2	+36.8

Source: U.S. Bureau of the Census, *Statistical Abstract of the United States, 1988,* p. 688, Table 1221.

risen steadily for over sixty years, from 45.6 percent in 1920 to 64.7 percent in 1983. What's more, blacks and other minorities (who tend to be disproportionately highly represented among low-income earners) increased their rate of home ownership more than twice as much as did whites. The rate of home ownership among whites climbed 40 percent from 48.2 percent in 1920 to 67.7 percent in 1983, while the rate among blacks and other minorities climbed 93 percent from 23.9 percent to 46.2 percent.[3]

4. Amenities in housing. The adequacy of housing for human physical comfort depends in part on the amenities in the structures, as my wife and I learned when we moved into our first house with nothing but two sets of dishes and utensils and an upside-down box for a dining table. The amenities in American housing have risen consistently over the years. From 1960 to 1983, the proportion of housing units with telephones rose from 78.5 percent to 90.4 percent; the proportion with air conditioning from 12.4 percent to 59.1 percent; the proportion served by a public sewer system from 70.2 percent (1970) to 74.3 percent; the proportion served by public or private company water systems from 81.7 percent (1970) to 84.4 percent;[4] the proportion with full plumbing facilities from 86.8 percent to 97.6 percent. The proportion without heating fell from 1.4 percent in 1950 to .8 percent in 1983.[5]

Newer housing also tends to be considerably better equipped than older housing. The proportion of new homes with central air conditioning rose from 34 percent in 1970 to 69 percent in 1986; with a garage, from 58 percent to 74 percent; with electric heating instead of gas (which, on the average, is more expensive),[6] from 28 percent to 44 percent; with a fireplace, from 35 percent to 62 percent; with two or more bathrooms, from 48 percent to 80 per-cent.[7]

5. Cost of housing as proportion of household income. Although current-dollar costs of housing, reflecting inflation, have risen precipitously in recent years (from $43,340 median in 1976 to $93,680 median in 1986), the costs adjusted for inflation, for increased living space per household, and for increased amenities tell a different story. Although the average monthly mortgage payment for recent home buyers rose from $329 in 1976 to $852 in 1986 in current dollars (an apparent increase of 159 percent), the rise in constant (1967) dollars was much smaller: from $193 to $259 (a real increase of 34 percent). Meanwhile, median household income for all Americans, in constant (1967) dollars, rose from $8,780 to $8,955, and for recent home buyers it rose even more, from $9,656 to $10,867. Thus the average monthly mortgage payment for recent home buyers, as a proportion of their income, rose only 19 percent in the ten years. In addition, the trend in the first half of the ten-year period was upward, while the trend in the second half was downward. Meanwhile, the average size of new homes was growing, from 1,644 square feet in 1976 to 1,825 in 1986, an increase of 11 percent.

Thus the average monthly mortgage payment for recent home buyers, as a proportion of their income and calculated per square foot of housing, rose only 8 percent. And it is likely that the value of the increased amenities (see item 4 above) more than makes up for that difference. Americans are getting more housing and amenities for their money, not less, despite appearances to the contrary.[8]

These are averages and medians. They do not mean that every American can afford average American housing. That is always the case with averages and medians; some people are above and some below. But rising averages and medians do tell us that, in general, housing for each relative segment of the income scale is improving. The average American consumer in 1985, for instance, spent roughly 30 percent of his after-tax income on housing (including shelter, fuel, utilities, public services, household operations, and furnishings); the average consumer in the bottom 20 percent of Americans' income devoted only a slightly higher proportion of his expenditures to housing—34 percent—and had he reduced his expenditures for alcohol, smoking, and entertainment by half, he could have devoted an additional 4 percent of his expenditures to housing.[9] To get some sense of what this means, a family spending 34 percent of its post-tax income of $10,000 per year on rent in 1986 ($1,000 less than average expenditures for the lowest 20 percent of incomes in 1985) could pay $283 per month in rent. That's about what average rent was at the time in metropolitan areas of northeast Pennsylvania, Seattle, Dallas-Fort Worth, and Minneapolis-St. Paul; significantly above average rent for Anchorage, Cincinnati, Denver-Boulder, Miami, Milwaukee, Portland, St. Louis, Atlanta, Buffalo, Cleveland, Houston, Kansas City, and Pittsburgh; and significantly below average in Boston, San Diego, Washington, D.C. and surroundings, Honolulu, and San Francisco-Oakland.[10] By shifting an additional 4 percent of expenditures from alcohol, smoking, and entertainment to housing, such a family could have paid above-average rent in any of those places but Boston and San Francisco-Oakland.[11] Inflation has pushed rents higher since then, but it has also raised incomes, in some places more than rent.

Housing Trends Worldwide

Evaluating trends in quality and quantity of housing worldwide is more difficult than evaluating them in the United States. Data are less readily available and less reliable for most countries, and almost completely unavailable for many low-income countries. Nonetheless, it appears that most countries around the world are, more or less rapidly, following the same path the United States have taken: from less-adequate to more-adequate housing. One fairly simple indicator of this is the extent of urbanization. Urban housing tends, on the average, to be better and less costly than rural, for a variety of reasons (economies of scale, availability of utilities and transportation, etc.). In every part of the world, proportions of populations living in urban instead of rural areas are growing, as shown in Table 5-2.

This indicates that, on the average and in the long run, housing is becoming more adequate, not less, worldwide. While it is possible to point to exceptions to this trend, it certainly seems unlikely that anyone would argue that housing in the less-developed countries is equal to or better than housing in the more-developed countries; yet urbanization is progressively higher as we climb the ladder of development, as the table shows. Whether increasing urbanization causes improved housing conditions or the two are both effects of some other underlying cause does not concern us here; what does is that there is a strong correlation between urbanization and improved housing.

TABLE 5-2

WORLDWIDE URBANIZATION OF POPULATION

	URBAN POPULATION			
	AS PERCENTAGE OF TOTAL POPULATION		AVERAGE ANNUAL GROWTH RATE (PERCENT)	
WORLD SEGMENT	1965	1984	1965-73	1973-84
Low-income economies	17	23	4.5	4.6
Middle-income economies	36	49	4.5	4.1
Lower middle-income	26	37	5.1	4.2
Upper middle-income	49	65	3.9	4.1
High-income oil exporters	36	70	9.2	7.7
Industrial market economies	72	77	1.8	1.2
East European nonmarket economies	52	64	2.6	1.8

Source: The World Bank, *World Development Report 1986* (New York/Oxford: Oxford University Press, 1986), pp. 240-1, Table 31.

The economies of scale made possible by the concentration of people in cities make it easier for many people to support themselves there than in rural areas. (This becomes increasingly apparent as food prices, reflecting the historic trend for agricultural productivity to outpace population growth, fall, making it increasingly difficult for people to support themselves by farming.) Thus many developing countries experience rapid migration from countryside to cities. On arriving in the cities, immigrants find that the best route to economic independence and self-sufficiency in housing is to start with a very small dwelling, often nothing more than a hut or a tent on a small piece of land (probably like what they lived in before they migrated). Once they have gained full title to that, they can sell it to new migrants and begin moving, step-by-step, up the housing ladder.

Why do they leave the country for the city when their first houses there are little different from what they leave behind? Partly, as we have already noted, to take advantage of the greater opportunities for work that the city offers (often self-employment as vendors, taxi drivers, or simple laborers). But there are two additional reasons: (1) Although the dwellings they first occupy in the city may differ little from, or perhaps be smaller or flimsier than, their homes in the country, they are more likely to benefit from services like roads, sewers, water, and trash pickup than they were in the country, and the degree to which those services are available plays a major role in determining how desirable and healthful housing is. (2) The greater job opportunities translate into increased likelihood that someday these people will be able to own their own homes, thus climbing out of the dependency of renting.

When we in developed countries see film of these sometimes vast "tent cities" in less-developed countries, we tend to assume that they indicate a problem. In reality, they indicate a problem being solved. The tents and huts massed together differ little, individually, from those scattered across the countryside that the urban immigrants left. Collectively, they appear to present a picture of desperate and hopeless poverty. The opposite, however, is more often true: they are the first step in an upward movement toward private home ownership and increasing adequacy of housing for those who never could have become economically productive enough in the country to make the same climb.

The development of "informal" urban communities in Peru's capital city of Lima illustrates the trend. In forty years, Lima's population has grown from about 560,000 to nearly 6.8 million—twelve times its former size. A majority of that growth has been in the form of informal urban communities, large clusters of huts built by migrants without permits from the municipal bureaucracy. Some migrants come from the surrounding countryside and some from the city's badly deteriorated slums. Just when the informal housing movement began in Peru is difficult to determine, but by 1940 it accounted for about 4 percent of all new dwellings in Lima, after which it climbed steadily as a proportion of new housing, to 15 percent in 1945, 28 percent in 1954, 57 percent in 1968, 62 percent in 1975, and 69 percent in 1985. By 1982, 47 percent of Lima's total population "lived in informal settlements, 45.7 percent in formal neighborhoods, and the remaining 7.3 percent in slum areas." During the same time, publicly subsidized housing has never accounted for more than 16 percent of new dwellings in the city.[12]

More important from the standpoint of quality of housing is the tendency for this informal housing to improve radically over time. While informal settlements may start out as simple huts, they don't stay that way. The fact that the homes are privately owned gives their owners incentive to improve them. Thus "the average value of an informal dwelling [in Lima in 1984] was $22,038 and the total value of the buildings located in Lima's informal settlements came to $8,319.8 million, an amount equivalent to 69 percent of Peru's total long-term external debt in that same year."[13]

The compelling force in this movement, according to Peruvian economist Hernando de Soto, is people's desire to own their own homes, to have secure, private property and the rights that come with it. "The history of the informal settlements," writes de Soto, "is the history of the informals' struggle to own private land."[14] The informals' success in the struggle is reflected in home ownership statistics for Lima:

In the period between 1961 and 1981, independently owned housing in Lima increased by 375 percent, while rented housing declined by 34 percent. This means that people abandoned rural areas or rental slum dwellings in formal [i.e., legally recognized] neighborhoods, to live in their own homes in informal settlements, thereby seeking to lay the essential basis for participating in the incipient market economy generated by Peru's people. As a result, in districts of Lima with a large proportion of informal settlements, the percentage of owner-occupied dwellings is greater than in formal neighborhoods. For instance, in Villa Maria del Triunfo, an informal neighborhood, over 99 percent of the homes are owner-occupied; in Breña, where there is virtually no informal housing, only 28 percent of all homes are owner-occupied. The development of informality has brought home ownership to a larger percentage of low-income residents than middle-income residents.[15]

Despite the risks and time-consuming delays inherent in the informal housing movement (because it operates largely outside the law), the disadvantaged people of Peru have shown a resolute willingness to beat the odds for the sake of a chance to lift themselves out of poverty.[16] And the city, the perfect setting for low-capital entrepreneurship, is where they find the greatest opportunities to better themselves, beginning with housing.[17]

POPULATION GROWTH, TRANSPORTATION, AND COMMUNICATION

Imagine for a moment that you're traveling by car. To your chagrin, you drive over a bunch of tacks that scattered over the road when a box dropped off a flatbed truck. All four of your tires are flat. Now, where you would rather be? (1) In a middle-class downtown residential or business section of most cities? (2) In a rural farming area where the nearest farmhouse with a phone is four miles away and the nearest gas station that sells tires is fifteen miles away? (3) In the wide-open stretches of New Mexico, where the nearest house might be fifteen miles away, and the nearest tire store a hundred?

If the answer is as obvious to you as it is to me, you have a sound intuitive understanding of the relationship between population, on the one hand, and transportation and communication, on the other.[18] The cost per capita of transportation and communication facilities (e.g., roads, gas stations, tire stores; telephones, radio stations, television stations) is always lower in densely populated than in sparsely populated regions. That's why major metropolitan areas can afford to build and maintain eight-lane freeways with their elaborate systems of interchanges, while rural counties, like the one I live in, have a tough time keeping their dirt roads graded. It's why large airports are located in or near cities, not in Montana's Glacier National Monument. It's why Contel of Arkansas is just now preparing to make all private phone lines available to rural customers in my area, while they've been standard service to in-town customers just five miles away for twenty years. It's why I can't get cable television service, but people in most cities have over fifty cable channels readily available to them. And it's why I can't receive a single twenty-four-hour radio news station, even though there is one in almost every major city in America. Far from putting a strain on transportation and communication services, population growth makes their cost per capita lower by multiplying the number of persons who can use them and thus share in bearing their costs.

Unfortunately, this fact often is obscured by reports of the huge price tags on urban transportation systems. For example, the 4.4-mile section of the Metro Rail system under construction in downtown Los Angeles has an estimated price of $1.2 billion. While that undoubtedly is a lot of money (and Metro Rail is not an economical way to solve the transportation problems that plague Los Angeles),[19] when viewed as cost per person in Los Angeles and compared with what it would cost per person if located elsewhere but built at the same price, the picture changes considerably. It amounts to $368 per resident of Los Angeles. If it were built to serve Nashville-Davidson, Tennessee—which covers almost the same land area as Los Angeles—it would cost nearly seven times as much per resident: $2,532.[20]

Another thing that often obscures the efficiency of transportation in heavily urbanized areas is the density of traffic that often significantly reduces average driving speeds. The Southern California Association of Governments predicts, for instance, that average speed on the Southern California freeway system will drop from 35 to 19 miles per hour by the turn of the century.[21] This problem, however, is more properly attributed to the failure of local governments to foresee and prepare for population growth patterns as quickly as they once did than to population density itself. State and local governments, largely in an effort to force Southern Californians to end their love affair with cars, put the skids on new freeway construction in the mid-1970s. Since then, with continued rapid population growth in the region, traffic volume has roughly doubled, but almost no new freeways have been built. Increased traffic congestion is an inevitable result. The solution is not to slow, stop, or reverse regional population growth (which would simply force people to move farther from their jobs, hence to drive more miles to and from work, and thus to exacerbate traffic congestion all the more), but to respond to population growth with increased freeway construction.[22]

Despite the maddening congestion of highways in some major city areas, however, a different perspective might lead to a more positive assessment of transportation in those areas. The key is to compare them with rural areas and to recognize the real purpose of transportation. *The real purpose of transportation is not to go fast, but to get where you're going safely and comfortably in a convenient amount of time.* These might sound like two ways of saying the same thing, but in reality they are not.

"Where you're going" is not so much a given address as it is a provider of a service (a place to work, shop, enjoy a concert). These places normally are much closer to the average resident in a major metropolitan area than to the average resident in a rural area. If a large shopping mall is just five miles away, it hardly matters if you can only drive thirty miles per hour; it takes only ten minutes to get there. But if you live in a rural area and the nearest shopping mall is twenty miles away, it will take twenty-four minutes to get there even at fifty miles per hour. If the Los Angeles Music Center is thirty miles away and you can average thirty miles per hour on the way there, you'll be there in an hour. But if the Tulsa Opera House is 120 miles away and you can average sixty miles per hour, you'll need two hours to get there.

Furthermore, safety and comfort are generally better on urban than rural roads and highways. While nonfatal injury accidents are about 60 percent more common on urban than on rural roads, fatal accidents are about 70 percent more common on rural than on urban roads.[23] And urban roads, because they are supported by bigger tax bases, generally are kept in better condition than rural roads, making for smoother, more comfortable rides.

No doubt the frustrations of slow driving in congested city areas are real, but the alternative of small-town or rural driving is not necessarily any better, and in most cases it is worse.[24]

Population has, in principle, the same relationship to transportation and communication all over the world that it has in the United States. Higher population densities make better transportation systems "both more necessary and more economical. Twice as many people in a small village implies that twice as many people will use a wagon path if it is built, and also implies twice as many hands with which to build the wagon path. . . ."[25] The effect is not merely a matter of convenience—how long it takes to go shopping or to a concert—but also, in many places, of life-or-death importance. The better and bigger an area's transportation system, the less expensive it is, per capita, to transport goods of all sorts. For farmers in less-developed countries, the difference between having and not having adequate transportation can mean the difference between using and not using fertilizer on their crops, or between having only a small local market or a large regional market (or even a world market) for their crops.[26] The same principles apply to communication systems as well.

Quite simply, more people mean more and better transportation and communication, not only absolutely but also per person, because people are not only consumers, but also producers of these services, and they tend to produce, directly and indirectly, more than they consume. As we will see in the next chapter, this is part of how a rising population improves a country's economy.

WHERE CAN WE GO TO PLAY?

It may be clear how transportation and communication, and even housing, improve with increasing population, other things being equal.* But what about recreation? Don't more people mean there's

---

*The qualifying phrase "other things being equal" is neither trifling nor disingenuous. It alerts us to the important fact that the beneficial economic effects of population growth (of which we will see more in Chapter 6) are not automatic—i.e., they do not occur under all circumstances. A population's worldview—including especially its

less space left for people to relax, to play, to enjoy the beauty of nature?

Yes and no. It's simple to see that 5 billion people in the world mean more people per acre of land than 1 billion, and it's tempting to conclude that space for play therefore is more scarce with 5 billion than with 1 billion people. But the temptation rests on a misunderstanding of the scarcity of recreational opportunities.

The Himalayan Mountains have a very low population density and are among the grandest natural wonders in the world, but they're not the greatest recreational attraction in the world. Why not? Because they're so hard to get to that few people ever visit them. And why are they so hard to get to? Because the transportation systems—airports, railroads, and highways—in and near them are minimal. Those systems, in turn, are minimal because the population density there is so low that it won't support more-developed systems. In contrast, Orange County, California, is one of the more densely populated regions in the United States. Yet its beaches, amusement parks, and cultural institutions attract millions of visitors annually. It is not the mere existence of recreational space (whether developed or natural), but its accessibility to people that is important.

As we saw in Table 4-2, recreational area (including national and state parks and forests, national wilderness and primitive areas, and wildlife protection and propagation areas) comprises nearly 40 percent of the total land in the United States—about eighteen times the "urban" area on which three-fourths of our people live. Historically, the trend is toward our having more, not less, open land like that.[27] The acreage in the national park system almost tripled between 1960 and 1986. More important, however, the land is becoming increasingly accessible. Visits to national parks climbed

---

understanding of the nature of man, morality, the animate and inanimate world, and the proper workings of civil government—has tremendous importance in determining economic well-being. While we can predict with confidence that economic growth will outdistance population growth in a society whose worldview remains largely Christian, abandoning that worldview might make the opposite occur. It should not be inferred from this, however, that population growth within the context of a continuously non-Christian worldview is necessarily harmful. While we can predict economic harm from replacing the Christian worldview with a non-Christian one, possibly even despite population growth's normal beneficial effects, those effects can cause economic betterment within a culture dominated continuously by a non-Christian worldview. The present point is simply that population growth is normally (i.e., other things being equal) helpful to an economy rather than harmful. (For the importance of worldview to economic performance, see Beisner, *Prosperity and Poverty*, Chapters 6, 7, and 14.)

from 79.2 million in 1960 (an average of slightly under one-half visit per person) to 364.6 million in 1986 (an average of over 1.5 visits per person), an increase of 360 percent (compared with population growth of 34 percent over the same period).[28] Similar trends have occurred in state park and recreation areas, with acreage increasing by 47 percent from 1981 to 1986 and visits by 23 percent from 1980 to 1986.[29]

TABLE 5-3

ATTENDANCE AT SPECTATOR SPORTS, 1960 AND 1986
(in thousands)

	1960	1986	% INCREASE
Total population	180,671	241,596	34
Sport			
Major league baseball	20,261	48,452	139
Professional basketball	1,986	11,491	478
Professional football	4,154	17,304	316
Professional hockey	2,387	11,621	386
Horse racing	46,879	70,580	51
Greyhound racing	7,924	25,759	225
College basketball	*29,104	37,106	27
College football	20,403	36,388	78

*1978 attendance.
Sources: U.S. Bureau of the Census, *Statistical Abstract of the United States, 1988*, p. 218, Table 372; U.S. Bureau of the Census, *Statistical Abstract of the United States, 1982-83*, p. 236, Table 401.

The majority of our recreation doesn't occur in huge natural parks, though. It occurs in our own homes and communities while we enjoy games, movies, sports, amusement parks, and reading. If money expenditures are any indication of the amount of time we spend on recreation and entertainment, Americans have been enjoying more and more of these lately. Total personal consumption expenditures for recreation, measured in constant dollars, tripled from 1960 to 1986, rising almost six times faster than population. It also rose in proportion to total personal spending, from 5.5 percent to 7.1 percent, an increase of 29 percent.[30] Attendance at spectator sports has risen several times faster than population, as shown in Table 5-3. Participation in recreational activities has risen right along with it, as shown in Table 5-4.

Rather than diminishing our opportunities for recreation, a

growing population increases them. Why? Partly because many of our recreational activities require our participating with other people; the more people there are near us, the more likely we are to find others who want to play jai alai or racquetball. Partly because a growing population causes a growing transportation system, which makes it easier for us to reach the wilderness regions in which we can enjoy nature. And partly, too, because some spectator sports simply are not economically feasible in locales with small populations. Professional football, basketball, and baseball teams can only operate in cities large enough to support them; the more such cities there are, the more teams there can be.

TABLE 5-4

PARTICIPATION IN RECREATIONAL ACTIVITIES, 1970, 1986
(in thousands)

	1960	1986	% INCREASE
Total population	205,052	241,596	17
Activity			
Amateur softball players	16,000	41,000	156
Golfers	11,245	20,200	80
Tennis players	10,655	18,017	70
Tenpin bowlers	51,800	67,000	29
Motion picture attendance	921,000	1,017,000	10
Bicycles purchased	6,900	12,300	78
Recreational boats owned	8,800	14,300	63
Sport fishing licenses sold	31,100	*35,700	15
Sport hunting licenses sold	22,200	*27,700	25

*1985 sales.
Source: U.S. Bureau of the Census, *Statistical Abstract of the United States, 1988*, p. 219, Table 373, p. 221, Table 377.

The same story could be told of Americans' participation in the arts and other leisure activities. More Americans are visiting more museums and art galleries, attending more live theatrical, symphonic, choral, and operatic performances, and reading more novels, plays, short stories, and poetry than ever before. Higher percentages than ever before are involved in leisure-time activities like swimming, jogging, camping, hiking, weight lifting, calisthenics, volleyball, aerobics, ping-pong, boating, and on and on.

CONCLUSION

A careful look at the relationship between population growth and crowding shows that more people do not necessarily translate into more crowding. In many instances, population growth increases people's ability to get away from crowds. Even where crowding occurs, it is not an unmitigated evil; its effects are mixed, and in most cases more people appear eager to enjoy its benefits despite its problems than are willing to forego its benefits to escape its problems. At least so far as mankind's need for space is concerned, the world is not overpopulated and shows no signs of becoming so. Housing, transportation, communication, and recreation all increase in both quantity and quality, not just absolutely but per capita, as population grows.

These empirical facts are consistent with the theological and moral lessons we discovered in Scripture at the beginning of the previous chapter: population growth is a blessing, not a curse. What Solomon called glory for a king—a multitude of people (Proverbs 14:28)—turns out to be a great benefit for his subjects as well.

MALTHUS UNDONE: HOW POPULATION GROWTH AND ECONOMIC GROWTH RELATE

Chapter 4 argued, on the basis of Biblical ethics and anthropology, that population growth is, in principle, desirable, and Chapter 5 that the world is not overpopulated. Aside from compelling reasons to the contrary, we ought to welcome new people. But increasingly in recent decades, people have argued that there are compelling reasons to limit population growth.

The essence of the growth-limitation argument is simple: while population grows geometrically, economic production increases only arithmetically. Only recurrent and severe famines will prevent population from outgrowing production. Compassionate people don't like to see others suffer, so we ought not to permit population growth to outpace production growth. It is not, however, clear why production should increase only arithmetically, while population increases geometrically (or, for that matter, why population should always increase; recall from Chapter 4 that population has fallen in some regions at some times and has, for most of human history, held almost steady worldwide). After all, every mouth born into the world normally comes with two hands. Why shouldn't those hands produce enough to satisfy that mouth—and other mouths too?

Proponents of the conventional theory have an answer: the productivity of labor (units of output per worker hour) rises or falls in direct proportion to the capital laborers can use, and the addition of new laborers diminishes the ratio of capital to labor, thus diminishing the average laborer's productivity.

But why should the ratio of capital to labor fall as population grows? Might it not rise? To this they have several answers: (1) The law of diminishing returns: the resources we turn into capital at a given time are those most cheaply developed; therefore, as time goes by, we turn to resources that are increasingly costly to develop. (2) The negative impact of added children on saving: each child reduces the proportion of income his parents are able to save, since they must devote more income to feeding and otherwise providing for him. (3) The negative impact of added children on time devoted to work: each new child increases the demand on her parents (especially her mother) for time spent in child-rearing, which diminishes parents' time available for productive work. (The extent of both the materialism and the shortsightedness of the anti-population-growth perspective is apparent here. If nurturing children made in the image of God, training them to love and serve others and to work hard, isn't productive work, what is it? And if children, once raised, become productive workers, how is it that raising them was not productive work?)

EFFECT OF POPULATION ON ECONOMY: MALTHUSIAN THEORY

The gist of this argument was clear as far back as the work of Thomas Robert Malthus, a minister and economist whose *Essay on the Principle of Population* (1798) set the tone for most considerations of population growth's economic impact.[1] Wrote Malthus in the first edition of his *Essay*:

> . . . the power of population is definitely greater than the power in the earth to produce subsistence for man. Population when unchecked increases in a geometrical ratio. Subsistence increases only in an arithmetical ratio. A slight acquaintance with numbers will show the immensity of the first power in comparison with the second.

Therefore,

Population does inevitably increase where there are the means of subsistence, the history of every people that have ever existed will abundantly prove.[2]

In other words, population will always grow to the limit of "the power in the earth to produce subsistence." Then it will be checked solely by the inability of some to survive—i.e., by starvation (or sometimes by war). Mankind must suffer regular, severe famines. Thus did economics acquire the reputation of "the dismal science."

Considering Malthus's theory from the perspective of the late twentieth century, it is easy to underestimate its persuasive power. Sitting atop the pinnacle of two centuries of rapid economic growth in both the developed and most of the less-developed world, we may be excused for protesting, "But look, there are many times more people now than there were in Malthus's day, and our income per capita is many times more. We enjoy far higher standards of living than most of Malthus's contemporaries could have dreamed of. He *must* have been wrong."

While that response may in the end be right—and we will argue that it is—it is not sufficient in itself. Malthusian theory will not succumb so easily. It can shift ground slightly, arguing that, until recently, total human population hadn't begun to press the limits of the earth's capacity to provide sustenance. Now, however, things are different, and Malthus is about to be vindicated.[3]

Critique of Malthusian Theory

Shortly we will see whether refinements to Malthus's theory are sufficient to save the general perspective. First, however, let's look at some obvious errors in the basic theory.

1. MAN'S PRODUCTIVE CAPACITY

Malthus mistakenly assumed that it was the earth that provided for man, not man himself—particularly not man under the loving care of an omnipotent and omniscient Providence. His central thesis, as we have just seen, was that "the power of population is definitely greater than *the power in the earth to produce subsistence for man*." Such language, if taken seriously and at face value, implies that man never progresses beyond hunting the game and gathering the fruits that naturally grow around him.[4] Yet hunting and gathering have not been the chief occupations of significant portions of mankind for thousands of years. Indeed, even the most hospitable locales could hardly support more than one or two persons per square mile by hunting and gathering. At that rate, the world's population must have peaked at 50 to 100 million, a height it topped over two thousand years ago[5] and now surpasses by fifty to 100 times. At the very least, then, Malthusian population theory must be drastically revised to account for man's own productive capacities.

2. THE EFFECTS OF CAPITAL AND DIVISION OF LABOR

Malthus largely ignored the multiplication effects of capital (tools) and the division of labor on workers' productivity. Bare hands attempting to produce everything a person needs from raw materials to finished product can achieve little. Adding even the simplest tools and slightest division of labor, however, greatly multiplies their productivity. Over two centuries ago Adam Smith showed that in the trade of pin making, for instance, the division of labor multiplied workers' productivity by 240 to 4,800 times.[6] If the economy at the dawn of the Industrial Revolution could multiply a worker's productivity that much, what effect must the economy of our day have? And of the future?

Suppose for a moment that hunting and gathering can support one person per square mile at subsistence and that the economic organization achieved by the beginning of the Industrial Revolution had multiplied average worker productivity by only 100 times (from 2 to 42 percent of its multiplication effect on pin making). That economy, then, could have supported the earth's 1989 population of 5.2 billion at subsistence.[7] Since then, increased capital and organization have multiplied the productivity of labor many times again. Malthus's neglect of these facts left a gaping hole in his theory.

3. DISCOVERY, INNOVATION, AND INVENTION

Malthus's theory, in this simple form, fails to consider the effects of discovery, innovation, and invention on economic productivity and welfare. We are thinking here not simply of the use of tools (covered under the previous point) but of finding (a) new resources to do the job of older ones, (b) new and more efficient ways and machines to use old resources, and (c) new sources of old resources. Rather than an unchanging supply of resources with which man can meet his needs, as assumed by Malthusian theory, history shows a constantly growing supply. Rather than dividing the same resource pie into smaller and smaller pieces as population grows, we bake more pies.

Coal offers a good example. W. Stanley Jevons, one of the finest social scientists of his day, predicted in 1865, as Julian Simon summarizes, "that England's industry would soon grind to a halt due to exhaustion of England's [domestic and imported] coal."[8] Jevons produced a chart showing past coal supply and use and projecting them into the future, purportedly "showing the impossibility of a long continuance of that progress." The perceived need for more coal, however, combined with the opportunity to gain profits, gave prospectors incentive to find new deposits, engineers incentive to find more efficient methods of transporting coal and converting it to heat, inventors incentive to find alternative methods to generate the heat coal provided, and so on. The results were that England not only exceeded the consumption of coal that Jevons had called "impossible," but also found huge additional domestic and foreign deposits, developed cheaper and faster ways to mine and import it, and developed ways to use oil and other resources (eventually nuclear fission) as substitutes. There now is no end in sight to England's access to whatever energy it needs from a wide variety of sources—including cheaper coal. The same holds true in the United States and elsewhere:

> . . . the proven U.S. reserves of coal are enough to supply a level of use far higher than at present for many hundreds of years into the future. And the use of coal is even being subsidized in some countries even though coal's labor cost per unit of output has been *falling* continuously . . . because the cost of *other* fuels has dropped even more. This suggests that *not enough* coal was mined in the past. . . .[9]

The supply of wood provides a similar example. In 1905 President Theodore Roosevelt warned Americans, "A timber famine is inevitable."[10] Yet by 1971 Sherry Olson could report that a "glut of low grades of factory lumber exists. . . . In spite of expanded uses of timber for pulp and paper, we are probably growing more cubic feet of wood annually than we were in 1910."[11] United States domestic timber production in 1970, a year before Olson wrote, was 11.1 billion cubic feet, up 24 percent from a decade earlier; by 1985 it was 12.4 billion cubic feet, up another 12 percent. Per capita consumption of timber products rose from 63.3 cubic feet in 1960 to 77.7 cubic feet in 1984.[12] While the inflation-adjusted price of wood and wood products in the United States rose slightly in that time,[13] indicating a slight increase in its economic scarcity,[14] there appears no likelihood of a shortage of wood in the foreseeable future.

Innovation, invention, and discovery have, in fact, made almost all natural resources less costly through the years, indicating that resources are becoming less scarce with time.[15] This is precisely opposite the results predicted by Malthusian theory.

4. ECONOMIES OF SCALE

Basic Malthusian theory ignores the effect on productivity of rising economies of scale engendered by increasing population. A region with high population can afford to build far more rapid and efficient transportation and communications systems than can a region of equal size with low population. These diminish the cost of moving goods and transmitting information. Businesses that cater to tens or hundreds of thousands of people can afford to live on smaller profit margins than businesses that cater to only scores or hundreds, making prices lower. Large numbers of people living near each other cause increased division of labor and accumulation of capital, multiplying labor's productivity. These and other economies-of-scale effects of population growth tend to increase productivity, offsetting the opposite tendency on which Malthusian theory focuses.

To summarize these four points, simple Malthusian theory fails to quantify and compare the positive and negative effects of population growth on economic productivity. Instead, it almost completely ignores the positive effects and overstates the negative.

5. DISTINGUISHING SHORT TERM FROM LONG TERM

One implication of the first four points is that basic Malthusian theory fails to distinguish between short-term and long-term effects of population growth on economy. By focusing on added people as consumers rather than producers, it implicitly focuses on their youth, the period when they consume more than they produce. Of course during their childhood added people represent a per-capita economic loss to society.[16] But children grow up to be productive adults.

Various economic analyses give different answers to the question, "What is the ratio of the average man or woman's production to his or her costs to society in a lifetime?" However, consistent with the historic and worldwide trend to higher and higher standards of living despite growing population, the studies all indicate that in their lifetimes people produce several times more on the average than they consume. One study, for instance, indicates that the average American male produces or occasions the production of 13.5 times, and the average female 6.5 times, as much material wealth as he or she costs in a lifetime.[17] While population growth spells a short-term decline in production per capita, it spells a long-term rise—i.e., a rise in production that outpaces the rise in population. The Malthusian focus on the short term is one facet of its failure to balance positive against negative effects.

Let's contemplate this point for a moment from an ethical perspective. Its factual implications are: (a) a decrease in population growth rate yields short-term per-capita economic benefit by reducing, short term, the ratio of consumers to producers. But (b) the same decrease in population growth rate yields long-term per-capita economic loss by reducing, long term, the ratio of producers to consumers. Conversely, (c) a steady population growth rate (not to be confused with a steady population size, = zero population growth) yields short-term per-capita economic loss (which may be either an absolute loss or a comparative loss—i.e., slower short-term growth than otherwise) by reducing, short term, the ratio of producers to consumers. But (d) the same steady population growth rate yields long-term per-capita economic benefit by reducing, long term, the ratio of consumers to producers.

In other words, slowing population growth now is enriching our own generation at the expense of future generations; sustaining growth now is enriching future generations at our own expense. As Julian Simon so aptly put it, ". . . we should remember that our long run will be someone else's short run, just as our short run was someone else's long run. Some measure of unselfishness should impel us to keep this in mind as we make our decisions about population policy."[18] The Biblical ethic of self-sacrifice for others' good (in addition to the Biblical notion of the value of human life in general, which we discussed in Chapter 2) certainly gives presumptive support to the idea that we ought to sustain rather than reduce population growth rates. "Greater love has no one than this, that one lay down his life for his friends" (John 15:13). The selfish generation, not the generous one, curtails population growth.

6. ECONOMIC FACTS CONTRADICT MALTHUSIANISM

Broad implications of Malthusian theory for local/regional economies, national economies, and the world economy are counterfactual. These implications are: (a) as population density rises, per-capita production should fall; (b) as population density rises, food provision per capita should fall; (c) worldwide per-capita production measured in real goods and services (or in inflation-adjusted monetary units) ought to decline as population grows. Let's look at each of these separately. (Detailed data and analysis on which the following discussion is based are to be found in Appendix 2. References to tables in the text of this chapter all are to tables in that appendix.)

6A. POPULATION DENSITY AND PER-CAPITA PRODUCTION

Rising population density does not consistently accompany falling per-capita production. On the contrary, low, moderate, and high levels of production per capita are to be found at all levels of population density. (See Table 6-1-A.) The lowest GNP per capita, on the average, is not among nations with the highest population densities, as Malthusian theory leads us to expect, but among nations in the third and fourth quintiles of density. (Quintiles are one-fifth subsets of a larger sample, defined in ascending or descending order. For example, in the numbers 1-100, the first quintile in ascending order is 1-20, the second is 21-40, etc.) Conversely, the highest GNP per capita, on the average, is not among nations with the lowest population densities, as Malthusianism suggests, but among nations in the highest quintile of density.[19]

Defenders of Malthus might respond that the high GNP's among high-density nations only prove Malthus's assertion that population grows to meet the capacity of production to provide for it, but the response misreads Malthus. What Malthus taught, and what basic Malthusianism has always held, is that population grows to meet the capacity of production to provide for its subsistence, and production's capacity to provide for population's subsistence is production's upper limit over the long term. In other words, Malthusianism adequately predicts that there must be a high GNP where there is a high density of population, but it also predicts that where there is a high density of population the GNP per capita must be low. That is inconsistent with the data.

Another way to see this weakness in Malthusianism is to compare individual nations of closely similar population densities. If Malthusianism is correct, their demographic and economic profiles should be closely similar. Mauritania, Botswana, and Australia all have 5 persons per square mile. Yet Mauritania's GNP per capita in 1984 was $450; Botswana's was more than double that, $960; and

Australia's was more than twelve times Botswana's, $11,740. Similar phenomena inconsistent with Malthusian predictions appear at all density levels.[20]

6B. POPULATION DENSITY AND CALORIE SUPPLY

Again, Malthusianism's prediction that as population density rises food provision per capita should fall is inconsistent with the data. (See Tables 6-1, 6-1-A, and 6-1-B.) The only one of the five quintiles of population density that provided, on the average, less than 100 percent of the calories necessary to sustain normal life was the lowest, consisting of nations with average density of 15 (see Table 6-1-A). The highest average calorie supply per capita was in the fourth density quintile.[21] And the twenty nations with less-than-required calorie supply had average population density of 133—nearly two-thirds lower than the average for all sixty-five nations. Contrary to conventional Malthusianism, this suggests that increasing population density may improve a nation's ability to provide food for its citizens. Later in this chapter we will see why.

Comparison of individual nations also shows wide variability in the relationship between population density and food provision. The four nations with the lowest densities had calorie supplies per capita ranging from 97 to 130 percent of daily requirement. The six with densities from 14 to 18 persons per square mile had calorie supplies per capita ranging from 68 to 134 percent of requirement. The five with densities from 42 to 52 persons per square mile had calorie supplies ranging from 85 to 112 percent of requirement. The three with population densities in the 60s per square mile had calorie supplies ranging from 82 to 137 percent of requirement.

Why should Burundi, with a population density of 466 persons per square mile, have been able to provide a daily calorie supply per capita of 102 percent of requirement, while Venezuela, with density of only 52 persons per square mile, could provide only 99 percent of daily calorie requirement per capita? Is it because Burundi had a higher GNP per capita? That seems like a good guess, but in reality Burundi's GNP per capita was only $220 per year, while Venezuela's was $3,410. Similar variability is apparent throughout Table 6-1.

6C. POPULATION GROWTH RATE AND GNP PER CAPITA

The one set of data that appears, at first glance, to confirm Malthusian theory is Table 6-2-A. The lowest, second, and third quintiles of GNP per capita all have significantly higher population growth rates (2.32, 2.85, and 2.43 percent per year average, respectively) than do the fourth and highest quintiles (1.65 and 1.83 percent per year average, respectively). This is understandable: the higher the population growth rate (assuming that the majority of it is attributed to births rather than to immigration),[22] the higher the proportion of young nonworkers to workers is likely to be. Hence production per capita is bound to be lower in a society with a high population growth rate than in one with a low growth rate, even if production per worker is the same. But this is true only in the short run. If both societies' population growth rates hold steady over two or three generations (a generation being defined as the average number of years from birth to the end of childbearing for women in the society), then the ratio of young nonworkers to workers in each will reach equilibrium, after which productivity growth rates in the two will tend to be equal as well (other things being equal; i.e., to the extent that they are determined by the ratio of young nonworkers to workers).[23]

Even the tendency of higher population growth rates to cause lower levels of GNP per capita should not be absolutized, however.[24] By ordering the quintiles according to ascending population growth rate rather than ascending population density, we see that the highest quintile of population growth rate in 1965-1984 had GNP per capita in 1984 slightly above the average for the sample as a whole and third of the five quintiles.[25] In addition, the quintile whose population growth rate matched the overall average had the lowest GNP per capita. The Malthusian theory would have predicted, other things being equal, that the lowest population growth rate would yield the highest GNP per capita, the second lowest the second highest, and so on. The predictions do not hold true consistently.

Comparing Past and Present: Individual Nations. We can make the same point in another way. Instead of comparing various nations with each other during the same time periods, we can compare different times in the histories of individual nations. Malthusianism predicts that the productivity of labor must fall as population density increases because the capital available for labor to work with must be divided among more and more people, resulting in diminishing ratios of capital to labor. If this is true, then historical data for individual nations should, at least in general, show a trend of diminishing GNP per capita.

(It is important to keep in mind the difference between GNP [gross national product] and GNP per capita. GNP per capita is the value of goods and services each person in a nation would enjoy if the entire nation's production were divided equally among all residents. GNP per capita may fall even while GNP rises if population rises more rapidly than GNP. A rise in GNP per capita, therefore, means not only that the total national product is rising, but that it is rising faster than population.)

The facts, however, are just the opposite of those predicted by Malthusianism. In the United States, for instance, growth of GNP *per capita* averaged roughly 1.8 percent per year from 1950-1981,[26] and 1.7 percent in 1965-1984. (Remember, this is not just growth of the total gross national product. It is growth of that product relative to total population. In other words, if the total gross national product were divided equally among all people in the population each year, each person would have 1.8 percent [or 1.7 percent] more wealth each year than he had the last,[27] despite there being more people among whom to divide the total wealth.) This growth is not peculiar to the United States. Fifty-six out of the sixty-five nations represented in Appendix 2 experienced a net increase in GNP per capita over the period 1965-1984; only nine experienced a net decrease.[28] Only one of the sixty-five nations experienced a net decrease in population during the same period. In thirty-eight of the sixty-five nations, the average annual growth rate of GNP per capita actually exceeded the average annual growth rate of population. Clearly, then, the historic trend is that GNP per capita has been increasing along with population, often faster.

Comparing Past and Present: Worldwide Trends. This is not an isolated trend—it is worldwide. In 89 percent of the 128 nations represented in the World Bank's *World Development Report 1986*, GNP per capita rose during the twenty years from 1965 through 1984. The average annual growth rate of GNP per capita (weighted by population) for the sixty-five nations represented in Table 6-1, including the nine with net losses in GNP per capita, was 3.45 percent (i.e., doubling, in constant dollars, every twenty-one years). If even half this rate continues during the next hundred years—and there is no apparent reason why it should not—worldwide GNP per capita (in constant 1984 dollars) will be over $18,000, over five times what it was in 1987—a forecast radically opposite that of the doomsayers who predict poverty for the world of the twenty-first century.[29]

These average growth rates are not skewed by disproportionate effect of the richest nations, either. They are fairly constant among all development classes. Average growth rate of GNP per capita among low-income economies (under $450 per year in 1984) in 1965-1984 was 2.8 percent (doubling every 25.7 years); among middle-income economies ($450 to $1,699 per year in 1984), 3.1 percent (doubling every 23.2 years); among upper middle-income economies ($1,700 to $8,000 per year in 1984), 3.3 percent (doubling every 21.8 years); among high-income oil exporters ($6,490 to $21,920 per year in 1984), 3.2 percent (doubling every 22.5 years); and among industrial market economies ($4,440 to $16,330 per year in 1984), 2.4 percent (doubling every thirty years).[30] (The popular belief that the rich are getting richer and the poor are getting poorer is, on the average and worldwide, simply not true. Both are getting richer.)[31] These facts are the opposite of what Malthusianism predicts.

Improving Standards of Living. One needn't turn to all these statistics, however, to get a simple grasp of what has been happening throughout history. Just imagine living at any time in the past, and compare it with living now. With isolated individual exceptions—exceptions that become fewer and farther between as we look farther into the past—almost everyone almost everywhere in the world is better off economically today than he would have been had he lived in the past, whether twenty years ago, fifty, a hundred, or a thousand.

The history of economics, indeed, hardly deserves to be called dismal, for it traces the rise of mankind from general destitution to general prosperity. The only thing dismal is thinking what life must have been like in the not-so-distant past. A typical Finnish farm near St. Petersburg in the late eighteenth century, for instance, merits this description by historian Fernand Braudel: it consisted of "a group of wooden huts, most of them in a state of collapse, that made up the farm: the house, with its single smoky room, two small byres, a Russian bath (a *sauna*), a stove to dry wheat or rye. The furniture consisted of a table, a bench, a cast-iron pot, a cauldron, a basin, a pail, some barrels, tubs, wooden or earthenware plates, an axe, a spade, a knife for slicing cabbages."[32]

Too easily we forget the great wealth we enjoy in our day, not comparing ourselves with ordinary people of the past, but with extraordinary people of the present. (How easily we succumb to discontent and covetousness!) A dose of economic history might sober us all up. Consider the typical possessions of the poor (and they were almost everybody) of Europe in the eighteenth century and before:

Inventories made after death, which are reliable documents, testify almost invariably to the general destitution. Apart from a
very small number of well-to-do peasants, the furniture of the
day labourer and the small farmer in Burgundy even in the eighteenth century was identical in its poverty: "the pot-hanger, the
pot in the hearth, the frying pans, the *quasses* (dripping pans), the
meix (for kneading bread) . . . the chest, the bedstead with four
pillars, the feather pillow and *gue'don* (eiderdown), the bolster,
sometimes a tapestry (cover) for the bed, the drugget trousers, the
coat, the gaiters, a few tools (shovels, pickaxe)." But before the
eighteenth century, the same inventories mention only a few old
clothes, a stool, a table, a bench, the planks of a bed, sacks filled
with straw. Official reports for Burgundy between the sixteenth
and the eighteenth centuries are full of "references to people
[sleeping] on straw . . . with no bed or furniture" who were only
separated "from the pigs by a screen."[33]

Are most ordinary people today better off economically than
they were in the sixteenth through eighteenth centuries? Certainly.
Scores, sometimes even hundreds of times over. Are there more people now than then? Of course. About a dozen times more. Has rising
population, then, been accompanied by rising or falling economic
prosperity? By now the answer is obvious.

SUMMARY OF THE CRITIQUE
Thus far we have argued against the conventional Malthusian view
of the relationship between population and economic welfare (1) that
it ignores the overwhelming positive effects of (a) man's productive
capacity, (b) capital and division of labor, (c) discovery, innovation,
and invention, and (d) economies of scale; (2) that it fails to distinguish between short-term and long-term effects; and (3) that economic and demographic facts and history are overwhelmingly
inconsistent with the theory.

We noted near the beginning of the chapter, however, that
Malthusians suggest three refinements to the theory by which they
hope to save it: (1) the law of diminishing returns; that is, as time
goes by, we turn to resources that are increasingly costly to develop;
(2) the negative impact of added children on saving; (3) the negative
impact of added children on time devoted to work. Are these
refinements sufficient to save the theory?

History provides a resounding answer: No. Whatever the causes, production per capita has increased steadily worldwide for centuries. Declines are the exceptions, not the rule. Whatever value there is in the claims about diminishing returns in resources and diminishing saving and work in relation to added children, the claims cannot negate the brute facts of history.

To develop a more sound understanding of the relationship between population and economics, however, we need to examine each of those claims more carefully and look also at other ingredients of the population/economy mix that Malthusianism tends to ignore. The following chapter will focus on the first refinement of Malthusianism, the claim that, with the passage of time, growing populations must depend on increasingly costly natural resources for their production. In what remains of this chapter we will compare the negative short-term economic effects of added children on parents' saving and work time with the positive short- and long-term effects of other elements.

THE IMPACT OF POPULATION GROWTH
ON ECONOMIC PRODUCTIVITY

In 1977, Julian Simon published a ground-breaking book on which he had been working for ten years, *The Economics of Population Growth*. When he began his work, Simon agreed with the conventional wisdom "that rapid population growth was the major threat to the world's economic development," a view he had championed in scholarly articles. But the more he studied historical data, the more convinced he became "that population growth can contribute to a better future."[34] In the book he explained why population growth and economic growth have coincided in the past and will do so in the future, despite Malthusian predictions to the contrary. What follows is a simplified summary of Simon's explanation.[35]

Underlying Values

"[T]he welfare judgment one makes about additional people depends," Simon wrote, "on such values as the importance of the short run versus the long run, whose welfare one wishes to take into account in which proportions, and what one believes is the importance to be attached to human life at poorer and richer standards of living."[36]

If we value the short run over the long run, then we will favor slow population growth, no growth, or even population decline over moderate to rapid population growth. Why? Because during the first eighteen to twenty years of their lives, new additions to the human race cost more (in material economic terms, not in spiritual terms) than they contribute. If we want to increase prosperity per capita, one easy way to do it is to stop having children for ten or twenty years. As the working-age population continues to grow but the under-working-age population declines, per-capita production will rise dramatically. The problem is that eventually we reach the point when a disproportionately high percentage of the population is too old to work very much, and there won't be young people to replace them. Then production per capita will fall drastically. The only way to avoid this is to maintain a birth rate at least sufficient to match the death rate. Declining population may well mean per-capita benefit in the short run, but it means per-capita loss in the long run.

If we value our own welfare over ensuing generations', then it makes sense to curb population growth. Indeed, on that basis it would make sense simply to sacrifice everybody but ourselves. If (God forbid!) you and I just killed everybody in the world but ourselves, we would fall heir to all the world's wealth. We would be enormously rich. But only for as long as we lived. When we died, it would all be over. Of course the Biblical ethic of love for neighbor can't permit such thinking.

If we value the lives of wealthy people more than those of poor or middle-class people, it might make sense, in the short run, for us to limit population growth. After all, the more non-wealthy people there are, the smaller is the proportion of wealthy to non-wealthy people. Why not, then, simply kill everyone whose annual income is below a certain limit? (And let's just hope we're the ones who set the limit!) Or if we can't quite stomach that, perhaps we should require certain levels of income before people are permitted to bear children. (This may sound preposterous, but various population-control advocates have offered it as serious policy advice.)[37] Aside from the simple fact that the very lives of the poor and middle-class among us are valuable at least to themselves and usually also to their families and friends, the Bible simply can't condone an ethic that values the wealthy more than others (James 2:1-9).

From a Christian standpoint, then, the presumption is in favor of a growing population. How, really, does population growth affect economic growth?

Growth Causes Growth

While population growth does have some negative effects on economic growth, its net effects (other things being equal) are positive, because it has more and weightier positive effects than negative.

The overall relationship between demography and economy is complex. We can view the relationship as having four levels. The primary level consists of population size, density, and growth rate. These all affect the secondary level, which consists of (1) the number of people, (2) health, (3) age distribution, (4) education, (5) perceived family needs, (6) saving, (7) perceived needs for production, (8) total demand, and (9) the number of inventors and adapters in the work force. These nine elements, in turn, affect the third level: (a) amount and quality of work done, (b) capital stock (tools, buildings, machinery, etc.), (c) social infrastructure (roads, communication systems, water and sewer systems, etc.), and (d) technological level and economies of scale. These four elements, joined by one additional function of the size of population—namely, the number of consumers—affect the fourth level, which is output per worker and income per consumer. That level, in turn, affects rates of fertility and mortality in the population, which determine ensuing population size, density, and growth rate. And so we come full circle.[38]

The two points at which it appears that population growth has a negative effect on production (aside from the diminishing-returns effect on resources alleged by Malthusians, which we will examine in the next chapter) are parents' work time and saving.

EFFECT ON PARENTS' LABOR-FORCE PARTICIPATION

Census studies show that, on the average, each new child a woman bears diminishes the time she spends working outside the home. By how much? Simon, in his analysis, suggests that we begin by looking not at the first child each woman bears, but at subsequent children.[39] The presence of a child in the home reduces the mother's time working outside the home significantly only during the first twelve years of the child's life. After that it has almost no effect. Assuming that each woman would have one child anyway, each additional child (assuming an average of two years between births) adds two years to the time mothers' labor-force participation is reduced. Each additional child beyond replacement birth rate costs society slightly under one-fourth of a worker in the labor force in each of two years by reducing its mother's outside-the-home work time.[40]

But what is the effect on the father's work time? The opposite:

the average father works an additional two-tenths of an hour per week outside the home for each child in the family throughout the twenty-five years after the child's birth.[41] Assuming an average work week of forty hours, then .2/40 x 25 = .125 additional work years for the father result from the birth of each new child to the family.[42] Subtracting the additional work years for the father from the lost work years for the mother gives a net short-run loss to the economy of .1 work year for each additional child born.[43]

Note that this is a short-run loss: since the average child eventually will spend forty-seven years in the work force, he or she actually gives a net long-term benefit to the economy of 46.9 work years (or 46.99 work years if we allow for the higher market value of male labor-force participation than female).[44] In short, the negative short-run effect of an additional child on parents' labor-force participation is minute and is offset many times over in the long run by the child's own labor in adulthood.

Even this analysis is both materialistic and shortsighted, however. The assumption that a woman's shifting her work from outside to inside the home is a cost to the labor market is highly suspect, to say the least. On the contrary, since her children will grow up to be productive workers outside the home, her work in caring for them should be considered a contribution to work outside the home as well. Furthermore, the inside-the-home/outside-the-home distinction is purely arbitrary. What we should be concerned about is the well-being of *people*, and people live and work in both places. The mother's shifting her place of work from outside to inside the home should not, in the final analysis, be viewed as a loss at all. Indeed, as one father who works at home, I can testify that mothers who work at home work considerably more and considerably harder than I've seen many men and women work outside the home.

EFFECT ON FAMILY SAVING

Since capital is the crucial element in multiplying the productivity of labor, and saving is a source of capital, whatever affects the amount of saving affects the amount of capital and, ultimately, the productivity of labor. It is often assumed that increased family size causes decreased saving, hence decreased capital for use by laborers, and hence decreased productivity of labor.[45] The reason seems simple: more children in the home create higher demand for expenditures, which, unless income rises enough to offset the higher demand, leaves less income to save after expenditures.

In actuality, however, the relationship of family size to saving is not nearly so simple. Some of the child's expenditure demands will be met not by diminishing the money set aside for saving, but by the parents' diminishing their own expenditure demands. (How many parents have gone without new clothes for years so their children could have the clothes, toys, books, and education they needed?) Some parents' commitment to saving rises when they add children to their families because they hope to send those children through college.

In fact, it is impossible to prove, over long enough time periods to be statistically significant, that an increase in childbearing causes a decrease in proportion of income saved. "The sharp decrease in family size in the last 100 or 50 years was not accompanied by an increase in the proportion of saving to income."[46] As Simon sums up the situation, "The general theory of consumption and savings is most complex and unsettled at present. One cannot say with much certainty what will be the effect of an increase in income of any sort (e.g., short-run, long-run, windfall) on saving and consumption. And in particular the relationship of family size to saving must be even more complex and unsettled than consumption theory in general."[47] Certainly for Christians who take seriously the Biblical value of leaving an inheritance not only to children but also to grandchildren (Proverbs 13:22), increasing family size should result in more, not less, saving (and hence perhaps less, not more, spending on oneself).

In addition, whatever effect children may have on their parents' saving is not directly proportionate on the economy as a whole. In other words, diminishing personal saving by, say, 25 percent does not diminish total investment in the economy by 25 percent. Why? Because personal saving makes up only a portion of total investment in the economy—19 percent in 1986.[48] So *even if* an increase in the number of children might diminish personal saving by 25 percent,[49] it would, in 1986 proportions, diminish total investment by only 4.75 percent.

Again, however—and *it is crucial in considering the relationship of population growth to economic growth that we keep this constantly in mind*—this analysis focuses on short-term negative rather than long-term positive effects. The long-term effects are opposite and many times greater in magnitude. The child who (hypothetically) diminishes his parents' saving will eventually become an adult who will (certainly) add his own saving to total economic investment. If he diminishes his parents' saving by 25 percent for each of, say, twenty years, he will do his own saving for two or three times that many years (the forty-seven years of his average working life plus some years of saving before he enters and after he leaves the work force). If his parents saved 4.3 percent of their annual income before his birth (average for 1986 in the United States),[50] they will save 3.225 percent of it for the twenty years after his birth; but after that he will add his savings on his income to their savings on their income, the combination being equivalent to 7.53 percent of the parents' income for the remainder of their working years (minus [hypothetically] 25 percent of his 4.3 percent savings rate each year for each dependent child he has). The short-term loss again translates into long-term gain for the economy as a whole.

Suppose we contrast the effects on saving by a couple with no children versus a couple with three children, each of whom grows up to have three children, each of whom in turn grows up to have three children. In our simplified scenario, the childless couple has after-tax income of $60,000 per year, and the couples with children have after-tax incomes of $40,000 per year as long as there are children under twelve in their homes and $60,000 per year thereafter (keeping dollar values constant over time).[51] All couples save at the 1986 average rate of 4.3 percent, minus 25 percent for each child born to each couple. Total savings, without interest, after the four generations will be: (1) childless couple, $121,260; (2) couple with three children, $1,632,014 (over thirteen times the other couple's savings).[52] Now, which of the two couples had the more beneficial impact on total savings in the economy in the long run?

Again, from the perspective of Biblical ethics, which enjoins personal sacrifice for the sake of others, it is clear after comparing the short-term and long-term effects of children on saving that a Christian worldview supports the choice for more children rather than fewer or none.

Summary of Impact of Population Growth on Economic Productivity

In these two elements of the relationship between population and the economy—parents' labor and family savings—population growth yields short-term losses but long-term gains. Earlier we saw that other important elements had similar results. Over their lifetimes, people tend to produce more than they consume; higher population density makes possible greater economic efficiencies from division of labor, economies of scale, and capital application; more people mean more and faster increases in knowledge and its application through discovery, innovation, and invention. These long-term benefits of population growth so far outweigh the short-term costs that economic production has consistently outgrown population. There is no reason to think this trend has ended or will end in the foreseeable future.

The specifics of these generalities vary from nation to nation, particularly between more-developed countries (MDC's) and less-developed countries (LDC's). The primary difference is in how we define short run versus long run. The short-term costs of moderate population growth (1.5 percent, or doubling about every fifty years) are transformed into long-term gains in MDC's in thirty to eighty years[53] and in LDC's in 120 to 180 years,[54] and that moderate population growth has better long-run effects on the productivity of labor (and hence average personal prosperity) than do declines in population, stable population, very slow population growth (.0036 percent, or doubling about every 2,000 years), or fast population growth (2 percent, or doubling every thirty-five years). Simon summarizes his findings:

1. In the context of MDC's: when the effects of knowledge, economies-of-scale, and natural resources are taken account of, together with the classical elements such as diminishing returns and the dependency burden, a simulation model shows that faster population growth has at first a negative effect on per-worker income than slower population growth. But after a period of perhaps 30 to 80 years, higher fertility and faster population growth lead to *higher* per-worker income. . . .

2. In the context of LDC's: moderate population growth leads in the long run to higher per-worker income than does a constant-size population *or* very fast population growth. . . .

The optimum LDC population growth rate differs fairly widely within the positive growth range depending upon [varying economic conditions within the respective nations], which suggests that no simple analytic model is acceptable and no single answer about the best rate of population goals is reasonable. . . .

3. Within a rather wide range of positive population growth rates in LDC's there is relatively little long-run difference in per-worker-output results—though *low or zero population growth rates do much worse, and very high population growth rates do somewhat worse, than do moderate rates.* . . .[55]

All of this is mere financial analysis, of course. It doesn't account for the inestimable value of people to themselves and those who know and love them. Who can put a dollar value on seeing a little girl take her first steps, or a son catch his first fish or his first touchdown pass, or a daughter say her wedding vows to a fine young man? People are worth more, far more, to all of us than the paychecks they draw, the goods and services they produce, the contributions they make to the economy. We should count their value in personal relationships and as bearers of the image of God as their primary value, and should see their ability to contribute to our material economy as a bonus.

CONCLUSION

The Bible's preference for large and growing population is consistent with what we discover upon a careful analysis of the economics of population growth. It is no mistake that we read, "And God *blessed Noah* and his sons and said to them, 'Be fruitful and multiply, and fill the earth'" (Genesis 9:1).

FROM SCARCITY TO UBIQUITY: THE CHANGING DYNAMICS OF RESOURCES IN THE MODERN WORLD

*P*roponents of slowing or stopping population growth believe that as population grows, productivity (production per worker) must fall, causing poverty and, ultimately, famine. Chapter 6 showed that children are not, as this position alleges, long-term drags on economic productivity by diminishing their parents' work or savings. The actual impact of population growth on economic productivity, other things being equal, is positive, not negative, because in the long run people tend to produce several times more than they consume.

Nonetheless, growth opponents assert that a growing population entails a law of diminishing returns from resources. After all, the earth is only so big. It contains only so many atoms of each resource. Therefore, the more people there are, the fewer resources there will be for each person to work with and the lower the quality of those resources will be. Hence productivity will be lower, poverty will follow, and the end will be famine.

To test this second argument, we will look first at its theoretical and empirical aspects on the broad scale: does it make sense and does it accurately predict what has happened in history? Then we will look at how it holds up in specific empirical tests related to four kinds of resources: food and agriculture, energy, non-fuel minerals, and wood. Finally we will suggest a different theoretical understanding of the relationship between population and resources and will venture forecasts for resources on the basis of that understanding.

THE THEORY OF DIMINISHING RETURNS IN RESOURCES

Building on Malthus's ideas in the *Essay on Population*, the nineteenth-century economist David Ricardo constructed a "law of diminishing returns" for resources. According to Ricardo, since people always seek the least costly ways to meet their needs, they will always use better resources before worse ones. In fact, they will bring new resources into use in constantly declining levels of quality. As a result, returns from the use of resources must become progressively worse.

In very simple theoretical models, Ricardo's idea seemed unassailable. It was especially appealing in a world dominated by agriculture.[1] It seems obvious, for instance, that farmers will choose agricultural land close to centers of population before land far from them, since it costs more to transport produce from far than from near, and that they will choose rich agricultural land before poor, since their crops will yield more in rich soil than in poor. As population grows and more food is needed, farmers will be forced to develop land farther from population centers, necessitating higher transportation costs, and to develop poorer soil, yielding smaller harvests. Hence yield per acre must fall. Eventually, unless population is held in check by some other means, it must be checked by farmers' inability to produce enough food: starvation lurks!

This model, however, is far simpler than reality.[2] One obvious flaw is its assumption that farmers won't, as they reach farther away for new land to cultivate, find richer land than they've been farming. But who would argue that the Mississippi lowlands and the Great Plains were not richer farmland than the rocky soils of most of the Eastern states? Yet those came into production long after the worse soils nearer America's first population centers.

Much more important, however, is the model's failure to take into account growing *knowledge* and its effects on tools and methods. This criticism was offered by John Stuart Mill in 1848:

There is . . . no possible improvement in the arts of production which does not in one or another mode exercise an antagonistic influence to the law of diminishing return to agricultural labour. Nor is it only industrial improvements which have this effect. Improvements in government, and almost every kind of moral and social advancement, operate in the same manner. . . . We may say the same of improvement in education.

The law of diminishing returns from resources, Mill wrote, "may . . . be suspended, or temporarily controlled, by whatever adds to the general power of mankind over nature; and especially by any extension of their knowledge, and their consequent command, of the properties and powers of natural agents."[3]

From Diminishing Returns to Multiplying Returns

What seemed a slight adjustment to Malthusian and Ricardian theory in Mill's day turned out to be its complete reversal. Adam Smith had pointed out, some seventy years earlier, how division of labor and adequate capital had multiplied workers' productivity in the pin making trade some 240 to 4,800 times. Other new inventions and applications, like steam engines, cotton gins, steel-bladed plows, reapers, combines, railroads with steam locomotives, and other machines and tools, had similar effects in other trades by Mill's time. The revolution in productivity surged ahead after that with the substitution of electricity for steam as a source of power as early as the 1880s. Instead of relatively inflexible drive shafts, gears, and pulleys determining where machines must be placed in a factory, the flexibility of electrical wiring allowed efficient work flow to determine factory layout.[4] The result was multiplied productivity.

What electricity did in all kinds of factories other processes and devices did in specific industries; they reduced the labor needed to produce practically anything. The cost of producing steel rails fell from close to $100 per ton to $12; of producing a gallon of kerosene from 1.5 cents to .45 cents; of refining aluminum from 87.5 francs per kilogram to 3.75 francs. "Overall, the American wholesale price index declined from 100 in 1880 to 82 in 1890—a change for which advances in technology were in good part, though not wholly, responsible."[5] Internal combustion engines, cars, and planes continued the revolution.

In our hurried admiration for innovative processes and tools, it would be easy to overlook an important parallel development: a change in the sorts of resources used. Nowhere was this more obvious than in energy. The switch from largely human and animal muscle to the mechanical transmission of energy from moving water in the eighteenth century was followed swiftly by the substitution of steam and then electricity. The order was precisely opposite what diminishing-returns analysis called for. Industry went from lower-quality to higher-quality resources. Indeed, that short-term trend reflected the long-term trend in energy resource use by mankind through history: from wood to "manure, peat, coal, oil, gas, uranium, and boron (and, in the future, possibly deuterium from the sea)[6]. . . . Does this suggest that, in the march of time . . . supplies of fuel have been progressively met by utilizing the fuels of higher economic quality first and then moving to those of lower economic quality?"[7]

A similar phenomenon occurred in metallurgy and all the industries dependent on it, marked by "the substitution of steel for cast iron, improvements in machining, and progress in mechanical engineering. The combination of steel with controllable metallurgical properties and advances in machining made possible the interchangeability of parts, which in turn made possible the mass production of agricultural machinery, sewing machines, typewriters, cash registers, bicycles, and, a little later, automobiles."[8]

The effect of all these changes on the overall economy was explosive. Workers' productivity multiplied. Goods and services became less expensive, while quality improved because of standardization and interchangeability of parts, and workers earned more income with which to buy them. Breakthroughs in medicine reduced mortality rates, especially in childhood. Population growth rates shot upward. The combination was what Malthusianism and Ricardianism thought impossible: rapidly growing population with rapidly growing productivity of labor.[9]

A Conflict of Worldviews

From the perspective of the Christian worldview, the diminishing-returns analysis rests on a false notion of reality. A monument to metaphysical materialism consistent with Marxism-Leninism but not with Christianity and the whole civil social order that grew from it, it focuses entirely on material things. It ignores the importance of mind and of the application of knowledge to the material world. Not what we find in nature, but what we can make of it defines true resource availability. As knowledge grows and changes, so does what we can make of nature. Solomon's praise to wisdom is a fitting response to the deadening ideas of Malthusian and Ricardian analysis of resources:

> Take my instruction, and not silver, and knowledge rather than choicest gold. For wisdom is better than jewels; and all desirable things can not compare with her. (Proverbs 8:10, 11)

Indeed, the Bible clearly presents knowledge, especially godly wisdom, as the wellspring of human prosperity:

> I, wisdom, dwell with prudence, and I find knowledge and discretion. . . . Riches and honor are with me, enduring wealth and righteousness. My fruit is better than gold, even pure gold, and my yield than choicest silver. I walk in the way of righteousness, in the midst of the paths of justice, to endow those who love me with wealth, that I may fill their treasuries. (Proverbs 8:12, 18-21)

The Geometric Growth of Knowledge

A Biblical perspective values knowledge over material things, recognizing that applied knowledge can work tremendous changes in the physical world. The more advanced any society's knowledge becomes, the less sensible is any diminishing-returns analysis of resources. "The supreme resource that human beings need to live good lives is not buried beneath the crust of the earth," wrote Ben Wattenberg. "The only real resource is the human intellect. When unfettered, the human intellect can create all the other resources, sometimes out of thin air!"[10]

In 1962, after 200 years of what seemed to be quantum leaps in technology, Barnett and Morse could write, "The plain fact . . . is that the acceleration of sociotechnical change has now become the dominant influence on economic growth. [Economic models that fail to account for this change] thus do not, and cannot be made to, represent twentieth-century reality"[11]—or any reality from now on, for that matter. Their observation becomes increasingly important as knowledge increases by leaps and bounds. From 1961 through 1986, for instance, 1.75 million new patents were awarded in the United States alone, and the annual number both here and worldwide is, on the average, increasing (up nearly 20 percent between the decades 1961-1970 and 1971-1980).[12] Who would have thought, in 1962, when the simplest hand-held calculators running on transistors were hailed as a great new technology, that in less than thirty years there would be microchips capable of thousands of calculations per second and computers the size of soft drink cans capable of 60 million calculations per second?[13] Yet those developments have occurred, and more will occur to dwarf them in significance, because they are themselves tools for acquiring yet more knowledge.

And let us not forget, while marvelling at the inventions that have multiplied human productivity and the output that can be gained from resources, that the inventions come from *human minds*. People created in the image of God, an image involving, in part, knowledge, are the spring from which these discoveries flow. The more people there are to think and exchange ideas, the more knowledge and innovation there will be. Not only the number of inventions, but also the speed at which they are applied throughout the economy increases as population grows, since more people take part in passing on newly acquired knowledge.[14]

A Biblical understanding of reality points not to a law of diminishing returns from resources, but to a *law of increasing returns*. Why? Because the growth of knowledge so outstrips the depletion of physical resources as to make each new resource or method yield higher output per unit of labor and capital than the one it replaces.

> [T]he cumulation of knowledge and technological progress is automatic and self-reproductive in modern economies, and obeys a law of increasing returns. Every cost-reducing innovation opens up possibilities of application in so many new directions that the stock of knowledge, far from being depleted by new developments, may even expand geometrically. Technological progress . . . appears to obey what [Gunnar] Myrdal has called the "principle of circular and cumulative causation," namely, that change tends to induce further change in the same direction.[15]

The old Malthusian and Ricardian views of the relationship between resources and population ultimately rest on the mistaken notion that there is no qualitative difference between men and animals. Animals are dependent on what they find in their natural environment. Their population is necessarily limited by what their environment can support.[16] But men, by applying their minds, can change their environment, making it support thousands of times more people (and animals) than it naturally could, at many times higher standards of living.

Precisely this distinction between men and animals, with its economic implications, appears in Scripture. It stands out clearly throughout Psalm 104. God provides directly for animals through the natural processes of the world, but provides indirectly for mankind through labor: "He causes the grass to grow for the cattle, and vegetation for the labor of man, so that he may bring forth food from the earth, and wine which makes man's heart glad . . ." (Psalm 104:14, 15a).

Far from a growing population's necessitating diminishing returns from resources, more thinking people devise more and smarter ways to develop and apply resources, causing increasing productivity. Furthermore, they increase the varieties and supplies of resources, making them less scarce, not more.

THE WORLD OF INCREASING RESOURCE SUPPLIES

We could as easily have made this heading, "The World of Diminishing Resource Scarcity." The two statements mean the same thing. The greater the supply of something, the less its scarcity; the less its scarcity, the greater its supply.

Common sense seems to tell us that the more we use of something, the less there must be left of it. But in the case of resources, what seems like common sense is common nonsense. Let's see why first, and then look at some representative historical data that illustrate the case.

Causes of Increasing Resource Supply

Why do resource supplies increase over time despite rising population and consumption? There are two chief reasons: substitution and transformation. Often these blend into each other.

SUBSTITUTION

Admittedly, substitution as an explanation for diminishing resource scarcity (increasing resource supply) is a bit of sleight of hand. It sidesteps the question, "Is oil (or tungsten, or tin, or bauxite, or coal) getting used up?" But sidestepping a question can be good if the question is the wrong one to ask. In this case, the right question is,

"Is there an increasing or decreasing supply of whatever we need at any given time to do the things we might do with oil (or tungsten, or tin, or bauxite, or coal)?" Or, to refine the question yet more, "Is there an increasing or decreasing supply of whatever it is we use oil (or tungsten, or tin, or bauxite, or coal) for (namely, in the case of oil, primarily energy and lubrication)?" And substitution answers this question.

Why is this general question more refined than the specific question we started with? Because resources are not physical substances but functions: energy, shelter, transportation, communication, rigid or flexible barriers, and so on.[17] What we care about is not really oil, but the service we get from it. If I figure a way to use Beisnerium twice as cheaply for the same purposes tomorrow, nobody is going to decry the demise of oil in the human economy, aside from those who presently make their living in the petroleum industry. And they, like whalers of old, will find new ways to earn their livings and will enjoy the benefits of Beisnerium just as much as their neighbors.

If, for instance, the supply[18] of oil is diminishing (a doubtful assumption), but we can substitute synthetic oil made from shale or coal or even from palm oil (a renewable resource!) for its lubricative functions, and hydrogen combustion, nuclear fission or fusion, or solar, geothermal, tidal, or wind generation for its energy uses, and there's plenty of stuff to substitute, then it makes little sense to weep about a diminishing supply of oil. After all, who weeps now about the almost complete end to whale oil production? Nobody. (Indeed, champions of saving the whales rejoice.) We just use something else for the same purposes—something better, in fact (more BTU's by weight and volume, lower labor-capital cost per unit of production, less pollution per BTU, etc.).

Substitution doesn't always mean switching from one substance to another, though. Sometimes it means switching from one grade of a substance to another or from one source of a substance to another. If oil runs out in a pool under Huntington Beach, California, but a bigger pool is found under New Brownsville, Texas, or if new technology is developed to pump water into the old oil pool to increase pressure and force more oil from what was once thought a dry pool, then the supply of oil is effectively increased.

What happens, for example, to the supply of copper as a resource if, at time T, the best technology permits us to produce industrial grade copper at X dollars per ton from 10 percent pure ore, and then at time T1 new technology permits us to produce the same grade of copper at 1/2 X dollars per ton from 1 percent pure ore, and we estimate that there is 100 times as much 1 percent pure ore as 10 percent pure? The supply of copper as a resource is multiplied by well over 200. Not just by 200, but by several (probably many) multiples of it, depending on how much ore there is at each gradient between 10 percent and 1 percent and on how much impact the new technology has on refining those purities of ore.

This is no fanciful example. Precisely this kind of technological advance has been occurring with monotonous regularity in regard to almost all of the minerals (including copper and other metals, as well as mineral fuels) we use as resources.[19] Our increasing ability to use low-grade copper ores economically is a good example: "In the 19th century . . . only copper ores containing 4 to 6 percent of copper were regarded as useful. At present, however, ores are worked with an ore content of as little as 0.4 percent. It is virtually certain that in 20 to 30 years ores with as little as 0.25 percent will be profitably exploited." The same is true of other ores as well.[20]

In short, substitution of different substances to do the same jobs or of lower grades of the same substances, refined to equal end products by less costly methods, greatly multiplies resource supply. The more knowledge increases, the more adept we will become at making such substitutions. On this ground alone we are justified in foreseeing an ongoing increase in resource supplies through time, one that will outstrip (and be enhanced by) growing human population.

TRANSFORMATION
Even more important than substitution, however, is transformation. Or perhaps we could simply say that transformation is substitution gone wild.

Generally when we speak of *substitution* we mean using one thing that we find in nature for the same purposes for which we used another thing we found in nature. But *transformation* means changing one thing into a different thing and using it accordingly. The key difference is the application of energy in chemical processes rather than in mechanical processes. Mechanical processes—the chief manipulative processes of the Industrial Revolution, marvelously fruitful in themselves—leave substances basically what they were. But chemical processes change substances completely: they work at molecular and elemental levels rather than gross levels. The result is the complete transformation not only of individual substances, but also of the whole resource/production/consumption equation. The breakthrough comes by way of the practical application of Einstein's discovery that energy and matter are different forms of the same thing. With sufficient energy to apply in chemical processes, we can make pretty much any resource we want in pretty much any quantities we need; natural amounts of particular raw materials become almost irrelevant.

The practical implication of this is a tremendous multiplication of the sources of resources. When chemical processes allow us to produce finished metals from ores of extremely low purity, they also allow us to produce the finished metals from ores of extremely widespread occurrence. As Barnett and Morse put it in the technological dark ages of the early 1960s, ". . . the newer technologies utilize very extensive, frequently ubiquitous, resources."[21] *Ubiquitous*: existing everywhere. From resource scarcity to resource ubiquity!

Are Resource Supplies Really Increasing?

Again, this heading could have been worded differently: "Is Resource Scarcity Diminishing?" Or perhaps better yet, "Are Resource Costs Rising or Falling?"

Are we playing games here, switching the question at the last minute? No, we're just paying attention to the real meaning of scarcity. Scarcity is a measurement of the ratio of supply of a good to the demand for it in the marketplace, and that ratio determines price. Hence price is a measure of scarcity. Greater scarcity equals higher price; lesser scarcity equals lower price. Other things being equal, rising prices mean increasing scarcity (diminishing supply); falling prices mean diminishing scarcity (increasing supply).[22]

Let's look. Are resources getting more expensive (more scarce) or less? We'll look first at the general picture over a long period, then at some individual examples in more recent history.

COST TRENDS IN RESOURCES

The three chief divisions of extractive goods (natural resources) are agricultural products, minerals, and forest products. The labor-capital cost per unit of agricultural output fell 50 percent between 1870 and 1957. The labor cost alone fell 65 percent.[23] The labor-capital cost per unit of mineral output fell 78 percent; labor cost alone, 84 percent.[24] Only in labor cost of forestry products (a labor-capital cost estimate was not possible because of the peculiarities of the industry) was there a weak indication of increasing scarcity: the inflation-adjusted price of sawlogs rose 83 percent from 1870 to 1920, but fell 17 percent afterward, leaving the 1957 inflation-adjusted price 50 percent above the 1870-1900 average price.[25] One recent study showed falling mineral prices relative to the average cost of labor in the United States from 1900 to 1970: copper, down 87 percent; iron, 62 percent; zinc, 79 percent; aluminum, 97 percent; and crude petroleum, 90 percent.[26]

TABLE 7-1

INFLATION-ADJUSTED FOOD PRICE TRENDS, 1870-1980
Prices Received By Farmers

COMMODITY	YEARS	% CHANGE
Wheat	1870-1980	-37
Rice	1870-1980	-10
Barley	1870-1980	-42
Corn	1870-1980	- 4
Sugar beets	1910-1980	-13
Sugar cane	1870-1980	-48
Cotton	1870-1980	+ 7
Beef cattle	1870-1980	+84
Hogs	1870-1980	- 6
Milk	1870-1980	+12
Chickens	1870-1980	-80
Eggs	1870-1980	-58

Source: Adapted from D. Gale Johnson, "World Food and Agriculture," in Julian L. Simon and Herman Kahn, eds., *The Resourceful Earth: A Response to 'Global 2000'* (New York: Basil Blackwell, 1984), Figures 2.1-2.12.

Data for extractive goods in the United States from 1870 to 1957 showed generally falling costs by all methods of measurement—a clear sign of diminishing scarcity. Average labor-capital cost of all extractive goods fell by one-half, labor cost by two-thirds, while the average labor-capital cost of nonextractive output fell by about one-half, and labor cost by 60 percent. Finally, the ratio of extractive to nonextractive output cost fell slightly as a function of labor and capital, but as a function of labor alone by nearly 80 percent.[27] The conclusion: from 1870 to 1957, natural resources, on the average, became significantly less scarce.[28]

The downward price trends of 1870-1957 have continued. Inflation-adjusted worldwide prices for the chief non-fuel minerals, ores, and metals taken as a group (iron ore, manganese ore, phosphate, aluminum, copper, lead, zinc, tin, and tungsten) fell by about 5 percent from 1950 to 1980. Prices of non-ferrous base metals (aluminum, copper, lead, zinc, tin, and nickel) fell by about 10 percent. Prices of crude fertilizers (phosphate and potash) fell by about 26 percent.[29] Aside from fuels (chiefly petroleum, coal, and uranium), these represent the vast majority of non-agricultural extractive resources used in the world. Similar declines have occurred in agricultural prices since 1870, as Table 7-1 shows.[30]

What are we to make of the three cases in which agricultural products showed a rise in price through the 110-year period? They indicate increasing constant-dollar cost. But they, like all the others, also need to be seen in light of changes in income during the same period. While cotton prices rose 7 percent, beef prices 84 percent, and milk prices 12 percent, average income in constant dollars multiplied many times over, making these increases, if you'll excuse the pun, easy to swallow. Thus, for instance, the price of wheat deflated by average wages in the United States plummeted by over 95 percent from the mid-1800s to the late 1970s.[31] Indeed, the same observation applies to all the price trends observed here. As income rises, even stable constant-dollar prices become easier and easier to afford. Falling constant-dollar prices, then, are all the better.

Petroleum seems to offer a different picture, at least in the last two decades. In the 1970s and early 1980s, because of the OPEC oil embargo, its price shot up and we all got mad waiting in long gas lines on odd- or even-numbered days. Everyone knew we were running out of oil. Were we?

Oil price trends appear to indicate increasing scarcity. The price of a barrel of oil at the well went from $3.89 in 1973 to $31.77 in 1981; but it fell to $12.66 in 1986. Adjusting for inflation, the story changes drastically: in constant 1967 dollars, oil at the well was $3.04 per barrel in 1973, $11.79 in 1981, and $4.37 in 1986. More important to most of us, who never see unrefined oil, but do burn lots of gasoline in our cars, the inflation-adjusted price of gasoline fell more than 10 percent from 1973, the year before the oil embargo, to 1986: from 29.1 cents to 26.1 cents per gallon.[32]

But things changed in 1987-1989. Iran and Iraq started attacking tankers in the Persian Gulf, and the United States sent its naval ships in to protect shipping, raising tensions in that volatile area and so causing a speculative boom in oil prices. OPEC, which had been plagued by members exceeding production quotas, got its act together in late 1988, reduced supply in the market, and pushed prices back up.[33] In early 1989, the *Exxon Valdez* ran aground in Alaska, spilling millions of gallons of crude oil and igniting a firestorm of price speculation. Several tanker accidents followed fast on its heels. Still, on August 21, 1989, as I write this, domestic crude oil stands at $18.90 per barrel (down 14 percent in three months from the year's peak of $22 on April 21), about $5.75 per barrel in 1967 dollars, 89 percent above its 1973 price, while gasoline is about 95 cents per gallon in current dollars, about 29 cents in 1967 dollars (almost exactly what it was in 1973) and is headed down.[34]

What can we learn from the recent history of oil prices? Not much about the actual scarcity of oil. The prices tell us that oil has swung wildly from lesser to greater scarcity and back in the market. But the chief causes of the swings have been hoarding by a cartel, war, and freak tanker accidents, not a genuine fall in the amount of oil producers can pump from the earth. After all, at the height of OPEC's embargo of the 1970s, most member nations were producing at only about 75 percent of capacity. "This means that among the OPEC nations alone there were an extra 8.6 million barrels per day available virtually at the throw of a switch."[35] Had they been pumping at capacity, prices would have continued their long-term fall.[36] The recent history of oil prices is a picture of a see-saw battle between non-economic factors (hoarding, war, accidents) and economic factors, the former trying to keep prices up and the latter pulling them down. If history is any indicator, the economic factors are going to win the war.

ESTIMATING RESERVES OF RESOURCES

Another way to look at the future supply of resources is to estimate the amounts that can be extracted and refined economically in the future. The metals that make up 95 percent of the world's annual consumption are "clearly inexhaustible" in supply: iron (85.7 percent of U.S. consumption, 89.83 percent of world consumption), aluminum (8.22 and 4.47 percent), silicon (1.05 and .71 percent), magnesium (.21 and .09 percent), and titanium (.02 and .01 percent). "The least abundant of these is titanium, which constitutes about 1 percent of the earth's crust. . . [!]" Metals that make up most of the rest of our use are "probably inexhaustible" in supply: copper (1.38 percent of U.S. metal consumption, 1.35 percent of world consumption), zinc (1.23 and .97 percent), manganese (1.19 and 1.76 percent), chromium (.5 and .45 percent), lead (.25 and .2 percent), nickel (.15 and .09 percent), and tin (.03 and .03 percent). Metals that are neither clearly inexhaustible nor probably inexhaustible make up only .07 percent of U.S. and .04 percent of world consumption, and in the few instances in which exhaustion might come in the next few centuries, substitutes are readily available at economically feasible costs.

TABLE 7-2

LAND AND SEA METAL RESOURCES (TONS)

	OCEAN NODULES	SEA WATER	EARTH'S CRUST*	RATIO OF ANNUAL USE TO RESOURCES^
Aluminum	——	18 bil.	80,000 tril.	1/5,759,649
Chromium	——	80 mil.	110 tril.	1/9,654,211
Cobalt	3 bil.	800 mil.	25 tril.	1/627,447,930
Copper	3 bil.	6 bil.	6 tril.	1/812,123
Gold	——	8 mil.	3.5 bil.	1/2,004,571,428
Iron	130 bil.	18 bil.	58,000 tril.	1/81,860,619
Lead	4 bil.	60 mil.	12 tril.	1/2,444,483
Manganese	160 bil.	4 bil.	1,300 tril.	1/48,666,118
Mercury	——	60 mil.	9 bil.	1/10,327,795
Uranium	——	6 bil.	180 bil.	1/3,883,090

*Upper layer only: 1 million trillion tons—about 4 percent of total.
^Compared with 1986 world production, computed from data in Susan Buchanan, Seymour Gaylinn, et al., eds., *1988 CRB Commodity Year Book* (New York: Commodity Research Bureau, 1988). To make the figures directly comparable with those in the previous three columns, some weight data had to be converted to short tons.
Source: Adapted from Kahn, Brown, and Martel, *The Next 200 Years*, p. 104, Table 13.

It's easy for nonspecialists to assume that most metals are rare. On the contrary, most are found nearly everywhere on earth: "A cubic kilometer of the earth's crust on average contains about 210 million tons of aluminum, 150 million tons of iron, 150,000 tons of chromium, 7,000 tons of uranium, 80,000 tons of copper, and so on."[37] Indeed, metals are not only in the earth's crust, but also in its sea water and on its ocean floors, as Table 7-2 shows. As extractive and refining technologies continue to improve, permitting us to exploit lower and lower concentrations of ores in increasingly remote locations, the scarcity of almost all extractive mineral resources will abate, not worsen.

Of course, we're not likely ever to mine and refine all of these metals. That would require sifting through the whole upper layer of the earth's crust, filtering all of the world's sea water, and mining all of the nodules from the world's ocean floors—unlikely tasks indeed. Not to fear. We won't need all of them. Suppose our mining ultimately comes to equal, as a proportion of these resources, the present extent of human settlements as a proportion of the land area of the world, which, as we saw in Chapter 4, was about 1 percent. That would mean the aluminum to be mined would be enough for 57,596 years at 1986 production levels, the chromium enough for 96,542 years, the cobalt enough for 6,274,479 years, and so on. We'd be in the biggest trouble with copper: at 1986 world production levels, we'd run out in just 8,121 years! (Assuming that we never recycled copper or substituted other metals, plastics, or not-yet-invented synthetics for it, or began mining it from the moon and other planets.)

These hopeful statistics are surprising to many of us who keep hearing in the media about dwindling reserves of resources. What's behind the confusion? Primarily a failure to understand the nature of resource reserves. The data shown in Table 7-3 give us as graphic a demonstration as any of the counterintuitive nature of resource reserves.

TABLE 7-3

PROVEN RESERVES OF PETROLEUM AND ANNUAL PRODUCTION, 1973-1986
(Millions of barrels as of December 31)

	RESERVES	PRODUCTION
1973	35,300	20,561
1975	32,682	19,301
1980	29,805	21,791
1981	29,426	20,404
1982	27,858	19,437
1983	27,735	19,342
1984	28,446	19,812
1985	28,416	19,328
1986	26,889	20,270

Source: U.S. Bureau of the Census, *Statistical Abstract of the United States, 1988*, p. 662, Table 1166.

Imagine that! Proven world reserves of oil at the end of 1973 were 35.3 billion barrels, and by the end of 1986 they were 26.9 billion. But did we use only 8.4 billion barrels in the thirteen intervening years (646 million barrels per year)? No. We used about thirty-one times that much: 20 billion barrels per year. At that rate, we should have run out in about twenty-one months. But we kept going that way for 156 months, using about 260 billion barrels, with no end in sight.

What does this tell us about "proven world reserves," not only of oil but of any natural resource? That they're a mere fraction of actual world reserves. That new reserves keep getting found. That nobody cares about finding all the oil (or any other resource) in the world, at least not now. Instead, it will be found shortly before it's needed.

Why isn't anybody interested in finding all the oil (or anything else) in the world? For the same reason many American farmers aren't interested in growing all the crops they could each year. If they did, they couldn't sell them all. Finding new resources costs money. If exploration costs can't be passed on to consumers fairly soon after they're incurred, oil companies are going to be in a tight spot. What's the use in finding all the oil in the world if it can't be sold for decades or scores or hundreds of years? Instead, oil producers have found that it's most economical, at least granted recent conditions, to explore just far enough in advance to keep proven reserves at about 50 percent above the previous year's production.[38]

Still, some of us would like to know when the world itself really will run out of oil. From an economist's standpoint, the answer is, "Probably never." Why? Because if recoverable oil ever begins to dwindle sufficiently, its price will rise enough that people will conserve more, find more efficient uses for it, and substitute other energy sources more. Long before it's all gone, it will be so little used that hardly anyone will think about it.

Nonetheless, some petroleum geology experts have tried to estimate future petroleum discoveries.[39] As of 1978, about 600 billion barrels of oil had been produced. About another trillion barrels of discovered reserves remained, enough for about fifty years at the average yearly rates prevailing during 1973-1986. About another 400 billion barrels of reserves, enough for another twenty years, were considered probably discovered. Estimates of *undiscovered* potential recoverable petroleum ranged from about 1 to 6 trillion barrels, or about enough for another fifty to 300 years after discovered and probably discovered reserves were used up.[40]

Actual world consumption is likely to increase considerably in the next hundred years as more nations become increasingly developed economically, but it isn't likely to exceed U.S. consumption per capita by much, if at all. In the years 1986-1988, U.S. consumption per capita averaged about twenty-five barrels per person per year.[41] Assuming that the world's population reaches 10 billion by the end of the next century (an assumption probably on the high side), at which time population will likely stabilize, and assuming that by that

TABLE 7-4

CHANGES IN KNOWN RESERVES OF RESOURCES, 1950-1970

ORE	KNOWN RESERVES IN 1950 (1,000 METRIC TONS)	KNOWN RESERVES IN 1970 (1,000 METRIC TONS)	PERCENTAGE INCREASE
Iron	19,000,000	251,000,000	1,321
Manganese	500,000	635,000	27
Chromite	100,000	775,000	675
Tungsten	1,903	1,328	-30
Copper	100,000	279,000	179
Lead	40,000	86,000	115
Zinc	70,000	113,000	61
Tin	6,000	6,600	10
Bauxite	1,400,000	5,300,000	279
Potash	5,000,000	118,000,000	2,360
Phosphates	26,000,000	1,178,000,000	4,430
Oil	75,000,000	455,000,000	507

Source: Kahn, Brown, and Martel, *The Next 200 Years*, p. 92, Table 8.

time most nations will be as wealthy, per capita, as the United States and will consume oil at about our present rate per capita, annual world consumption will reach and stabilize at about 250 billion barrels per year. At that rate the 1 to 6 trillion barrels of undiscovered potential petroleum reserves would be used up in about four to twenty-four years—i.e., about A.D. 2100 to 2125. But that scenario is highly unlikely for several reasons: (1) world population probably won't reach 10 billion by that time, because we're on the tail end of the demographic transition;[42] (2) industrial, transportation, and domestic energy users will become increasingly fuel-efficient because of continued technological improvements; (3) nuclear fission and fusion, solar, hydrogen combustion, and geothermal energy sources will be used increasingly as substitutes for petroleum, and will be cheaper, cleaner, and safer.

What is more likely is that by the late twenty-first century petroleum will be a fairly minor source of the world's energy. Not long afterward it (along with coal, of which there are far greater supplies)[43] will be remembered the way we now remember wood, manure, and peat: as a primitive stepping-stone to far more efficient energy sources.

Petroleum is the pessimist's example, so far as proven reserves are concerned. As Table 7-3 shows, proven reserves of oil have, on the average, shrunk over the years since 1973. Historical trends differ significantly for others, as we see in Table 7-4.

Similar trends have continued for these and most other minerals. With the exception of tungsten, for which there are plenty of substitutes, proven reserves keep increasing.

WILL WE HAVE ENOUGH ENERGY?

Despite all that we have seen about resource availability, concern continues, particularly in the popular media, that we are running out of energy. To address that concern, let's look at just one likely energy resource for the future, one that uses present technology: nuclear fission. Other sources—nuclear fusion, solar radiation (which will last as long as the sun keeps shining), geothermal, hydrogen combustion, and so on—will become increasingly economical as time passes and technological improvements are made, but presently nuclear fission is our best non-fossil fuel source.

The amount of practically minable ore of sufficient quality for use in nuclear power generation is enough to last for thousands or even hundreds of thousands of years. The actual cost of nuclear power generation tends to be about equal to that of oil and coal power generation, and as the use of nuclear power plants increases, the costs are more likely to go down than up. At any rate, there is no reason to doubt the economic feasibility of using nuclear power as the world's chief energy supply for thousands of years to come—unless another source, using another technology, becomes cheaper.

The chief objection to nuclear power, however, is that people fear that it is dangerous. Just how safe is it? The important question is not, "Is nuclear power absolutely safe?" but "How safe is nuclear power compared with alternatives?" The answer to that is quite clear: it is much safer.

In America's worst nuclear accident, at Three Mile Island in 1979, no one died or was injured, and there is no evidence of increased radiation-induced illness in the area. Residents were exposed to less than 100 millirems of radiation from the accident, about what they'd get in two or three X rays, or what they'd suffer if they moved to Colorado, where background radiation is higher.

Over 600 plant years of nuclear reactor operation in America have caused not a single civilian death (though three military personnel died in an accident at an experimental reactor in 1961), although it is estimated that the average nuclear plant might cause from .6 to four deaths per year through normal operation and hypothetical accidents. By comparison, the average coal-fired generating plant causes somewhere between twenty-five and 257 deaths each year.[44]

Even the anti-nuclear Union of Concerned Scientists estimated in 1977 only about 120 deaths per year from all causes related to all nuclear power generation in the U.S.: mining uranium ore, building generating plants, radiation from the plants, and exposure to radioactive wastes. More scientifically qualified government-sponsored research programs estimated deaths at about ten per year. Coal power generation, in contrast, accounts for about 10,000 deaths per year in America due to air pollution alone (which, interestingly enough, contains more radiation than is expelled from nuclear power plants), not counting deaths of coal miners from lung disease and mine accidents.

Probably what people most fear is a catastrophic accident, a meltdown. What are the dangers from that potentiality? The Nuclear Regulatory Commission estimates that a meltdown might occur, on average, once in every 20,000 years of operation per nuclear power plant or, with about eighty plants operating in the U.S., about once in every 250 years. The NRC estimates that the typical meltdown would cause about 400 deaths. This estimate of the *hypothetical* danger from meltdowns indicates about 400 deaths every 250 years, or 1.6 deaths per year—only .016 percent of *actual* deaths each year from coal power generation.

The Union of Concerned Scientists (an anti-nuclear lobbying group with very few members with expertise in nuclear technology) disagrees. It paints a gloomier picture. It estimates an average of one meltdown for every 2,000 plant years, or one every twenty-five years with eighty plants operating (hardly persuasive since, with over 3,000 plant years of operation so far worldwide, no meltdown has occurred yet).[45] It also estimates that each meltdown would cause about 5,000 deaths, meaning that, in 100 years, 20,000 deaths, or 200 per year, should result from meltdowns in the U.S. Yet air pollution alone from coal-burning plants already causes an estimated 10,000 deaths *per year*. Even by the anti-nuclear UCS's estimate, then, nuclear power generation is at least fifty times safer than coal.

Indeed, even if all of the roughly 400 coal-fired plants in the U.S. were replaced with nuclear plants, then, according to the UCS's estimates, a meltdown would occur every 4.17 years, each meltdown killing 5,000 people, for an average of 1,199 deaths per year—about 12 percent (one-eighth) of current yearly deaths by pollution from coal-fired plants. If we assume the NRC's estimates instead of the UCS's, then with 480 nuclear power plants there would be one melt-down every 41.7 years costing 400 lives, or an average of 9.6 deaths per year—about .096 percent (less than one one-thousandth) of yearly deaths caused by pollution from coal-fired plants.[46]

Not only the operation of nuclear plants, but also the disposal of their waste frightens some people. How much danger is there from nuclear waste? After a careful analysis of the technology of nuclear waste disposal, Bernard Cohen, former chairman of the American Nuclear Society's Division of Environmental Sciences, estimated that nuclear power generation is likely to cause .0001 deaths per power plant per year due to high-level waste and another .0001 due to low-level waste, a combined .0002 deaths per plant per year. With eighty plants, that yields .0016 deaths per year, or .00016 percent of the 10,000 deaths caused by air pollution from coal. With 480 plants, that would yield .096 deaths per year, or .00096 percent of the deaths from coal pollution.[47]

Another way to look at the question, "How safe is nuclear power compared with alternatives?" is to ask, "How many lives would be saved if the nation's roughly 400 coal-fired plants were all replaced by nuclear plants?" Recall that the NRC estimates that .6 to four deaths per year might be caused by operation and accidents at the average nuclear power plant, while twenty-five to 257 deaths per year are caused by pollution from each coal-fired plant. This means that replacing all 400 coal-fired plants with nuclear plants would save from 8,400 (taking the low-risk estimate for coal and the high-risk estimate for nuclear) to 102,560 (low-risk estimate for nuclear, high-risk estimate for coal) lives per year. Comparing the UCS's esti-mate of 120 deaths per year from roughly eighty nuclear plants and the NRC's low-risk estimate for coal plants, replacing the 400 coal plants with nuclear plants would save 9,400 lives per year.

Will we produce enough energy in the future, and will we pro-duce it at an acceptable risk? Yes.

CAN FOOD SUPPLY KEEP UP?

So far, except for our brief look at agricultural price trends, we've focused primarily on mineral resources. But people can't eat bauxite, petroleum, and iron ore. Food is essential to survival. Can we grow enough of it in the future?

Quite simply, yes. Indeed, as more of the world's nations advance economically, growing enough food will become one of the least of mankind's problems. In the United States, which provides something of a model for the future pattern of other nations' economies, agriculture—including forestry, fisheries, and farms—amounts to just barely over 2 percent of gross national product, and food accounts for only about 15 percent of personal consumer expenditures (and about two-thirds of expenditures on food actually are for the processing, packaging, and marketing, not for the food itself).[48] Agricultural employment has fallen steadily, not only since the nineteenth century, but even in very recent years, and is likely to continue to fall: from 4.3 percent of all employment in 1970, to 3.4 percent in 1980, to 2.9 percent in 1986, and to a projected 2.2 percent in the year 2000.[49] Improving technology and increased capital are enabling food production to outpace population growth many times over.

What are the prospects for increased food production in coming generations? Two chief factors are involved: the number of acres of land that can be harvested, and the amount of food that can be taken from each acre.

Increasing Land Under Cultivation

The amount of land harvested can be increased in two ways: bringing new land under cultivation, and increasing the number of crops harvested each year from presently cultivated land.[50] The former method, it is estimated, can multiply the number of acres harvested two to three times—from the present 2.8-3.5 billion acres[51] to 7-8.5 billion.[52] The cost of developing the land would, on the whole, be minor:

> About one third of the land that is not already being used for farming would cost less than $500 per acre (in 1981 dollars) to make ready; about one third would cost around $1,000 per acre; and the worst third would cost close to $2,000 per acre. This money would pay for things like clearing forests, soil conserva-

tion, terracing, leveling and/or draining, etc. These costs are not decisively different than the current costs of agricultural land. Paying such costs would not multiply the cost of food, indeed might not increase it at all.[53]

Sequential cropping (two, three, or even four crops per year from the same land) "could add as much grain-equivalent as an additional 4,000 million [i.e., 4 billion] acres with a single crop."[54] Max Singer sums up the enormous potential for added cropland:

> We now grow our food on [2.8 billion] acres. We can add [5 billion] acres of land not now used as farmland, and we can add the equivalent of [4 billion] acres by the use of sequential cropping. This is a total potential increase of [9 billion] acres of food harvest. If we used all these additional acres, we would be harvesting more than four times as many acres to grow food as we do now.[55]

Increasing Crop Yields

The yield of each harvest from a given acre of land can vary widely depending on the methods used by the farmer. Yields can be increased "through improved varieties, fertilization, pesticide control, water management, research and technology transfer." The difference in crop yield and labor cost of production between advanced and low- or even moderate-level cultivation can be huge, as Table 7-5 shows. As less-developed countries become wealthier, their crop yields can increase as yields have done in the United States.

> While both developed and developing countries produced around 1.15 tons of grain per hectare in the period 1934-38, the developed countries had lifted yields to 3.0 tons by 1973-76 while the developing countries had attained only 1.4 tons (the U.S., 3.5 tons for all grains and 5.0 tons for corn while some countries have attained 6 tons for rice).[56]

In other words, by using only current technologies already in use in developed countries, developing countries could double or even triple their grain yields.

TABLE 7-5

INCREASING U.S. AGRICULTURAL YIELDS, 1960-1986

CROP	1960-1964	1970-1974	1982-1986
Corn for grain: hours per acre	7.0	4.3	3.1
Yield per acre (bu)	62.2	84.0	109.3
Hours per 100 bushels	11	5	3
Wheat: hours per acre	3.0	2.9	2.6
Yield per acre (bu)	25.2	31.0	36.9
Hours per 100 bushels	12	9	7
Hay: hours per acre	5.0	3.7	3.0
Yield per acre (short tons)	1.77	2.12	2.45
Hours per short ton	2.8	1.8	1.2
Potatoes: hours per acre	48.0	41.6	32.6
Yield per acre (100 lbs.)	195	234	284
Hours per short ton	5	4	2
Cotton: hours per acre	47	18	5
Yield per acre (lb.)	475	470	581
Hours per bale	47	18	5
Milk cows: hours per cow	93	62	24
Yield per cow (100 lbs.)	75	101	127
Hours per 100 lbs. of milk	1.2	.6	.2
Cattle, except milk cows:			
Hours per 100 lbs. of beef produced	2.6	1.7	.9
Hogs: hours per 100 lbs. produced	1.9	1.0	.3
Chickens (laying): hours per 100 layers	126	78	44
Rate of lay*	212	225	246
Hours per 100 eggs produced	.6	.3	.2
Broilers: hours per 100 birds	3	1	.4
Hours per 100 lbs. produced	.8	.3	.1
Turkeys: hours per 100 lbs. produced	2.4	.8	.2

*Eggs produced during year divided by average number of hens and pullets of laying age on hand during year.
Source: U.S. Bureau of the Census, *Statistical Abstract of the United States, 1988*, p. 624, Table 1090.

As of 1983, the low- and middle-income economies of sub-Saharan Africa—the poorest economies in the world—produced, on average, 90 percent of the calories per capita they needed. The three worst countries in the world—Mali, Ghana, and Chad—produced over two-thirds of the calories their people needed.[57] Improving yields alone could enable all of the countries that now produce less than the required calorie supply to surpass it comfortably.

Another factor closely related to improving yields is reducing waste through spoilage and damage by rodents and birds. In developing countries, roughly 10 percent of each year's crops are lost to these causes.[58] Cutting that loss in half would raise calorie supply provision in the world's poorest nations from an average 90 percent to almost 95 percent of requirement.

Why, then, aren't the developing countries producing enough food for their people? The means exist and are not too expensive to be used. The chief problem seems to be that their governments, which tightly control their economies, underemphasize agriculture and place restrictions on it that prohibit its growth. They have subsidized urban growth, expanding military institutions, and monuments at the expense of agriculture. They have set legal maximum prices on agricultural commodities that are below world prices, reducing the incentive for farmers to bear the costs necessary to increase their productivity.[59] Often forced collectivization of agriculture has severely reduced agricultural productivity in developing nations. Reversing these and similar governmental policies in developing nations would quickly resolve most of the difficulties those nations have in providing enough food for their people.

Max Singer reports on studies that indicate "that the amount of food grown on the average acre used all over the world could be increased by 80% just by using more inputs [fertilizers, pesticides, herbicides, machinery, and labor] according to the best practices of today's farmers. In other words, just by using more stuff on the same land we could multiply food production by almost two times." In addition, the use of improved seeds (called "high-yielding varieties," or HYV's) could roughly "double average worldwide yields per acre." Again, "increased use of practical irrigation [i.e., "without use of groundwater, desalination, or diversion of major rivers from their basins"] could add about 15% to the average yield per acre."[60] The use of improved inputs and techniques could also increase yields per acre, though it is more difficult to calculate just how much. In summarizing the potential for increasing yields, Singer writes:

> . . . a potential multiplication by 5.4 times seems roughly correct. A potential gain in average yields of close to five times today's average is entirely consistent with past experience, recent trends, and the current momentum of agricultural technology. . . . In the

most recent decade grain yields for the world as a whole continued to grow at over 1.9% per year. Improvement is continuing.

We can have very high confidence that a tripling of worldwide average grain yield per acre over the next century or so is
entirely feasible. We can also have substantial, but slightly less,
confidence that current agricultural science could also increase
average yields by at least half again, if that were needed. . . . In
[two to three hundred years] there is good reason to believe that
a further doubling of agricultural yields per acre—to ten times
the current world average—would be possible if there were a
demand for it.[61]

Finally, in summarizing the potential of both increasing the
land cultivated and increasing the yield per acre, Singer writes:

> With conventional agriculture we can at least triple the number
> of acres harvested for food, and we can at least triple the effective
> yield of the average acre. . . . Therefore there is good reason to be
> confident that we can grow nine or ten times as much food as we
> do now, using only conventional agriculture—without damaging
> our environment and without spending more than a percent or
> two of our income. Over the very long-term it is quite reasonable
> to believe that we could grow or produce enough food for high
> quality diets for 100 billion people.[62]

I doubt, however, that it will ever be necessary for mankind on
earth to grow that much food. It's more likely that human population will level off at 10 to 20 billion.[63]

CONCLUSION

Resources of all sorts will be less scarce in the future than they are
today. Most will cost less in constant dollars. Almost all will cost
much less as shares of personal income all over the world.[64]

Yet in one important sense it hardly matters whether resources
are getting more or less scarce, more or less costly. Why? Because they
are coming to constitute less and less of our total economy. As our
economy grows and our incomes rise, we will be better able to afford
the resources we need, regardless whether their costs rise or fall. In the
nineteenth century, for instance, raw materials (food, fuels, drinking
water, metals, wood, miscellaneous minerals, stone, sand, and gravel)

constituted the greater part of most people's cost of living in America. But by 1980, all these raw materials accounted for only about $1,620 per capita, or 13.5 percent of U.S. GNP per capita.[65] Natural resources make up less and less of our cost of living.[66]

We are moving from a world dominated by nature to a world dominated by mankind, from a human population overwhelmingly poor to one comfortably wealthy, from an economy dominated by material resources to a world dominated by human (chiefly mental) resources. We aren't all there yet. Some nearly are, others are well on their way, a few trail far behind (but still, mostly, rise faster than developed countries rose from the same low levels).[67] Barring major catastrophes there is little reason to doubt that the vast majority of people will be comfortably wealthy in a few generations.

But we must not confuse increasing material prosperity with all-around human progress. The "human world" into which we are passing will not, barring some special divine intervention, be any better morally or spiritually than the "natural world" we are leaving behind. After all, it was the fall of *man* that brought God's curse on the earth (Genesis 3:17), and nothing man, by himself, can do will ever deliver him from his fallen nature. It is the faith of the Enlightenment, not of Christianity, that predicts utopia just over the horizon.[68]

Christian faith cannot embrace such an idea. Whatever his material progress, man's moral problems will remain. The great challenge will be to build moral character without most life-threatening natural challenges. Wealth cannot ennoble the spirit. It may merely enable that fallen spirit to act out its evil intentions more effectively. Perhaps material prosperity will show better than anything has yet shown that man does not live by natural resources alone, but by every word that proceeds out of the mouth of God.

POPULATION GROWTH AND THE GOOD LIFE: CAN QUANTITY AND QUALITY COEXIST?

Okay, so mankind can, by knowledge and hard work, make a world of plenty for far more people than there are today. Will it be the kind of world any of us would want to live in? What we've seen so far makes an interesting economist's case in favor of population and economic growth. But what about clean air, clean water, uncrowded beaches, wide-open spaces, livable communities? Have we merely crunched numbers at the expense of our souls? Can there be weal as well as wealth? Must prosperity be built on pollution that will kill us all in the end?

So far we've looked mainly at *quantity* of life and property. What about *quality*? There is more to stewardship of the earth than multiplying people and wealth. God has told us not only to cultivate, but also to guard the earth (Genesis 2:15). Conscientious Christians cannot settle for doing only the former and neglecting the latter.

In this chapter we'll look at some environmental issues—chiefly pollution—related to health. In Chapter 9, we'll discuss what resource management policies best comport with Biblical ethics of liberty and property, economic productivity, and mankind's safety. In Chapter 10, we'll look at environmental issues—chiefly associated with crowding—related to aesthetics. Admittedly there is some overlap between the groups of issues treated here and in Chapter 10. The traffic congestion we'll discuss in Chapter 10 can cause unhealthy stress, and smog can ruin an otherwise pleasant view. But the hypertension caused by stress is an indirect effect of the displeasure caused by gridlock, and smog's offense to our aesthetic sensibilities is surely not so important as its effect on our lungs.

COUNTING COSTS AND ACHIEVING HISTORICAL PERSPECTIVE

Before we get to specifics about pollution, though, let's look briefly at two principles that apply to all types of pollution.

First, we need to bring some economic reality to our thinking about pollution. Nobody in his right mind would say he isn't in favor of having cleaner air, water, and land. Pollution is no one's best friend. Everyone considers it, at best, an unavoidable evil. All of us would like to see it banished from the earth. (And perhaps, with improving aerospace technology, we can banish some of it someday by sending nuclear waste, for instance, into the sun.)

But reducing or eradicating pollution is more easily said than done. Like most things in life, pollution abatement costs something. It is not an unmitigated good. And if pollution abatement is not an unmitigated good, then pollution itself must not be an unmitigated evil. After all, pollution costs something to produce. It's expensive to mine, transport, and burn coal and oil; to make insecticides, herbicides, fungicides, and rodenticides; to build, drive, and fuel cars and trucks. No one would bear the costs without expecting benefits.

Reducing pollution, then, costs us something. More expensive electricity, food, and transportation are just a few examples. Admitting that there are costs as well as benefits to pollution abatement doesn't mean we aren't sincere about ridding ourselves of the hazards of pollution. It just means entering the battle with our eyes open.

The relevant question is not, "How much pollution would we like to have if getting rid of it cost us nothing?" but "What is the appropriate combination of environmental purity and all the other desirable things we enjoy, given that we can have more of one only at the cost of sacrificing some of the others?"[1] And the answer is quite likely not one that any individual or committee can determine in a manner that fairly represents all the interests of all the people in the community—whether the community be a town, a metropolitan area, a state, a region, a nation, or the world. (Appendix 3 suggests methods of making pollution cost/benefit analysis efficient.)

Second, any sensible approach to pollution thinks with historical perspective. The important question is not so much, "How much pollution is there now?" but "What are the historical trends in pollution? How much has there been, how much is there now, and how much will there be?" Just as a hospital patient might seem at first glance to be in horrible shape, but turn out to be very much on the mend, so the environment might be getting better, not worse, despite how bad it appears when we look at it without historical perspective. Historian Daniel Boorstin put the point well:

> We sputter against The Polluted Environment—as if it was invented in the age of the automobile. We compare our smoggy air not with the odor of horsedung (sic) and the plague of flies and the smells of garbage and human excrement which filled cities in the past, but with the honey-suckle perfumes of some nonexistent City Beautiful. We forget that even if the water in many cities today is not as spring-pure nor as palatable as we would like, for most of history the water of the cities (and of the countryside) was undrinkable. We reproach ourselves for the ills of disease and malnourishment, and forget that until recently enteritis and measles and whooping cough, diphtheria and typhoid, were killing diseases of childhood, puerperal fever plagued mothers in childbirth, polio was a summer monster.[2]

Merely reading the description by French historian Fernand Braudel of the role famines and epidemics, especially the plague, played in shortening and making loathsome the lives of all people before the nineteenth century cannot fail to make us appreciate the healthier environment we enjoy today—an environment made that way largely by the introduction of chemicals that kill pests and germs and protect crops.[3] Is it sensible to consider these chemicals only as pollution?

DOMAINS OF POLLUTION

Let's look now at trends in the three major domains of environmental pollution: air, water, and land. Are these getting cleaner and safer, getting dirtier and more dangerous, or holding steady? Furthermore, what effects does pollution have on mortality and health?

Air Pollution

You wouldn't guess it from media reports, but air in the United States is getting cleaner, not dirtier. From 1976 to 1986 average carbon monoxide levels at monitoring stations fell 36 percent; ozone levels, 20 percent; sulfur dioxide levels, 40 percent; total suspended particulates levels, 24 percent; nitrogen dioxide levels, 11 percent; and lead levels, 80 percent.[4] Not surprisingly, air pollutant emissions also fell nationwide, despite a 60 percent increase in industrial production. From 1970 to 1985, annual emissions of carbon monoxide fell 32 percent; of sulfur oxides, 27 percent; of volatile organic compounds, 22 percent; of particulates, 60 percent; of lead, 90 percent. Only emissions of nitrogen oxides rose: up 10 percent (but down 1.5 percent 1980-1985).[5]

Improved gas mileage in motor vehicles, a chief source of air pollution, has been a major contributor to cleaner air. Despite a 64 percent increase in the number of vehicle miles driven between 1970 and 1985, motor fuel consumption rose only 32 percent. The reason? Average mileage for all vehicles on the road improved by 22 percent.[6] And there's better news to come. The older cars and trucks are the bigger gas guzzlers. As they wear out and leave the roads, average fuel consumption will decline further, reflecting the near doubling of fuel efficiency in new cars from 1970-1982.[7] And continued improvements in pollution control devices will help, too.

While these data apply only to the United States, similar trends are occurring in all the more-developed countries. The less-developed countries, however, face a period of increasing pollution while their economies catch up. Yet it is hardly fair to criticize them for putting wealth before the environment just now. After all, increasing wealth is the fastest way to increase health and longevity: more wealth makes food, medical care, safe transportation, sanitation (especially water and sewage treatment), and everything else that contributes to better health more affordable. There is every reason to believe that as they approach the levels of wealth we enjoy now, they will change the way they stack environmental and economic issues against each other, just as we did. Perhaps, just as they are climbing out of poverty faster than we did, they will also climb out of pollution faster than we're doing it when the time comes, for in pollution control, just as in economic improvement, they will benefit from our prior development of technology.

Water Quality

The recent history of water quality in the United States is similar to that of air quality. Ten and twenty years ago we were warned that Lake Erie was dying (or dead), but now it's thriving with fish and has "extensive recreational use."[8] Safe drinking water is no longer a concern in any but tiny, isolated locations in America; the same is true in all of the more developed countries of the world.

Water pollution, on the average (and there are some exceptions, mostly in heavily industrialized areas), is going down in the United States. The Environmental Protection Agency has set maximum standards for various water pollutants (and in the case of dissolved oxygen, which decreases as biodegradable pollutants like human waste, paper, and food products increase, a minimum standard). The violation rate for fecal coliform bacteria declined by 23 percent from 1975 to 1986; for dissolved oxygen, by 60 percent; for phosphorus, by 20 percent; for lead, by more than 90 percent; and for cadmium, by more than 75 percent.[9]

Equally important, the percentage of the U.S. population served by sewer systems has increased dramatically: from 61 percent in 1960 to 75 percent in 1986, an increase of over one-fifth. More important still is the percentage served by sewage treatment plants: up from 22 percent in 1960 to 74 percent in 1986, an increase of 236 percent.[10] Some cities and towns are even finding that treated sewage can be used to create wetlands, where plants and natural bacteria further process biodegradable wastes and form habitats for wildlife.[11]

Drinking water supply in the world's less-developed countries is improving. Urban dwellers served by water systems in developing countries rose from 67 to 75 percent, an increase of 12 percent, between 1970 and 1980. The increase for rural dwellers was 107 percent, from 14 to 29 percent. With the rapid shift of population from rural to urban, however, sanitation service in developing countries dropped significantly during that period. While 71 percent of urban dwellers and 11 percent of rural dwellers were served in 1970, only 53 and 13 percent respectively were served in 1980.[12] As economic growth continues in those countries, though, it is certain that they will improve both their drinking water supplies and their sanitation services. Yet the improvement will not be without its ups and downs:

When a country moves from primitive, very poor conditions to the very first stage of economic development, pollution usually is reduced as plumbing and sewer systems and other basic measures for cleanliness become understood and affordable. The next stage of development often brings industrialization and increases in pollution. Later the industrialization often produces enough wealth so that the country wants to, and can afford to, take control measures that reduce pollution.[13]

Improvements in air and water quality in the United States have not been without cost. Air pollution abatement expenditures, in constant (1982) dollars, totalled over $254 billion in 1975-1985, while water pollution abatement expenditures totalled over $262 billion.[14] The willingness of Americans to expend that much money indicates their commitment to maintaining or even improving their environment. As wealth grows over the years, a clean environment will become increasingly affordable. The same will be true for the rest of the world.

Land Pollution: Problems of Solid Waste

Americans generate a lot of trash: about 3.5 pounds per person per day lately, or 150 million tons per year, not including junked cars, obsolete equipment, and a few other types of waste. About 96 percent of our wastes are either biodegradable (paper and paperboard, 37 percent; textiles, 2 percent; wood, 4 percent; food, 8 percent; yard wastes, 18 percent; total, 69 percent) or recyclable (glass, 10 percent; metals, 10 percent; plastics, 7 percent; total, 27 percent), and some are both (paper, paperboard, and wood, 41 percent). But so far, we've found it most cost effective to put most of it into sanitary landfills (what we used to call garbage dumps), though some is incinerated. As of 1984, only about 15 percent of all wastes (by weight) were recovered.[15]

Landfills, however, take up space, and handy locations for landfills are dwindling. About 40 percent of the country's dumps will reach capacity in the next five years.[16] If that rate keeps up, they'll all have to be replaced every 12.5 years. Still, we're not about to be buried in trash. With total U.S. land area of 3.5 million square miles, all of the country's current 6,034 municipal solid waste landfills, even if they averaged a square mile apiece, would fit on .17 percent of U.S. land, or about one-seventh the land presently covered by rural roads and highways, railroad right-of-ways, and airports. Even if we assumed, absurdly, that we'd continue to use up .17 percent of U.S. land every 12.5 years for landfills, it would take 213 years for the land covered by landfills to equal the cropland currently used only for pasture (2.9 percent of U.S. land area, about double the urban land area).[17] That's a long time for us to figure out other things to do with trash than bury it.

RECYCLING

And we have an economic incentive to do just that. As land for landfills becomes increasingly scarce, it also becomes increasingly costly. During 1986 and 1987 alone, average dumping fees nation-wide increased 30 percent to $13.43 per ton, and in the northeast, the most densely populated region of the nation, where landfill scarcities are most critical, "dumping fees of more than $50 a ton are common, and municipalities that must haul trash long distances may pay as much as $140 a ton."[18] The rising costs of disposal are reflected in rising rates of recycling: from 7 percent in 1975 to 10 percent in 1984, an increase of 43 percent in just nine years.[19]

What can or might we do with our trash other than burying it? Lots of things. Philadelphia has contracted with New Jersey farmers who "collect food waste from curbs and backyards and haul it back to their farms to feed their hogs. They are paid about $40 a ton to remove and dispose of 115 tons of waste daily, saving the city roughly $60 per ton."[20] With about 11 million tons of food wastes going into landfills annually, we could feed a lot of hogs and perhaps bring down the price of pork while we're at it.

Already in some areas incineration has become less expensive than burying garbage. Methods have been developed to turn biodegradable garbage into energy.[21] Over 40 percent of municipal waste could be composted. The New Alchemy Institute in Massachusetts uses composted waste to make energy and carbon dioxide to heat a huge greenhouse and grow plants and tree saplings at 20 to 40 percent higher yields than normal, a process that could be duplicated almost anywhere.[22]

Some 21 percent of annual paper and paperboard wastes already are being recycled, as are 30 percent of aluminum wastes, 3 percent of ferrous metals, and 7 percent of glass wastes.[23] Jerry Powell, editor of *Resource Recycling* magazine, estimates that over 50 percent of current garbage could be recycled if buyers could be found for it.[24] New ways are found to use recycled materials all the time. As landfill costs increase, alternatives become increasingly attractive.

Plastics, which account for about 7 percent of our trash, had little recycling market as recently as 1986. But since then some plastics recycling processes have become profitable. Dow Chemical Co. began a joint project with Domtar Inc., a Canadian company, to recycle plastics; Mobil Chemical Co. and Genpak Corp. began recycling plastic fast-food containers into pellets from which insulation, flowerpots, clothes hangers, and industrial packaging can be made; Wellman Inc. has greatly increased its recycling of plastic pop bottles into polyester fibers to stuff jackets, bedspreads, and furniture cushions; and Plastic Recycling Inc. has begun recycling plastics into "plastic lumber" for fence posts and other materials.[25]

Aluminum has long been one of the most economically rewarding recyclables. Since it takes only about 5 percent as much energy to recycle aluminum as to process raw ore, there are strong economic incentives to increase its already 30 percent recycling rate. Glass is marginal since energy and raw material savings in recycling are slight to nonexistent, and paper recycling has an up-and-down market.[26] Glass recycling could be increased, though, if more states would adopt laws requiring bottle deposits—a measure citizens support, according to polls.[27]

Educating citizens is an important part of recycling. In May 1985, San Jose tried a pilot recycling project with curbside pickup. Where brightly colored containers were provided for recyclable materials, participation was about 70 percent; without providing containers, it was 35 percent. Still the city saved about $20 per ton of trash collected.[28]

TOXIC AND NUCLEAR WASTES

A special concern for many people is toxic wastes. They, too, are recyclable. Marine Shale Processors, Inc., in Louisiana, has pioneered a super-hot (over 2,000° F.) incineration technology that changes the molecular structure of the wastes and turns them into rocks, a process that company founder Jack Kent calls "glassification." The resulting product keeps the toxic wastes, mostly metals like cadmium and lead, from migrating. The gravel-like end product can be used as base for roads. The process isn't just marginally economical; it has earned its company fast-climbing revenues: up from $5.5 million in 1986 to about $40 million in 1988.[29] Genetic engineers are designing bacteria and fungi that digest toxic wastes and excrete safer substances.[30]

Another cause for concern is radioactive wastes.[31] The United States produce about 1,400 metric tons per year.[32] Some can be recycled in various ways: e.g., to sterilize raw sewage, food, and surgical dressings. Americium is used in smoke detectors. And plutonium and uranium have important industrial and energy uses.[33] Wastes not recycled can be disposed of safely by solidification and deep burial.

Misconceptions abound regarding nuclear waste. A common notion is that radioactive materials are the most deadly known to man; yet plutonium, on an equal-molecular basis, "is 80,000 times less toxic than botulism virus."[34] Furthermore, although materials remain radioactive for thousands of years, their toxicity decreases fairly rapidly during the first several hundred years, a period for which safe containment, while obviously more difficult than short-term storage of other toxic materials, is both technically and economically feasible.

When some people hear that nuclear waste must be carefully isolated for a few hundred years, they react with alarm. They point out that very few man-made structures, and few of our political, economic, and social institutions can be expected to last for hundreds of years. Such worries stem from our experience on the surface of the earth, where most things are short-lived. However, 2,000 feet below the surface the environment is quite different. Things remain essentially unchanged for millions of years.

Devoting 1 percent of the revenues from a typical nuclear power plant to processing and burying its wastes would be sufficient to make the waste safe throughout its dangerous radiation lifetime.[35]

In addition, it is unrealistic to suppose that future generations will be helpless to protect themselves should some nuclear waste somehow be released from its deep-burial storage location:

We have accepted without debate a patronizing view of our descendants. According to the EPA we must protect them for 10,000 years from the consequences of their posited unawareness of radioactivity. No other activity, from oil drilling to water engineering, has a 10,000-year planning horizon. The addition of one more function to a digital watch would make the measurement of radioactivity as commonplace as time-keeping, and eliminate the most extreme human intervention scenarios. Is this unlikely in 100 years? Will the consequences of a given dose of radiation be unreduced by 100 years of medicine, not to say 1,000? It was only slightly over 100 years ago that the germ theory of disease was discovered.[36]

WASTE OR RESOURCE?

As technology increases, we are finding more and more ways to turn more and more things into resources. Just as petroleum was not a resource but a nuisance as little as 200 years ago, so many things long considered useless trash are becoming valuable as we learn how to use them. It's time we learned to see our landfills, our auto junk-yards, and our sewage sludge as banks where resources are deposited until it's economically efficient to use them.

A friend of mine, Tom McAlister, is water and sewer superin-tendent of Rogers, Arkansas. His treatment plant sterilizes raw sewage, after which it is mixed with water and sprayed over fields. The hay grows faster and greener there than anywhere nearby. That is done by hundreds of sewage facilities nationwide already. Thirty years ago sewage was merely a nuisance. The city of Cambridge, Massachusetts, is working on converting its landfill into a park with football fields, softball diamonds, nature walks, and picnic grounds.[37] The same can be done with many, if not most, landfills. With imagination and investment, we can keep pollution to tolerable levels and turn some of it from bane to boon.

FOUR CURRENT WORRIES

When I discuss the environment with friends, four problems come up again and again: global warming (the "greenhouse effect"), depletion of the ozone layer, acid rain, and radon gas poisoning. The media have had a field day emphasizing these, making them topics of everyday conversation. Just when I thought I'd escaped discussing them for a while, when I was flying recently I opened the in-flight maga-zine and found myself staring at an excerpt from a book by Walter Cronkite that beats the drum on all four of them. People are gen-uinely frightened. They think these problems are dreadfully danger-ous, and they're convinced that we have no workable solutions. Because they are matters of such intense concern, let's look at each one specifically.

Global Warming

Climatologists have long been aware that an increase in certain gases in the atmosphere, particularly carbon dioxide (CO_2) but also hydrocarbons and methane, might cause an increase in global temperatures. These gases allow heat from the sun to reach the earth's surface, but trap reflected heat, thus moderating earth's temperatures the way the glass walls and ceilings of greenhouses moderate temperatures inside them. Without this greenhouse effect, the earth's surface temperatures "would be like the moon's, bitterly cold [-270 degrees Fahrenheit] at night and unbearably hot [+212 degrees] during the day."[38] Increasing these gases in the atmosphere would trap more heat at the surface of the earth. All else remaining the same, global average surface temperatures would rise.

In recent years some climatologists have become alarmed at the increase of the greenhouse gases in the atmosphere.[39] The amount of CO_2 has increased by about 20 percent since 1850, from 290 to 340 parts per million; on that everyone is agreed. But on everything else related to the greenhouse effect there is, as two investigators put it, a "cascade of uncertainty."[40] Some scientists claim average global temperatures already have increased significantly, others deny it. Some claim that an increase in atmospheric CO_2 will cause an average temperature increase of 2 to 4 degrees centigrade, others that it will cause an increase of less than 1 degree. Some claim that the greenhouse effect has already started, others that we're experiencing a slow decline in temperatures.[41]

What we *don't know* about future CO_2 buildup and its effect on global climate is as important as what we think we know (and most of that is debatable).[42] We don't know what average global temperatures really are (most monitoring stations are on land, not oceans, which cover 73 percent of the earth's surface),[43] or how much, if at all, they have changed over the last century and a half. We don't know how atmosphere, land, and oceans interact to determine climate and the extent to which some interactions might be self-regulating (e.g., increased CO_2 could cause increased growth of phytoplankton in oceans, which would absorb huge amounts of CO_2, creating a new steady state, or increased surface temperatures could cause increased evaporation, making more clouds, which could reflect more incoming heat from the earth). We don't know how much CO_2 is trapped in the atmosphere and how much is reabsorbed by photosynthesis, or how great the heating effect from CO_2 is.

We don't know how much the world's forests, which are important absorbers of CO_2, will expand or contract; whether the best response to a real increase in temperature would be to reduce fossil fuel consumption, plant more forests, adapt to the new climate, or some combination of these; the effect of varying rates of sunspot activity on global climate; the effect of volcanic activity on atmospheric CO_2 (we know it's huge, but don't know how huge). We don't even know whether an increase in temperature would, on balance, harm or help mankind.

Nonetheless, there are some things we do know about global climate, and they don't support the global warming/greenhouse effect hypothesis. One is that the computer models used to simulate the effects of increased greenhouse gases are grossly oversimplified and don't come close to reflecting the complexities of global climate.[44]

Another thing we know is that natural global climate variability unaccompanied by identifiable causes yields decades-long temperature variations big enough to explain all of the temperature patterns of the past century. In addition, the rising and falling (up .4° C 1880-1940, down .2° C 1940-1970, up .3° C 1970-1980) "global average temperature patterns" in the past century are closely correlated to increases and decreases in sunspot activity, an indicator of fluctuations in the sun's energy output, but are sometimes opposite of what would be predicted if the unvaryingly rising amounts of greenhouse gases in the atmosphere were the sole or major cause of global temperature changes.[45] Fluctuations in the sun's energy output may well account for most or all of the apparent global temperature increases, leaving greenhouse gases to account for at most a negligible amount.[46]

As often is the case, a longer historical view can help us evaluate the possibility of anthropogenic global warming and its import for civilization a little better. Historical studies of sunspot activity indicate that it goes in cycles, "with periods of low activity every 200 years or so during the last thousand years—midway between the 10th and 11th centuries, and in the 13th, 15th, 17th and 19th centuries"—with another low period due in the next century. These cycles of lower-than-normal solar energy output have correlated with cooler-than-normal global temperatures. "If the 21st-century cooling is comparable to the Little Ice Age [of the 17th century], the earth will be about 1° C colder as a result of natural factors alone than it has been in the 1980s."[47]

An even longer perspective reminds us that ice ages occur about every 10,000 to 12,000 years, and the last one was about 11,000 years ago.[48] We're due for another soon. This raises the possibility that whatever slight warming might result from increased anthropogenic greenhouse gases could help mitigate the effects of the next ice age rather than overheating the world. No wonder one recent study warned that much more reliable computer modeling of climate should be done before policy makers undertake "corrective programs that could turn out to be unnecessary—or even harmful if a substantial natural cooling occurs in the 21st century."[49]

The point is not to deny that global warming is occurring or might be soon (although I doubt it). It is to suggest that we humbly acknowledge our limited understanding of God's amazing creation and be patient and deliberate in thinking about it, particularly when important and costly policy decisions are at stake.

What might we do to prevent or mitigate global warming? If it's largely due to natural phenomena, not much. We'll have to adjust. But if it's largely due to human activity (which is highly unlikely), there are sensible and affordable steps to take. First, we can convert oil and coal power plants to nuclear, a step that even the anti-nuclear Sierra Club, in its August 1989 world assembly, acknowledged could help.[50] Second, we can harvest mature forests (which metabolize CO_2 slowly) and plant new ones (which metabolize CO_2 rapidly). Third, we can use fuels like hydrogen and electricity for transportation.[51]

Of course global warming, man-made or natural, might occur anyway. The polar ice caps might melt—a process that would take centuries—causing sea levels to rise. Some coastal cities might have to be abandoned, although most probably could cope with the rising sea level, as Holland, Venice, and New Orleans have coped with their situations for generations. There would be no hurry. (And modern technology and greater wealth would make it easier.) Weather patterns might change. Some agricultural regions might become deserts, but some deserts could get all the rain they'll need for year-round farming. Areas presently too cold for significant agriculture could become tremendously fertile.

Despite all the uncertainties, futurist Max Singer calls the possibility of the greenhouse effect "[p]robably the main physical danger to the world now in sight. . . ." Nonetheless, he estimates that the cost of responding, including changing living patterns and moving some populations away from seacoasts, "will probably not be disastrously onerous" and "is unlikely to [be] as much as 5% of Gross World Product (GWP)"[52]—a price that the wealthy world of the twenty-first or twenty-second century will be able to afford without dire stress.

Ozone Depletion

Another cause of concern lately has been an alleged depletion of the stratospheric ozone layer that surrounds the earth. Ozone absorbs ultraviolet radiation, which may cause skin cancer. Ozone is depleted when chlorofluorocarbons (CFCs), nitrous oxides (N_2O), and some other chemicals react with it in the stratosphere. The less ozone there is, the more ultraviolet radiation people will be exposed to, and hence the more skin cancer they might suffer. This scenario is a legitimate concern. Nobody likes skin cancer. But the scenario rests on shaky foundations. That doesn't mean it's wrong; it just means it needs careful analysis and may not be adequate basis for stringent policy measures.

First, there is the empirical problem of determining the extent, if any, to which the ozone layer has been depleted. Unfortunately, it's hard to tell. The amount of ozone in the stratosphere naturally and commonly fluctuates by about 5 percent.[53] That makes it difficult, if not impossible, to see whether any trends of less than 5 percent are occurring. The much-publicized "hole" in the ozone layer over Halley Bay, Antarctica, is not really a hole, but a temporary thin spot (the depletion is only about 50 percent) that occurs annually in September and October. It was initially detected when the station there was first set up in 1956 (long before CFC and other suspect chemical levels would have reached high enough densities to have caused it), and does not seem to reflect global ozone changes.

Second, empirical difficulties extend to understanding how the ozone layer is formed and how resilient it is. In 1908 "an immense meteor exploded over the Stony Tunguska River basin of Central Siberia with the force of a ten megaton explosion. . . . [I]n its passage through the Earth's atmosphere this meteor would have generated about thirty million tons of nitric oxide. This nitric oxide would probably have removed 30% to 45% of the ozone in the Northern hemisphere. There is evidence that the ozone was depleted about that much in 1909, and that it took several years before the ozone level of the atmosphere returned to normal."[54] If the ozone layer could recover from that in "several years," might it recover from a much smaller pollution-engendered depletion equally quickly?

Third, as with the effect of greenhouse gases, there are theoretical difficulties in understanding how CFCs and other chemicals interact with the ozone layer. Studies have rendered widely divergent results, with one National Academy of Sciences study in 1980 predicting 18 percent depletion, a rerun of the study in 1982 predicting 7 percent depletion, and a rerun in 1984 predicting 2 to 4 percent depletion, all from the same CFC standard. We are only beginning to understand "the counteracting effects of other pollutants: methane, nitrogen oxides, and carbon dioxide," gases which, although they might contribute to a greenhouse effect, could mitigate ozone depletion. Again, just as alleged global warming trends tend to "disappear in the noisy climatic temperature pattern" of history,[55] minute ozone fluctuations predicted by the models (in the range of .2 percent per year) may be impossible to verify granted natural variations, "some of them as large as 50 per cent within a few months, at a given station."[56]

Fourth, the effects of ozone depletion on human health are generally exaggerated. Despite claims to the contrary, skin cancer rates are not directly correlated to ultraviolet exposure. Since 1935, skin cancer rates have increased 800 percent, while UV-B (the biologically active form of ultraviolet light) reaching sea level has declined. Finally, "a 5 percent decrease in the ozone layer, as calculated by some of the more pessimistic scenarios, would increase UV exposure to the same extent as moving about sixty miles south, the distance from Palm Beach to Miami, or from Seattle to Tacoma. An increase in altitude of one thousand feet would produce the same result."[57]

Ozone depletion could really be happening, but at least until now the data are not sufficiently clear to justify an unequivocal judgment. CFCs could be partially responsible, but so could natural factors like chlorine from volcanoes and salt spray, or solar-cycle variability (in which case we might be observing simply a downward swing in a cycle; ozone observations don't go back far enough to be sure). The point is not to deny the reality of the phenomenon (though it is questionable), but to suggest, as with global warming, that costly policy decisions should be based on more persuasive evidence.

How costly would it be to stop using CFCs? Available substitutes wouldn't work as well, might be toxic, flammable, or corrosive, would "reduce the energy efficiency of appliances such as refrigerators, and they'll deteriorate, requiring frequent replenishment." Of course, this doesn't mean that better substitutes won't be developed, substitutes as good as CFCs or better. Even so, making the trade will be costly: "About $135 billion worth of equipment uses CFCs in the U.S. alone, and much of this equipment will have to be replaced or modified to work well with the CFC substitutes. Eventually, that will involve one hundred million home refrigerators, the air conditioners in ninety million cars, and the central air-conditioning plants in 100,000 large buildings."[58]

Some Americans and Europeans criticized developing nations, particularly India and China, for refusing, at an international Conference to Save the Ozone Layer in March 1989, to agree to ban CFCs. But granted the tentative nature of the evidence, might they not have been making a prudent cost-benefit analysis? After all, they are not so well equipped as the more-developed nations to afford the costs of banning CFCs. It is only reasonable that they should demand more convincing proof than we might before taking those costs on themselves.

At any rate, it seems unlikely that depletion of the ozone layer will be irremediable; that depletion will harm human health seriously before it is detected and countermeasures are taken; and that in the long run, granted increasing wealth, whatever costs must be borne will be disastrous.

Acid Rain

During 1989, the Environmental Protection Agency, spurred by environmentalists and President George Bush, announced a $3 to $4 billion program to diminish acid rain. Its method is to reduce sulphur dioxide (SO_2) emissions from coal-fired generating plants, emissions believed to be the chief cause of acid rain. Acid rain, in turn, is thought to be killing forests and raising the acidity of lakes and streams in the northeastern United States so much that it reduces fish and other aquatic life. But proponents of the program overlook a few facts:

(1) The volume of growing stock of forests in the northeast has increased steadily since 1952, up 79 percent (up 72 percent for softwoods, allegedly most affected by acid rain). That's hardly consistent with the notion that acid rain is killing forests.

(2) There is no statistically significant correlation between acid rain and the acidity of lakes and streams. Indeed, only 10 percent of the lakes in the Adirondacks region of upstate New York, which has the highest acid rain readings in the country, are acid; 12 percent of the lakes in Florida, which has precipitation acidity only 15 percent of the Adirondacks' rate, are acid; and 47 percent of the lakes in Nova Scotia are acid, although the acidity of precipitation there is only one-fifth of that in the Adirondacks. On Frazier Island, Australia, 79 percent of the lakes are acid, although the island gets no acid rain.

(3) The real cause of acidity in lakes and streams is not precipitation, but acid leached by surface runoff (the source of over 90 per-

cent of lakes' and streams' water) from surrounding soil. "For New England, the correlation between acid rain and acid lakes is less than 0.16 (statistically insignificant), compared with a correlation of acid lakes with soil chemistry of nearly 0.80."

(4) The acid in the soil is caused primarily by decay of vegetation, and more vegetation decays when forests aren't harvested than when they are. Lake sediment analysis shows that the lakes that are acidic today were acidic in preindustrial times.

(5) The real cause of increasing acidity in northeastern American lakes and streams in recent years is maturing forests, not SO_2 emissions from coal generating plants. Acid lakes and streams result not from man's activity, but from nature's doing its thing. Acidity is simply returning to historic levels, from which it fell early in this century when many forests were clear cut for timber, removing acid from the surrounding soil. The decaying forests that have been offered as evidence of the effect of acid rain are really forests that have matured recently and have begun the normal cycle of decay and replacement. Immature forests in the same areas are healthy, showing no ill effects from acid rain.

(6) Resuming harvests of the forests in the region would do far more to reduce the lakes' and streams' acidity than reducing SO_2 emissions and would have the happy side effect of making lumber for housing construction less costly.

(7) The acidity in the lakes could be neutralized without reducing SO_2 emissions (which are almost certainly not causally related to the acidity anyway) by adding lime to the lakes instead, at about .025 percent (using boats) to .125 percent (using helicopters) of the cost of reducing the SO_2 emissions.[59]

Nonetheless, environmentalist groups don't like the lumber industry; they want the forests left in their natural state (but not the lakes and streams, it seems!). And they want SO_2 emissions reduced anyway. So they still push for the EPA's program instead of the less expensive and more effective solutions. And because they are the loudest and most persistent lobbyists, they are more likely to sway regulators than those who could benefit from the more sensible ways of dealing with the problem.

As if this weren't enough to demonstrate the self-defeating nature of some environmentalist ideas (a phenomenon we'll see more of in Chapter 10), reducing SO_2 emissions could exacerbate, however slightly, the alleged greenhouse effect. Sulphur dioxide brightens clouds, increasing the rate at which they reflect heat from the earth.

Its presence in the air mitigates the heat-trapping effect of carbon dioxide. Taking it out could increase the greenhouse effect, while doing nothing to reduce the acidity of lakes and streams.

Radon Gas Poisoning

Lately Americans have been alarmed by news of dangerously high levels of radioactive radon accumulating in their buildings. As with acid rain, nature, not man, is the culprit: radon is a byproduct of the decay of radioactive minerals in the ground. Man's attempts to reduce energy consumption have exacerbated the problem: tighter housing construction and more insulation have trapped radon released from the earth inside our houses. As a result, some experts warn, we risk radiation exposure that could cause lung cancer.

But as frequently happens, facts don't quite fit theory. If the theory is correct, locales with high radon levels should have higher lung cancer death rates than locales with low levels. But no such correlation exists. Instead, a comparison of radon levels and lung cancer death rates in 411 U.S. counties showed, "Lung cancer rates in counties tend to strongly *decrease* as average radon levels increase and vice versa. The effect seems to be statistically unquestionable. This is in sharp contrast to the (EPA) prediction that lung cancer rates should *increase* substantially as average radon levels increase."[60]

Why the discrepancy? The prediction was based on a 1968 study of uranium miners, most of whom were heavy smokers. Radon gas is a byproduct of uranium decay, so uranium miners are exposed to higher doses than are found in buildings. The EPA estimated that it took 2,500 "working level months" of radon exposure to produce one lung cancer death among these heavy-smoking uranium miners. From this it extrapolated that four picocuries of radon per liter of air was dangerous, requiring "remedial action." Yet that level would produce a lifetime exposure equivalent to only fourteen "working level months" for uranium miners, which "translates into a six-tenths per cent risk of dying from lung cancer from residential radon, or slightly less than the risk from drinking tap water in normal quantities."[61] The radon menace appears to be empty.

VIEWING THE BIG PICTURE

While it's important to look at specific domains and types of pollution, the more important question is whether the environment as a whole is getting safer or more dangerous to human health and life.

If we define pollution chiefly as byproducts of human activity that increase our risks of disease and death, life expectancy trends in the United States indicate that the balance of pollution versus the benefits of the polluting society is getting better, not worse. Average life expectancy at birth rose from fifty-four in 1920 to seventy-five in 1986.[62] Granted that average life expectancy until the eighteenth century was about twenty-eight years, and that the normal human life span (the age at which most people die of old age) is about eighty-five,[63] this means that life expectancy increased almost as much in the fifty-six years from 1920 to 1986 as it did in the 220 years from 1700 to 1920; that it rose about 46 percent of the way from the pre-Industrial Revolution average to actual life span between 1700 and 1920; and that it rose another 37 percent of the way between 1920 and 1986.

More impressive are statistics about adult life expectancy—the additional years an adult of a given age can expect to live. In 1940, the average forty-year-old American could expect to live another thirty-one years; in 1950, another 32.8 years; in 1960, another 33.8 years; in 1970, another 34.6 years; in 1980, another 36.7 years; and in 1985, another 37.3 years,[64] an increase of 20 percent in forty-five years, the most rapid increase occurring from 1970 to 1985. Sociologist and statistician Ben Wattenberg calls these "Super Numbers," numbers that tell us something tremendously important about our lives. Writing of this period, he asks,

> Wasn't this . . . when headlines were proclaiming that air pollution was frying your lungs, radiation was corroding your innards, carcinogens were everywhere, even popping up in your genetic structure? Wasn't this the same decade when Rachel Carson's grim prophecies were supposed to come true, when low-level radiation, high-level radiation, eutrophic water, and floating particulates were about to cut our time short? After all, the premise of the whole environmental legislative thrust—clean air, clean water, and so on—was that our health was in grave new danger, that the quality of our lives was eroding.[65]

Whether we do or don't have "too much pollution," then, it is clear that at least the balance of pollution versus the life-preserving benefits of the polluting society has improved dramatically. In other words, regardless what absolute levels of pollution exist, the overall environment today is healthier than it was in the past.[66]

LEGAL RESTRAINTS ON POLLUTION

Granted that progress is being made in many areas of pollution and that on the whole our environment is getting safer, not more dangerous, problems still can and do arise. Sometimes pollution really does hurt people. What can be done about it then? There is a Biblical remedy: just restitution.

Holding polluters liable for damage is largely the responsibility of civil courts enforcing tort law. Scripture supports the principle of restitution for negligent and malicious damage to persons and property and reveals principles to ensure that the restitution is just (Exodus 21:26-36; 22:5, 6).

First, under ordinary circumstances, compensation should be neither more nor less than necessary to restore the injured party, so far as possible, to his prior condition (Exodus 21:18, 19, 33-36). If the damage was unforeseeable, the victim and the tort-feasor were to divide the loss evenly. Even if the damage was foreseeable, its accidental nature meant that compensation was only to be equal, not multiple, as in the case of theft (compare Exodus 22:4).[67]

Second, fault (culpable negligence) exists only when past experience (including that embodied in statute law, like laws requiring railings around balconies [Deuteronomy 22:8]) has established the dangerous nature of an object or activity in someone's control and therefore has created the *a priori* assumption of foresight. Without fault, compensation is limited to dividing the loss evenly (Exodus 21:28, 29, 35, 36). Fault does not exist without clear historical precedent (either in personal experience or statute law); what can only be seen to have been "foreseeable" through hindsight must not be confused with what was reasonably foreseeable prior to an accident.

Third, the state cannot set a monetary value on a human life. Someone who is legally liable by culpable negligence for another's death must pay with his own life unless the survivors of the victim offer to accept a ransom instead—however high it might be, including perpetual servitude (Exodus 21:30).[68]

Fourth, one is liable only for persons and things over which he has—or at least should have—control, and then only if others do not interfere with his control so as to negate it. He is not liable for others' acts outside his authority. If someone let an ox out without its owner's knowledge, and the ox killed a neighbor, the person who opened the gate, not the owner, would be liable. Similarly, a company whose facility was sabotaged, releasing a dangerous chemical, would not be held liable for resulting damages; the saboteur would be. Scripture forbids punishing someone for an act he did not commit and for which he had no responsibility (Deuteronomy 24:16). Thus clear proof of causality is imperative if liability is to be adjudged and compensation assessed.

Fifth, punitive damages should be added to compensation only if property damage resulted from deliberate sabotage (i.e., if there was "malice aforethought"), and even the value of the punitive damages should be small compared with the actual compensation (Exodus 22:5). No punitive damages should be assessed atop equal compensation without proof of malicious intent (v. 6).

Thus Biblical Law requires strict restitution in cases of liability. But it also makes proving liability difficult. The plaintiff must prove fault, which means the combination of both causation and foresight. Foresight is not assumed, but must be proved by reference to past experience or statutory law. Even when liability is proved, compensation normally is limited to restoring what is lost, though when culpable negligence is proved small punitive damages may be added. (There is no provision for compensation for grief or for pain and suffering.) The Law protects both parties in a liability dispute, and the presumption is that in most cases victims are to bear accidental loss. Biblical tort law does not presume that every loss must be recoverable from someone else.

Where persons can prove clear, measurable injury to themselves or their property, can prove that the injury was caused by some pollutant,[69] can prove who produced the pollutant or released it into the environment, and can prove that reasonable foresight based on prior experience or statutory law would have informed the polluter to restrict the pollutant lest it harm someone, then they can and should receive compensation through the tort process.[70]

EARTH: CURSED BUT RESILIENT

Following the account of Creation, Scripture says, "And God saw all that He had made, and behold, it was very good" (Genesis 1:31). Some people assume on this and other bases that whatever is natural is good. But a short while later Scripture gives a different message. After the Fall, God said to Adam, "Cursed is the ground because of you; in toil you shall eat of it all the days of your life. Both thorns and thistles it shall grow . . ." (Genesis 3:17, 18). Because of the curse, "the creation was subjected to futility"; it "groans and suffers" (Romans 8:20, 22). The best way to fulfill the mandate to guard the earth (Genesis 2:15) is not always to preserve it untouched; often it is to modify it. There is a redemptive aspect to man's work (Genesis 3:18, 19).

In many important instances, nature is not best unchanged by man. Prudent forest management, including regular harvesting and reseeding, can reduce soil acidity and thus reduce naturally high levels of acidity in lakes and streams, as well as diminish risks from forest fires. Rivers that regularly flood and change course, destroying forests, fields, and human habitats, can be tamed by careful placement of dams, yielding a safer, healthier environment for man and beast while providing valuable recreation areas and reliable water resources to counteract the effect of droughts. Dangerous diseases like plague and malaria can be reduced by reducing the populations of disease-carrying vermin and insects.

The assumption that whatever is natural is best is wrong. Only people far removed from the age-old struggle to survive against the dangerous forces of nature can forget that. Botulism virus is natural, as are smallpox, plague, malaria, and polio. Floods and droughts are natural. Unpasteurized milk is natural and spoils fast. It is natural for insects and rodents to damage crops, sometimes enough to cause a high risk of famine. These and myriad other natural risks to human, animal, and plant populations are all natural, but not good. They can be, have been, and ought to be controlled by human action for the protection not only of human life and health, but also of the natural world.

Interdependence and Resilience

A common theme of environmentalism is that the ecosystems of the world are closely interdependent. From this it has been inferred that the environment must be excruciatingly fragile. Yet that is not the only inference that makes sense.

Not long ago I had the fun of jumping on a large trampoline. The tarp was secured to the frame by scores of ropes passed through rings sewn into the fabric, evenly distributing the stress of each impact, making the strain on each connection light. At one point I bounced, accidentally, directly on a connection rather than on the tarp. The direct impact tore it. But because there were scores of other connections, the stress of succeeding impacts was redistributed and the tarp remained fully usable. Over time, a rope will deteriorate here, another there, and eventually the owner will repair them. But it's not likely that enough ropes will deteriorate at once to make the trampoline useless.

The interdependence of the world is like that, only inestimably more complex. While individual ecosystems can be fragile, the capacity of the environment as a whole to compensate for damage here and there is astounding, especially when man applies his God-given intelligence to help out.

Yes, let us guard as well as cultivate the environment. But let us also redeem it. And let us remember that its Maker foresaw all that mankind could ever do, and made the world fit to sustain us as long as He intends us to be here. Without minimizing concerns about the environment or shirking our call to guard as well as cultivate it, we should not be surprised that the environment God created is not so fragile as we thought. The God who created and sustains all things by the word of His power (Genesis 1:1; Colossians 1:17; Hebrews 1:3) is infinitely wise. He has designed a world with numerous safety valves.

MANAGING THE RESOURCES OF THE EARTH

*T*oward the end of the parable of the laborers in the vineyard, Jesus portrays the landowner—who represents God—as saying to a grumbling laborer, "Friend, I am doing you no wrong; did you not agree with me for a denarius? . . . Is it not lawful for me to do what I wish with what is my own?" (Matthew 20:13, 15). The phrase "doing . . . no wrong" translates the Greek *adiko*, a form of the verb *adikeo*, "to wrong [by] any violation of human or divine law," to "treat someone unjustly," to "injure."[1] *Adikeo* signifies action opposite to *dikaioo*, to "show justice, do justice."[2] The stem of both verbs is *dike*, "justice,"[3] meaning whatever is in accord with the law, whatever is right according to the authoritative standard of right and wrong. Hence we should find it no surprise that *adikeo* may be translated "injure," a word derived from the Latin privative prefix *in-* and the stem *jus* or *juris*, "right, law," the same stem that we find in our words *just, justice, judge, judgment, jurisprudence*, and *jurisdiction*.

What the landowner said amounts to, "Friend, I am not violating the law in my action toward you. . . . Is it not [therefore] lawful for me to do what I wish with what is my own?" The comment rests on the fundamental principle that one may lawfully do whatever he wishes with what belongs to him so long as he does not in so doing violate God's Law in relation to someone else. So long as we use our property consistently with the Fifth through Tenth Commandments, civil law should protect our liberty rather than limiting or infringing it.

In the midst of writing this chapter, I talked with my friend Wayne Weatherford, a man well read in economic theory. "What are you writing about?" he asked. "Managing the resources of the earth," I said, to which he replied with a frown and a raised eyebrow, indicating the dubious virtue of the subject. "By which I mean," I hastily added, "you manage yours and let other folks manage theirs, and we'll all get along okay." Wayne's frown turned to a smile.

Perhaps it is oversimplifying things a bit to say, "You manage yours and let other folks manage theirs, and we'll all get along okay." But that simple statement probably is closer to the truth about resource management than any other statement as concise. Within the limits of God's moral Law,[4] the best policy of resource management is to permit every individual to use what belongs to him as he pleases. When violations of that Law occur, they are to be prosecuted by civil or criminal action, including tort litigation for recovery of injury. Aside from that, Biblical ethics insists that we cannot limit our neighbors' use of their property.

This perspective runs contrary to popular thinking today. No doubt it will take a good deal of time and persuasion to attract many people to endorse it. But I hope, in this short discussion, to suggest a few justifications for it.

DEFINING THE SUBJECT

The title of this chapter is "Managing the Resources of the Earth." The surface simplicity of such a title quickly gives way to deep complexities upon analysis. It will be instructive to look at those complexities. Let's take each element of the title in reverse order.

In What Sense Does the Earth Have Resources?

What does it mean to speak of resources *of the earth*? Should we take *of* as a possessive preposition: resources that belong to the earth, that are its property? No doubt some idolaters of the environment think of resources that way, seeing even man as belonging to the earth. But Scripture doesn't see things that way. It sees the earth and everything in it as belonging to God, and God as having entrusted all of this to man as His vice-regent, giving to man some strange thing called "rule" or "dominion" over everything in the earth, instructing man to "fill the earth, and subdue it" (Psalm 24:1; 8:3-8; Genesis 1:26-30). The earth owns nothing. So what we mean when we speak of resources *of the earth* is not resources belonging to the earth, but resources that we find here.

But that in its turn is misleading. To put it rather crudely, we don't *find* resources anywhere on, in, or over the earth—at least not in their natural state. For in their natural state things are not resources at all. Indeed, they often are obstacles, sometimes dangerous ones. No, the earth—poor as it is, owning nothing—is not generous. It gives us no ready-made resources. Instead, we find *raw materials*. And these are to be distinguished most carefully from *resources*.

Raw Materials vs. Resources

Raw materials *become* resources only by the application of human ingenuity to them. Until then they contribute little or nothing to our needs—with the important exceptions of things like air and gravity,[5] from which we benefit without conscious action. Pretty much everything else in our environment becomes a resource to us only when we have developed it in some way. In other words, we don't *find* resources, we *make* them.

Take petroleum, for instance. No less an authority than the *Encyclopedia Britannica* (1969 edition) declares this invaluable resource, for the control of which major military strategy in this century's two world wars was largely devised, "practically useless." "Practically useless," that is, "in its crude state." But when refined—when turned from a raw material into a resource—"it supplies fuels, lubricants, illuminants, solvents, surfacing materials and many other products," including plastics, inks, fabrics, and dyes. I daresay most of this book's readers are wearing a fair amount of that sticky black stuff that our ancestors less than two centuries ago considered, at best, an ugly, smelly nuisance and, at worst, a dangerous, bubbling pit into which to fall.

Now, this distinction between raw materials and resources is not a mere academic nicety. It is of essential importance to our whole approach to the question of managing resources. It has at least three major implications in this regard:

(1) Nothing is a resource until someone has thought of a way to use it, and usually the use requires some modification of it. Both the thinking and the modifying are costly procedures: they take time, energy, and often the application of costly tools and processes. Human nature being what it is, few people are willing to incur such

costs without some prospect of reward—reward of which Scripture clearly approves (Leviticus 19:13; Deuteronomy 24:15; Matthew 10:10; Luke 10:7; 1 Corinthians 9:14; 1 Timothy 5:18). Raw materials, therefore, will not normally become resources unless people expect some reward for applying their minds and bodies to them, and it is right that they should receive some reward.

(2) Lots of things may be resources tomorrow that are not today. This seemingly simple statement has profound implications for any discussion of *managing* resources. At the simplest level, this means that the resources we'll be managing ten or twenty years from now might be very different from the ones we're managing now. Predicting the changes is risky at best, impossible and counterproductive at worst. At a more complex level, this means that many feared shortages of resources will never occur because substitutes will be found that reduce or even eliminate the demand for the resources we fear running out of.[6] Who would have thought, sixty years ago, that we might generate electricity more cheaply, and at less risk to human health and life and to the ecosystem, by harnessing the energy released in the decay of radioactive materials than by burning either coal or refined petroleum?[7]

(3) Discoveries of new supplies of raw materials for which we already have found valuable uses may at any time turn sober and respected projections of future supplies into bad jokes. For instance, in 1981 leading geologists from around the world congregated at the Massachusetts Institute of Technology to discuss future prospects for world energy supplies. According to economist George Gilder, "These experts all solemnly decided that by 2015 a total of 70 trillion cubic feet of natural gas would be discovered in North America. Their book was published [in 1982] under the title *Energy in Transition*; by the time it came out, there were two finds in Canada believed to represent some 440 trillion cubic feet of natural gas [over six times the experts' projections of finds in the coming thirty-five years for all of North America]. And then in Louisiana and the Tuscaloosa trench there were further immense discoveries of geopressurized methane that are now being delivered for the first time."[8] And lest you think that this is an anomaly and that most forecasts of future energy availability are more reliable, consider the history of predictions of U.S. petroleum reserves. William M. Brown catalogues numerous predictions by petroleum experts, particularly by the United States Geological Survey, all of which called for declining production, imminent shortages, and the rapid depletion of petroleum

reserves. All of the predictions were wrong, mostly by many multiples. What's more, all of them were wrong on the *short* side.[9]

This strange phenomenon—that the errors almost always are in underestimating rather than overestimating future resource supplies—deserves careful consideration. The old legal principle, *Cui bono?*—"Who benefits?"—certainly suggests that we ought at least to look for some ulterior motive when people do something so improbable so consistently. I have no doubt that the root of the problem is that the "experts" who make such a prediction generally foresee themselves as playing an integral role in the civil government's response to the impending crises of resource shortages. Considerable money, prestige, and power are available to people assigned authority to make and enforce resource distribution policy. It is therefore to the advantage of these "experts" to create apprehension of shortages among government officials, even if no such shortages really are likely. Not that the authors of such predictions are dishonest; rather, their own biases can prevent their seeing facts clearly.[10] This is not to say that *all* such mispredictions stem from such bias; many undoubtedly stem from the simple difficulty, if not impossibility, of predicting the astounding results of the application of human minds to physical problems.[11]

Resource Management Policy Must Be Elastic

These three points, when brought together, have two important implications of their own. First, any resource management policy that restricts the elasticity of the resource marketplace or slows the adaptation of society to new knowledge and states of affairs regarding resources is necessarily harmful to society. While this point in itself deserves extensive discussion, let me simply say for the moment that this means, in general, that making resource management primarily, or even significantly, the responsibility and authority of civil government is inherently harmful, for the civil government, by its very nature, lacks the ability to respond quickly and innovatively to changing circumstances.[12]

Second, resource development—the extraction and manipulation of raw materials so as to make them useful to man—will happen most rapidly and on the largest scale in a society in which people are rewarded for contributing to it and are not restricted from using their inventiveness. In other words, free societies, where legal restrictions are placed only on such things as fraud, theft, and violence, are likely to progress more rapidly in the development of resources than centrally controlled societies, where restrictions apply to far more activities than fraud, theft, and violence. Societies, of course, tend to fall somewhere on a continuum between free and centrally controlled, but in general we can infer—and empirical investigation confirms—that the freer a society is, the more rapidly and comprehensively it will develop resources. Anyone who doubts this might try comparing the number of international patents originating in free societies with the number originating in centrally controlled societies.

But this is to run ahead of ourselves. We're still trying to define our subject. For the moment, it is sufficient to reiterate that there is a vast and important difference between raw materials and resources. Nonetheless, since few people are conscious of this distinction, and since we need to discuss both raw materials and resources, this discussion will assume that both are in mind.

Management Must Be Central or Diverse

Thus far we have determined that we are trying to discuss managing both the raw materials and the resources that are found and developed on, in, and over the earth. Now we come to the first word of the title: What do we mean by *managing* the resources of the earth?

The verb *to manage* comes to us from the French *manege*, which referred originally to the training of a horse in his paces. While etymology is not the be-all and end-all of definition, this insight does give us a helpful picture of what it means to manage something. It means to bring what is otherwise unwieldy and out of our control under our control, to cause something that once acted (or lay dormant) without regard to our desires to serve them. Tracing it back to its root in the Latin (*manus*, "hand"), *to manage* means to handle, to wield, to control or guide something.

The closest New Testament term to *manage* is *oikonomeo*, a verb meaning "to be a manager" or "to manage, regulate, administer, plan." The noun form of *oikonomeo* is *oikonomia*, meaning "management," particularly "management of a household" or "arrangement, order, plan." And one who performed the task of *oikonomia* was an *oikonomos*, a manager, administrator, or steward.[13] From these, of course, we get our words *economize, economy, economics,* and *economist.* Fundamentally these refer to the management of a household, including the household's physical objects (house, furniture, lands, and so on), its family members and servants, and its money. By extension they refer to the management or ordering or administering of anything.

When we think, then, of managing the resources of the earth, we have in mind taking them in hand—manipulating them (another word rooted in the Latin *manus*) so as to make them serve the needs of man, for whose service God made them (Genesis 1:26-30), in some orderly, designed, planned fashion rather than permitting them to act—or not act—willy nilly or of their own accord.

In this, the ideas of planning and control are prominent. Here the perennial temptation for human society has been to assume that what is necessary is some *central* plan. Often people mistakenly think that without a central plan there can be no plan at all, or they think that without a central plan there can be only chaos. On the contrary, the real choice facing every society is the choice between a centrally planned society and a society that results from the millions of diverse and constantly changing plans of its inhabitants. As the great Austrian economist Ludwig von Mises put it:

> The dilemma is not between automatic forces and planned action. It is between the democratic process of the market in which every individual has his share and the exclusive rule of a dictatorial body. Whatever people do in the market economy, is the execution of their own plans. In this sense every human action means planning. What those calling themselves planners advocate is not the substitution of planned action for letting things go. It is the substitution of the planner's own plan for the plans of his fellowmen. The planner is a potential dictator who wants to deprive all other people of the power to plan and act according to their own plans. He aims at one thing only: the exclusive absolute preeminence of his own plan.[14]

Whoever opts for the central plan must do so in full awareness that that option means both overruling most of the millions of individual plans and adopting a planning system that, because of its centrality and gigantic size, is inherently incapable of responding quickly to changing circumstances—the very sorts of changes that occur when free people make their free choices and change the availability of various resources. The proverbial surpluses and shortages endemic to communist states are not accidents; they are the inevitable results of central instead of diversified planning.

In contrast, the routine ability of free-market economies to maintain fairly steady supplies of products despite even most major calamities bespeaks the great flexibility of the free market and hence its ability to manage resources well. The fact that no industrialized, free-market state has suffered a famine in the past 200 years, while famines have occurred regularly and frequently in communist lands, illustrates this difference.[15] Adam Smith explained the difference on the basis of private incentives in his *An Inquiry into the Nature and Causes of the Wealth of Nations* (1776), in the "Digression concerning the Corn Trade and Corn Laws," where he noted that sellers of products have the greatest incentive to stretch out supply as long as possible while still meeting the demands of buyers, and therefore they achieve the goal best. Indeed, he argued—compellingly, I think—that governmental interference in the free market was the only means other than war or major natural catastrophe of turning a shortage into a famine:

> Whoever examines, with attention, the history of the dearths [shortages] and famines which have afflicted any part of Europe, during either the course of the present or that of the two preceding centuries, of several of which we have pretty exact accounts, will find, I believe, that a dearth never has arisen from any combination among the inland dealers in corn, nor from any other cause but a real scarcity, occasioned sometimes, perhaps, and in some places by the waste of war, but in by far the greatest number of cases, by the fault of the seasons; and that *a famine has never arisen from any other cause but the violence of government attempting, by improper means to remedy the inconveniencies of a dearth.*[16]

PRINCIPLES OF RESOURCE MANAGEMENT

Managing the resources of the earth, then, means planning and controlling how the raw materials we find about us are developed and used for the benefit of mankind. How best to do that is a question that can be analyzed in several ways: (1) What theological and moral standards should guide and limit the use of resources? (2) Who should do the planning and controlling? (3) What ends, or goals, should be pursued in managing resources? Let's look briefly at each of these questions.

Theological and Moral Standards

Five chief standards appear in Scripture for the management of resources:

THE DOMINION MANDATE

In what theologians have long called the "dominion mandate" in the opening chapter of Genesis, God says, "Let Us make man in Our image, according to Our likeness; and let them *rule* [or "have dominion"] over the fish of the sea and over the birds of the sky and over the cattle and over all the earth, and over every creeping thing that creeps on the earth." And, having made man male and female, He says to them, "Be fruitful and multiply, and fill the earth, and subdue it; and rule over the fish of the sea and over the birds of the sky, and over every living thing that moves on the earth" (Genesis 1:26, 28, emphasis added). Let me suggest three observations about this mandate.

First, the dominion mandate, or cultural mandate, as it is also called, is, as Old Testament scholar R. Laird Harris put it, "far from specific. To have 'rule over' the earth might as easily refer to the free use and development of resources as to our responsibility for their conservation. To 'rule over' the animals does not specifically say high dams for power should be rejected so as to avoid bringing an exotic type of little fish to extinction."[17] In other words, the dominion mandate cannot be packed as a pistol in the holster of either the devotees of untouched nature or the rapists of mother earth.

Second, while it may be ambiguous about other things, the dominion mandate clearly means that the earth, with everything in it—though it all belongs to God (Psalm 24:1)—was intended by God to serve man's needs. Man was not made for the earth; the earth was made for man. It is man, not the earth or anything in it, who was created in the image of God. To make man subservient to the earth is to turn the purpose of God in creation on its head.

Third, the dominion mandate does not tell us what particular uses of the earth are best suited to man's service. From this we can legitimately infer two things: (a) that God intended there to be considerable liberty regarding the ways in which we rule the earth, particularly since we differ about how we want the earth to serve us; (b) that difficult scientific and practical issues are involved in determining how best to make the earth serve us. From these two inferences we can derive a third: that we owe it to each other to be moderate and humble in our judgments of each other's views about resource management lest we mistakenly impose our own standards rather than God's.

PRIVATE PROPERTY

Scripture clearly approves of the ownership of private property, forbidding, as its does, all forms of theft (Exodus 20:15). In the context of resource management, granted the prevalence of statist attempts to control people's uses of property, it is particularly important to note that the Bible assigns to the owner of property absolute control over it within the limits of God's moral Law (Acts 5:4; Matthew 20:13, 15). This principle tells us that owners of resources may use them as they wish so long as they do not violate the rights of others—rights delineated in the Ten Commandments and the case laws derived from them.[18]

JUSTICE

The third theological and moral standard governing our use of resources is the broad Biblical principle of justice. It is important, however, that this principle be rightly understood. Biblically considered, *justice* means rendering impartially to everyone his due in accord with the right standard of God's moral Law revealed in Scripture.[19] What the Law prohibits, we should neither do nor permit others to do; what the Law permits, we may not prohibit.

Furthermore, the principle of justice prohibits force for any purpose other than to prevent or punish violations of God's moral Law. Force may not be used to induce compliance with anyone's wishes outside those countenanced by that Law. Reward, not punishment, is the proper incentive to lawful economic action; punishment should be restricted solely to violations of Biblical moral Law.[20]

LIBERTY

From these first three theological and moral principles follows a fourth: liberty. If God's instruction that we "rule over" the earth and everything in it is far from specific, and if a Biblical understanding of justice prohibits the use of force except to prohibit, prevent, prosecute, and punish violations of God's moral Law—the doing of *in*justice—then it follows that in all activities not proscribed by God's Law we have, and are to grant to others, liberty.

This brings us back to the observations with which we began, based on the landowner's comments in the parable of the laborers in the vineyard. So long as we do no injury (literally, *in-justice*) to another, we may use what belongs to us as we please—at least, we may do so without fear of human judgment. (God's judgment is another thing. He looks on the heart, not only on the outward action. He knows whether we have done something just from an unjust motive, and He judges us for that motive as well as for the act. But such judgment is impossible for human minds.)

But liberty does not mean license to do whatever we please. Others' rights define our liberty, put outside boundaries on it. Liberty means the freedom to do what is lawful, not what is unlawful, as the Apostle Paul makes clear in Romans 6. The person who has been set at liberty from sin has been made a slave of righteousness. Thus sin—which Scripture defines as lawlessness (Romans 6:19)—is not an option within real liberty.[21]

LOVE

But the dominion mandate, private property, justice, and liberty do not exhaust the Biblical principles governing resource management. A final principle is love, the selfless act of caring for the needs of others in conformity with the requirements of God's Law (Romans 13:8-10). While justice gives us the minimum standard of action, love is the high goal toward which every child of God is called to aim.[22] It is not enough that we should refrain from injuring our neighbors; we must do them positive good.[23]

This said, however, it is essential to note that love cannot be forced. It must be voluntary. Hence no appeal may properly be made to civil government to force actions above and beyond the minimum standard of justice. Because civil government is by nature an entity of force, the principle of love falls largely outside its capacities. It exists to enforce justice, not love.

Applying Principles to Resource Management

How might these general principles be applied to problems related to resource management? Let's look briefly at two basic points. These do not comprise an exhaustive list, but they do suggest some directions in which we might go.

First, the dominion mandate means at least that man, not the environment, is primary. Certainly the environment should be protected, but it must be protected for the sake of man, not for its own sake. Anything else is idolatry of nature.[24]

Second, the Biblical principles of private property, justice, and liberty mean at least that no entity, private or public, has proper authority to restrict others' use of property—including any resources they own—in any way other than that required by God's moral Law. Civil law should prohibit and punish actual injuries (injustices, violations of God's moral Law); it has no authority to use its legal monopoly of force for any other purpose.[25]

This does not mean, however, that just anything goes. Pollution—whether toxic chemicals, noxious odors, bothersome noises, or solid waste—that causes injury to others or their property should be subject to redress through the courts. The redress, however, should be in the form of restitution to those injured, not of fines to the state, which exists to protect and vindicate citizens' God-given rights, not to usurp those rights and the reparation for their violation to itself. Scripture provides for restitution of losses due to misuse of property (see, for example, Exodus 21:28-36; 22:6). However, real damage to or trespass upon property or person—not just diminution of exchange value of property (or labor)—must occur in order for restitution to be justified.[26] The mere fact that someone's offering a competing product reduces the market value of a product I offer is no cause for restitution.[27] Similarly, someone's locating a new housing development close to one in which I live, and so increasing the local supply of housing relative to demand and therefore reducing the market value of my house, is no injury to me, and I should have no coercive means of preventing it.

Some major difficulties arise at this point. Since the Industrial Revolution, civil courts have adopted conflicting notions of property rights and pollution-related torts. Furthermore, ever-growing state ownership of property—public lands, in particular—sometimes obscures the identities of both perpetrators and victims of pollution-related torts. In addition, technology has enabled us to observe and measure levels of physical invasion—by sound, light, and liquids, solids, and gases—heretofore unnoticed and thought inconsequential. Finally, determining actual causation in some cases of injury to property and person simply can be beyond our technical capacity, particularly when several different agents can have the same effects and it is impossible to determine which was the agent responsible for the effect in a given instance. In such cases, mere demonstration of correlation should not be accepted as an adequate substitution for proof of causation, and where causation cannot be proved, liability should not be adjudged. These four facts greatly complicate problems related to pollution tort policy.

Extensive discussion of these problems is, of course, impossible in this context. However, both Biblical principle and prudence indicate that they are better solved by tightening up the understanding of private property and its attendant rights and responsibilities than by transferring such rights and responsibilities increasingly to the state—the latter being the tactic of choice for many theorists and courts.[28] Further, *the current crisis in tort actions in our nation's courts cannot be overcome until Americans learn to trust anew in the loving providence of God* and so to accept most of life's inevitable suffering as from His gracious hand rather than thinking all of it must be blamed on someone else who must make restitution.

Let us turn briefly, now, to two final questions: (1) Who should plan and control resource use? (2) What should be the goals of resource use?

Who Should Plan and Control Resource Use?

Planning and control of resource use should, except perhaps under the extremities of war,[29] be left to the owners of the resources, within the limits of Biblical moral Law. There simply is no Biblical justification for civil government's attempting to control the use of private property, including natural resources, beyond those limits.

Making this work is not always simple. Problems arise in which property rights are difficult to define and determine. Ownership of water in aquifers or running streams or rivers, for instance, is difficult to define, as is ownership in lakes, oceans, and the atmosphere. In some instances, it seems that the state, acting on behalf of its citizens, must take on the role of owner of some such resources. In those instances, however, the state must function as nearly as possible the way private persons function as owners of property. If it fails to enforce its own property rights vigorously enough, its citizens will suffer losses due to abuse. If it exercises too vigorous control over the resources of which it asserts stewardship, its citizens may be deprived of considerable economic advantage and production.

Devising appropriate policies in this regard is not easy, but keeping three fundamental principles in focus should at least provide a sound basis for formulating policy: (1) Resources exist to serve man; man does not exist to serve them. Therefore they should be used, to the greatest extent possible, in manners best suited to the desires of the greatest numbers of people. Those desires should be measured largely by market forces: willingness and ability to pay.

(2) The state is a monopoly of force. Therefore it always faces the temptation to exert its will beyond proper boundaries. Safeguards against this must be built into every policy. (3) State officials and employees are subject to the same moral frailties as private persons. Their access to the coercive capacities of the state, however, makes them potentially more dangerous to others' rights than most private persons. Strict systems of accountability, therefore, must always be part of policy.

An implication of these three principles is that policy ought to aim toward the least possible state possession and control of resources, not toward the most possible, and toward the constant reduction of state ownership of resources as technical and legal means of defining and protecting property rights advance.

What Should Be the Goals of Resource Management?

Consistent with the dominion mandate's insistence that the earth, with everything in it, was made for man, not man for the earth, the goal of resource management should be to increase the degree to which the world serves man. Since, however, different people have different needs and desires, no generalization is possible regarding what particular uses serve that goal and what ones don't. Within the limits of God's moral Law, any use of resources that serves people is permissible; the more efficiently it serves them, the better it is. But any policymaker who thinks he can determine in advance what uses are best is a sad victim of *hubris*. Freedom, not constraint, must be the rule here.

What sort of public policy will best serve this principle of resource management? In general, expansion—not contraction—of private property rights, and even the transfer of more and more property into private rather than state hands, should be the goal of resource management policy. Such a policy will tend to keep the power of the state within its proper bounds, and so will diminish opportunities for oppression. It will also increase people's liberty within the bounds of God's Law and, simultaneously, increase their enjoyment of the goods and services that can be provided by the creative imagination as it seeks ever more ways to use resources.[30]

GROWTH AND PLANNING

*A*s we saw in Chapter 7, barring major catastrophes, there is little reason to doubt that the vast majority of people will be comfortably wealthy in a few generations. What kinds of major catastrophes might foil the world's progress, and how might we prevent or, failing that, recover from them?

Some we could do little to prevent and little to recover from. A comet or large meteor crashing into the earth could destroy the whole planet. A stray star could pass through our solar system, upsetting all the planets' orbits.

Some we couldn't prevent, but might recover from reasonably well. A natural ice age or natural global warming, for instance, would require some migration and changes in living patterns over a period of several centuries, but there's good reason to think we could cope with the new conditions fairly well.

Some we might prevent or, failing that, still recover from fairly well. Evangelism, diplomacy, economic development and trade, and deterrence, for instance, might long prevent another war as destructive as World War II.[1] Nonetheless, wars might still occur, as they presently do in various places around the world. Yet, as we learned following both world wars, recovery comes faster than building wealth for the first time.[2]

THE IMPORTANCE OF ECONOMIC GROWTH

We can have confidence of economic recovery in the face of most disasters partly by considering the effects of exponential economic growth. The 3.45 percent growth rate of annual gross world product per capita of 1965-1984 is enough to double GWP per capita every twenty-one years. At that rate, we can restore wealth lost to disasters pretty quickly, especially by historical standards.

But there is a much more dangerous kind of disaster. It's more dangerous because it doesn't look like a disaster. It happens too slowly, too quietly, too peacefully for most people to recognize it as a disaster. Its great danger springs from its effect on economic growth rates. If those fall even a little for very long, the improvement in material standards of living for many people can be delayed significantly, aborted altogether, or even reversed.

Compare, for instance, hypothetical economic futures for several low-income countries with different economic growth rates: Zambia, Mauritania, India, Burma, and Yemen. Assuming that they sustained their 1965-1984 growth rates for a century after 1984, what would be the results? (What follows is not intended as a prediction for these countries; it is offered merely to illustrate a point. Because economic growth rates rise and fall over time, straight-line extrapolation of these growth rates for other than illustrative purposes is misleading.) Zambia, with starting GNP per capita of $470 and a growth rate of -1.3 percent, would wind up with GNP per capita of $128, a devastating loss. Mauritania, starting at $450 and with a growth rate of 0.3 percent, would wind up at $607—an improvement but nothing to boast about. India, starting at $260 and with a growth rate of 1.6 percent, would wind up at $1,288, a fivefold increase. Burma, starting at $180 and with a growth rate of 2.3 percent, would wind up at $1,795, a huge (tenfold) improvement. And Yemen, starting at $550 and with a growth rate of 5.9 percent, would wind up at a staggering $200,770.[3]

Or compare hypothetical economic futures for the world as a whole at different economic growth rates. Average gross product per capita in 1984 for the sixty-five countries represented in Table 6-1 of Appendix 2 was $3,244. The average 1965-1984 GNP per capita growth rate was 3.45 percent. If that rate continued for a century, gross product per capita in 2084 would be $102,187. Cut the growth rate in half and you cut the resulting figure to less than a fifth: $18,207. Cut it to a fourth and the result is less than a thirteenth: $7,685. Make it equal to Zambia's, -1.3 percent, and the result is $884, a tragic loss of 73 percent. (While $102,187 GWP per capita may seem to us impossibly high, and GWP per capita may not reach that height in the next century, it doesn't hurt to remind ourselves that production per capita of $3,244 probably would have seemed impossibly high to the world of 1884 too, when GWP per capita was probably under $100. If world production per capita could multiply thirty-two times from 1884 to 1984, why couldn't it multiply thirty-three times from 1984 to 2084?)

History shows that increasing wealth is key to increasing human material well-being. Life expectancy, health, housing, sanitation, transportation, communication, education, recreation, enjoyment of books and music and art—these and a multitude of other tangible and intangible elements of human welfare tend to increase quantitatively, though not always qualitatively, as wealth rises. Significantly slowing the rate of growth of wealth for many people, therefore, can mean drastically slowing long-term improvement of their material well-being. Serious downturns in growth are more dangerous to material economy than any other likely man-made disaster. If we care about our neighbors near and far, present and future, we must care about the future of economic growth.

Yet a note of caution: Economic growth, much as it promotes material well-being, cannot guarantee spiritual, intellectual, moral, or aesthetic well-being. Scripture views material wealth, when properly gained through conscientious, ethical work in service to others, as a blessing from God (e.g., Deuteronomy 28:1-14; 30:9, 10). But it warns against prideful feelings of self-sufficiency that can lead the wealthy to forget God and their obligations to Him. God warns of decay and destruction for any society that forsakes Him and His Law (Deuteronomy 8:1-20). The history of Israel illustrates the common problem that wealthy societies often become morally complacent and bring upon themselves God's judgment.

Alexander Solzhenitsyn reflected this Biblical view when he said in his Templeton Address, ". . . if I were asked today to formulate as concisely as possible the main cause of the ruinous Revolution that swallowed up some sixty million of our people, I could not put it more accurately than to repeat: 'Men have forgotten God; that's why all this has happened.'"[4] Just so, Moses warned that when God would judge and ruin Israel for its apostasy and the surrounding nations would ask, "Why has the LORD done thus to this land?" men would say, "Because they forsook the covenant of the LORD, the God of their fathers, which He made with them when He brought them out of the land of Egypt" (Deuteronomy 29:24, 25).

Material prosperity is a good thing, but it is not all there is to man's well-being. It can enhance our opportunity to pursue holiness and happiness, but it does not render them automatically. Man is not merely physical, but also spiritual.

WORLDVIEW AND FREEDOM

Many factors affect economic growth rates. Inflation and deflation; interest rates, unemployment rates, and investment rates; rates of invention, innovation, and technological application; population growth rates;[5] foreign trade policies, educational levels, and transportation and communication infrastructure are just a few. These fluctuate in response to people's changing needs and desires and to governments' changing policies. But one overall structural factor and one worldview factor are particularly important to sustained long-term economic growth: economic freedom and a generally Biblical worldview. Countries with free markets tend to outperform those with controlled markets; countries where the predominant view of reality is consistent with the Biblical worldview tend to outperform those with anti-Biblical worldviews.

Biblical Worldview and Economic Growth

In an earlier book I discussed the importance of religious worldview to economic performance, so I'll only touch on the matter here.[6] The metaphysical idealism of the pantheistic, panentheistic,[7] and mystical atheistic religions (of which Hinduism and Buddhism are the most prevalent) and the magicalism of the polytheistic and spiritistic religions undercut the rational development of knowledge and resources. The dehumanizing influences of Marxist/Leninist and secular humanist atheism undercut the motives to service that lie at the root of long-term productivity. The Biblical worldview, whether explicitly or implicitly embraced, provides the best philosophical basis for rapid long-term economic growth. As economic historian Max Weber put it years ago, "Since Judaism made Christianity possible and gave it the character of a religion essentially free from magic, it rendered an important service from the point of view of economic history. For the dominance of magic outside the sphere in which Christianity has prevailed is one of the most serious obstructions to the rationalization of economic life."[8]

Scripture teaches that a rational God created a rationally ordered universe that is knowable and predictable in its functions. This metaphysical and epistemological worldview made possible the development of science and technology,[9] which have contributed so greatly to increased economic productivity. Scripture also teaches that God has set forth a moral pattern for human relationships and that following that pattern leads to mutual service and benefit. Further, it teaches that the physical and moral aspects of God's creation are consistent, so that moral acts have beneficial physical consequences and immoral acts have harmful physical consequences, at least in the long run.[10] Economies tend to be more productive where this general metaphysical, epistemological, and ethical worldview plays an important role in shaping general behavior than where it does not.

For this reason, two of the most important steps toward sustaining or improving economic growth anywhere in the world are evangelism and discipleship. Imparting and perpetuating the Biblical worldview provide the intellectual basis from which people can order their economic lives for the greatest benefit to their neighbors and themselves.[11] The other side of the coin is that abandoning the Biblical worldview would have disastrous consequences for long-term economic welfare all over the world. Alarmingly, the Biblical worldview is being undermined in precisely the countries that in the past four centuries have been most influenced by it: the industrial market economies of the West. New Age magicalism and pantheism threaten the rationality of the West's dominant worldview, and Marxist and secular humanist atheism threaten its ethical foundations.[12] It is crucial, therefore, that Christian families and churches improve and expand their efforts at truly Christian education, education that applies all of the Bible to all of life.

The Imperative of Economic Freedom

One aspect of the Biblical worldview particularly important to economics is the ethic of property and liberty that forms the foundation of the free market. Various economic historians have argued, compellingly I believe, that the development of this ethic was a crucial step on the way to the historically unprecedented, explosive economic growth that swept the now-developed world during and after the Industrial Revolution.[13] Without the promise of reward for self-sacrifice, people are slow to invest the effort and take the risks involved in producing more than their own basic needs. The Biblical ethic of property rights underlies that promise. Without the liberty to produce and trade at will within the bounds of justice—the information-processing system we call the market, which with its price mechanism sends billions of signals to and from producers and consumers all over the world—the amazing economic efficiency necessary for high productivity could not be achieved. The Biblical ethic of liberty undergirds this freedom.[14]

Whatever diminishes responsible, Biblical freedom in the use of property in the marketplace, then, diminishes economic growth as well. Elsewhere I have discussed various trade regulations (price controls, wage controls, occupational licensure, trust and antitrust laws, quotas and tariffs, and subsidies) that harm the economy by attacking liberty and property and so disrupting the price mechanism.[15] In the previous chapter I pointed out ways in which governmental regulation of resource management would be harmful. In Chapter 8 and Appendix 3 I suggest ways to bring market and legal forces to bear on pollution problems. For the remainder of this chapter, let's look at policies with direct application to population growth and regional economic growth.

TO BEAR OR NOT TO BEAR? POPULATION PLANNING

Christian morality, as we saw in Chapter 4, puts a high value on people. New people are to be welcomed with joy, not viewed as a population plague or people pollution. Multiplying reflects God's blessing, not man's curse (Genesis 1:28; 9:1). Solomon captured the spirit of Biblical population ethics when he wrote,

> Behold, children are a gift of the LORD;
>   The fruit of the womb is a reward.
> Like arrows in the hand of a warrior,
>   So are children of one's youth.
> How blessed is the man whose quiver is full of them;
>
> They shall not be ashamed,
>   When they speak with their enemies in the gate.
>   (Psalm 127:3-5)

When my wife and I were newlyweds, we attended a Presbyterian church in Colorado Springs. There were lots of other young couples in the church, and for some reason, although many wanted to have children, they were having trouble conceiving. It became a joke in the church: something wrong with the water! Then, within a few months, nearly a dozen pregnancies (including our first) got started.

About six months later, when many of the pregnant wives in the church were showing pretty obviously, the church hosted a candidate for the pastorate. From the pulpit he remarked jokingly on the profusion of births we were about to experience: "Must be something in the water!" "It's our new theology of church growth," I said. Everyone laughed, and the candidate, who with his wife already had two children, replied, "I'm sure you won't mind if my wife and I don't buy into your theology of church growth!" The humorous exchange has stayed in my mind ever since.

But there's a serious side to it, especially from the perspective of Covenant Theology, which sees God's promises as belonging in some sense to believers and their children (Acts 2:39; Genesis 17:7) and in light of the Great Commission, in which Christ assigned to the Church the task of making disciples of all nations, teaching them to obey Him as Lord (Matthew 28:18-20). Millions of Christians have accepted uncritically the anti-natalist propaganda of organizations like the Worldwatch Institute, the National Family Planning and Reproductive Health Association, Planned Parenthood, the Population Council, the Population Crisis Committee, and Zero Population Growth.[16] As a result, many have chosen, like our unbelieving neighbors, to have fewer children.

But having children is one important way for Christians to multiply spiritually as well as physically. We Christian parents can instruct our children in the faith from birth to adulthood. We can't do that so easily with the children of Muslims, Hindus, and secular humanists. Christian parents' children are more likely to grow up to be missionaries, Bible teachers, and pastors than are Buddhist parents' children. By choosing to have fewer children, we not only turn down what Scripture calls a blessed gift and reward from God (Psalm 127:3), but also reduce the number of most likely candidates for service in obeying the Great Commission. Christians need to remember that plenteous offspring are a blessing from God, not a curse (Deuteronomy 30:9).

Economic Consequences of Low Fertility

There are economic consequences of falling fertility rates, too. Total fertility rates (TFR) in industrialized countries (average about 1.9 children per woman) already are below replacement level.[17] Only three of the world's nineteen industrial market economies have TFR at or above replacement level. As a result, a reverse demographic transition is in store for the industrialized world: population will begin to shrink (aside from what is made up by immigration), and it will shrink geometrically. Just as surely as 1 percent annual population growth will double a population in seventy-two years, 1 percent annual population decline will halve it in seventy-two years. And just as surely as population growth fuels economic growth over the long term by making higher ratios of working to nonworking members of the population, population decline will fuel economic decline over the long term by making higher ratios of nonworking (retired) to working members.

To get an idea of the magnitude of the different effects of above- and below-replacement-level fertility rates, imagine two groups of 100 couples each (200 persons each). Group A has TFR of 1.9 children per woman, infant mortality rate (IMR) of 9 per 1,000, and child mortality rate (CMR) of 1 per 1,000 (about average figures for the industrial market economies in the 1980s). Group B has TFR of 5.0, IMR of 86, and CMR of 9 (Turkey's figures for the 1980s). The offspring of the sixth generation will number, for Group A, 137, and for Group B, 26,910.

If we think we've had a tough time keeping Social Security afloat in the 1980s, just wait till all the children not born to the population-bomb-conscious young couples of 1960 through 1990 start not bearing children from 1990 through 2020.[18] The baby boomers of the forties and fifties will reach retirement age with precious few working-age people to support them. Watch for a growing push for euthanasia. Former Colorado Governor Richard Lamb's comment that the elderly have a "duty to die and get out of the way" will take on an ominous ring.[19]

What does all this mean for population policy? Certainly the Biblical preference for childbearing should mean no state ought to discourage fertility. Not only coercive birth prevention (which is used in China and even in some American states with laws permitting involuntary sterilization of handicapped people), but even state-sponsored "education" programs that discourage childbearing must be resisted by knowledgeable Christians prepared to stand firm for their God-given right to liberty and to put the relationship between population and economy in a proper light.

In addition, Christians themselves need to rethink carefully their attitudes toward childbearing in light of Biblical teaching.[20]

Pro-life must come to mean more than just *anti-abortion*: it must describe Christians who rejoice in God's gift of children, who welcome them, who count it a blessing to be fruitful and multiply (Genesis 9:1).[21] Furthermore, it must come to describe Christians who are ready and eager to open their own families and homes to adopt children of unwed mothers who are persuaded by our anti-abortion reasoning not to abort, but who are not prepared to care well for their children.[22]

Ethics and Economics of Immigration

Above I mentioned that the populations of industrialized nations will, *aside from what is made up by immigration*, begin to fall because of low fertility rates. Immigration, however, promises to keep at least some of their populations growing, though it may radically change their cultures. (What might West Germany be like, for instance, if its native population were to shrink from 62 million to 40 million [a likely result of current demographic trends there],[23] and the loss were made up by immigrant Turks, who would then constitute more than a third of the population of Germany? The change would not necessarily be for the worse, but it certainly would be a change.)

Some people, including some Christians, resent or fear immigrants.[24] But there is little Biblical or economic basis for their resentment. Scripture abounds with exhortations to care for resident aliens, to defend them against injustice, and to make sure they aren't overlooked when they need charity (Exodus 22:21; 23:9; Leviticus 19:33, 34; Deuteronomy 1:16; 10:19; 23:7; 24:14, 17; 27:19; Jeremiah 7:6; 22:3; Ezekiel 22:29; Malachi 3:5; Matthew 25:35, 38, 43). It does, however, warn against extending full citizenship privileges to immigrants too quickly, insisting that they be ethically enculturated first (Deuteronomy 23:3-8).[25]

From an economic perspective, too, immigrants should be welcomed, not rejected. One very simple observation gives the first reason why immigrants tend to be good for the economy: they normally enter after they're already of working age. This means the economy gets new workers without having to support them (either at all or so long) during their childhoods.[26] In addition, immigrants tend to be highly self-motivated, thus making conscientious and productive workers. Often they come from poor circumstances and so are willing to do the kinds of jobs many Americans, because of sinful pride, are unwilling to do.[27] Typically they move upward on the economic ladder rapidly, within a generation or two arriving at or above average income levels.[28]

Some people find another basis for their fear of immigrants. They believe immigrants will undermine the political integrity of America by bringing with them their old political ideas. But while there is plenty of reason to believe that cultural customs will change with increasing immigration (just think of the cultural diversity already evident throughout this nation of immigrants), there is little reason to think newcomers will be less committed to the basic American principles of government. "If anything, recent arrivals to America may be even more patriotic than natives," writes Ben Wattenberg. "Remember that immigrants, unlike natives, choose to come here."[29] In the words of Jean Nguyen-Doyne, the first Vietnamese woman to graduate from West Point, "When you come from another country without the freedoms there are here, you work as hard as you can to make sure you never lose those freedoms. I want to contribute as much as I can to the Army and the country. I don't take the word freedom lightly." (Her sister is a cadet at the Air Force Academy.)[30]

A Biblical immigration policy that was economically and politically sound would permit anyone to immigrate who was not known to be a political subversive. It would wed the Biblical care for sojourners with the economic realization that voluntary migration means people go from where they were to somewhere they consider better for them, and once there they become productive.[31] But it would also require ethical and civic acculturation before immigrants could enjoy all the privileges of citizenship, particularly voting and holding public office.[32]

TO GROW OR NOT TO GROW? GROWTH CONTROLS

The story is told that when Cornelius Vanderbilt, the great railroad magnate of the late nineteenth century, decided to build his mansion near Asheville, North Carolina, he went to the building site, scanned the magnificent view of the forests of the Blue Ridge Mountains, and pointed at a peak far in the distance. "I don't want anything spoiling my view of that mountain," he said. "So I'll buy everything from here to there." Had Vanderbilt been alive today, he might have taken advantage of a less expensive—and less ethical— way to preserve his view.

The Nimby Phenomenon

In the last decade or so a new word entered the English language: *nimby*. An acronym for "not in my back yard," *nimby* neatly describes a prevalent attitude among opponents of regional population and economic growth. It means a variety of things:

"Go ahead and build your new house, but not in my back yard."

"Go ahead and live in a mobile home, but not in my back yard."

"Go ahead and build your new office complex, but not in my back yard."

"Go ahead and build your new sports stadium and hotel, but not in my back yard."

"Go ahead and build your new freeway, but not in my back yard."

As expressed, of course, *nimby* says nothing objectionable. Scripture upholds property rights, including rights against trespass (Exodus 20:15; Deuteronomy 19:14; 27:17; Proverbs 22:28; 23:10). The problem is, the way it's expressed isn't quite the way it's applied, for "my back yard" turns out to mean a lot more than "my back yard." In practice it means:

"Go ahead and build your new house, but not in my neighborhood."

"Go ahead and live in your mobile home, but not within my field of vision."

"Go ahead and build your new office complex, but not in my city."

"Go ahead and build your new sports complex, but not on the hillside where I like to go for walks."

"Go ahead and build your new freeway, but not through my county."

The *nimby* phenomenon makes all the sounds of defending people's property, but extends people's claim to control other people's property—and the one who can control the most is the guy with the most political clout, not the one who owns the most.[33] *Nimbyism* manifests itself particularly in powerful movements to limit or stop local and regional growth of housing, business and industry, and transportation facilities. It wraps around itself the cloaks of democracy (majority rule),[34] environmentalism, and concern lest living conditions become "too crowded" or highways "too congested." And it expresses itself chiefly in urban planning and zoning laws.

Nimbyites use city, county, and regional planning commissions to force their own notions of the good life on everybody around them and to exclude those who have different notions. They push for large minimum housing lot sizes to keep the wrong kind of people (low-income people) from moving into their neighborhoods. They complain of too much traffic, forgetting that traffic means people going where they want to go. They resent the development of shopping centers, insisting that their solitary enjoyment of the back bay area of Newport Beach, California, takes precedence over the satisfaction of the hundreds of thousands who would patronize a mall.

Normally *nimbyites* use the language of diplomacy. Rarely do their exclusivist motives come out in public. But occasionally they do. A classic case is Dr. Elizabeth Brown, president of Laguna (California) Greenbelt Inc., an anti-growth lobby that seeks to block new housing developments in the Laguna Beach area. Testifying in 1988 against a proposed single-family housing development with small lots and houses affordable to the non-rich, she said:

> The kinds of people that are going to be buying little, teeny lots, it is obvious we are going for, you know, close to what one might try to call affordable, and that is laudable, but the people who will come and buy those lots are not people who have one small BMW that they park in the highway [sic]. These are people that tend to be blue collar workers. They have big trucks. They have more than one truck if friends come over. I live a couple of blocks away from such a neighborhood and if you get into affordable housing you get into affordable housing lifestyle, and it is not a neat lifestyle. You need more space not less. You cannot just continue to crunch them into small spaces and expect to have anything of a quality lifestyle.[35]

Marie Antoinette couldn't have put it better. If they can't afford big houses on big lots with BMW's in their driveways, they'd best not live around here. Keep the low-life somewhere else.

Or take Tom Rogers, formerly a cattle rancher in the once-rural canyons of booming Orange County, California. Rogers was a major mover behind a growth-limitation initiative in 1988. Why? Because he didn't like seeing the land around him developed. Rogers told an interviewer during the 1988 campaign, "When people accuse me of being a conservative and bailing out, they miss the whole point. Private property is the very essence of this thing. I have a right to the peaceful enjoyment of my surroundings."[36] In reality, Rogers isn't concerned only about the peaceful enjoyment of *his* surroundings, but of everybody else's too. He insists on keeping development not only off his property, but also off his neighbors' property, even when his neighbors want the development. And contrary to his claims, private property is the very essence of what growth-limitation is against: people using what belongs to them as they see fit, so long as they don't actually injure others (Matthew 20:13, 15).

The *nimby* phenomenon has its alter ego. I call it *oimby*: "only in my back yard." This shows itself in the attempt by business people who own stores in downtown areas to prevent new commercial development in outlying areas, development that could draw traffic away from their stores. For example, when the Orange County Board of Supervisors approved 470,000 square feet of shopping space for Laguna Canyon, downtown merchants hired an attorney to stop the project. Why? They'd lose business. "It's probably going to kill the rest of our business downtown and change the character forever," attorney Belinda Blacketer explained. And Michael Patrick Lawlor, a member of the Connecticut General Assembly, decried the tendency for suburbs to develop their own commercial and cultural centers: "Towns the size of East Haven are beginning to acquire all of their own urban amenities. That is the trend that concerns me because once that is allowed to reach its ultimate point, where every city of medium size has everything it needs, then the urban core, the center cities, are going to die, because there's going to be no reason to live there."[37] Of course, no one notices that the suburbs' having all their own amenities means life is more convenient for people living in them.

Whether *nimby* or *oimby*, the basic thrust is the same: people intent on controlling what they don't own. It is un-Biblical (Exodus 20:15; Matthew 20:13, 15; Acts 5:4). And interestingly enough, it usually defeats itself in its attempts to control urban sprawl.

How Growth-Limitation Defeats Itself

For instance, when planners set maximum housing densities, they intend to prevent crowding and traffic congestion. But what happens? Reducing the number of dwelling units permissible in a given area doesn't reduce the demand for homes. It just relocates some of it, at the same time driving up the prices of the homes in the restricted area by limiting their supply and requiring larger, more expensive lots and floor spaces. What happens to the unmet demand? It moves farther out from the business center. Then people who live farther out drive through the planned communities closer in, increasing traffic congestion. But their property taxes go to their own communities, not to the communities experiencing the traffic congestion. So the congested roads don't get broadened, and new roads don't get built to relieve them of some of their burden. Pretty soon pressure builds to restrict housing density in the farther-out communities, raising housing prices there. People move even farther out, urban sprawl enlarges, traffic congestion gets worse, and people complain more about crowding. It's a vicious circle.

Growth opponents also resist building new freeways and other roads that could reduce traffic congestion because the roads would take up some treasured open space or encourage additional development in areas they service. Yet their resistance simply compounds the congestion problem. People have to go from where they live to where they work and shop. When where they live is forced farther and farther away from employment and shopping areas, their need to travel increases. Keeping down the number of roads merely means more traffic delays.[38]

Growth-Limitation versus Families

Particularly hurt by the slow- and no-growth movement are prospective home buyers. Because growth-limitation legislation reduces the supply of houses relative to the demand for housing in a given area, it forces the price of houses to rise. But that isn't all. The legislation also imposes an almost never-ending series of bureaucratic delays on home building, requiring multitudes of permits for every step in the process. The resulting delays jack up the price of housing even more.

In the 1930s, the Empire State Building was built in about a year. Hoover Dam took 21 months. Yet today, one single-family home [in Orange County, California, and other highly regulated areas] easily takes two years. A subdivision project can take two-and-a-half years—just to get a building permit. Major commercial projects routinely stagnate in the regulatory process for *five* years. . . .

Each day of delay means opportunity costs lost, i.e., units not built and money not earned (which would then have been reinvested in new projects) because developers' resources are consumed by delay-induced operating expenses, land costs, loan and tax payments, professional fees, and inflation. . . .[39]

Consequently, new single-family home prices in Orange County ran around $200,000 in 1988, compared with a national median of $93,000. About $25,000 to $40,000 of the difference was chalked up solely to the delays and other costs imposed by the regulatory process. "You can thank building regulations and our current policy makers for creating a governmental system that forces you to shell out an extra $8,000 down payment, and an extra $200-400 a month in mortgage payments."[40] Of course, because growth controls so increase the time and expense involved in building anything they affect, they also reduce overall economic productivity and growth.

Hardest hit by the housing crunch brought on by the growth-limitation movement and government regulations it has managed to push through are families with children. Why? Because they typically need the most living space in their homes, but can't afford it because they tend to be young couples not yet high on the salary scale. The skyrocketing prices of housing in growth-controlled regions like Southern California force these families to live far outside the major population and commercial areas. Only there can they find housing they can afford. But as a result they are stuck with one- to two-hour commutes to work. It seems hardly a coincidence that the very people who are most likely to consider human beings a threat to the environment rather than a blessing also support the growth-limitation regulations that make it increasingly costly for couples to decide to have children.[41] The anti-natalist and growth-control movements are natural allies.

Opposing Philosophies of Government

Some government agencies resist growth because it doesn't fit the services they're prepared to provide: roads, water systems, sewers, police and fire protection, waste disposal, etc. But their ability to provide services is restricted by the impact of growth restrictions on their revenues. The lower the density in an area, the lower will be tax revenues, and hence the lower will be the ability of governments to provide services. Their attitudes are precisely opposite to those of the free market. Producers and sellers in the market don't tell customers, "Look, this is what we want to provide, take it or leave it." Instead, they do constant market research to find out what people want, and then they produce and sell it. The bureaucratic way is inflexible and pays little heed to the wants and needs of the public; the market way responds flexibly to them.

In the past three or four decades, local government agencies with responsibilities related to housing and commercial growth have shifted their focus from facilitating to planning. Once it was assumed that the purpose of local government was to facilitate people's choices. But now it is assumed that local governments should decide what services they want to provide and where they want to provide them, and plan people's living and working choices accordingly. Thus local governments have changed from servants to masters, a change opposite the direction of both Biblical and historically American notions of governing.[42] Says Steven Hayward, a growth policy analyst with The Claremont Institute in Southern California:

> Government is supposed to serve the needs of the people; it is supposed to take the necessary steps to accomodate [sic] growth. But what the slow-growth movement proposes is exactly the opposite understanding of how government should work: *the natural growth of the economy is to conform to the needs and abilities of government.* Development is made to serve the government, rather than the other way around. And to do so, the movement seeks to transform our government by giving it significant new regulatory power. This new power will make it more intrusive and less effective. Most importantly, *it will transfer power from people to the governing class.*[43]

A Biblical understanding of government sees it as the servant, not the master, of the citizens, and sees its taxing and law-enforcing authority as properly used only to facilitate its service (Romans 13:1-6). From this perspective, the market—which reflects free people's choices—should determine the direction, rate, and type of growth, and civil government should respond to that by providing the necessary services.

Similarly, the Biblical ethic of property undercuts the *nimby* and *oimby* phenomena. Scripture sees owners of property as free to do with it what they will within the limits of God's moral Law (Matthew 20:13, 15; Acts 5:4).[44] *Nimby* and *oimby* both are attempts to wrest control of property away from property owners and vest it instead in bureaucratic agencies. The Biblical standard is, "If you want to control it, own it. If you don't own it, don't try to control it." Because it responds to decisions by owners about property rightly in their control, the market, not bureaucracy, is best equipped to guide property use, including patterns of housing, commercial, and other land development.[45]

One might object to a market-driven land-use policy, "But then what happens to parks, wilderness areas, scenic rivers and mountains and forests? What happens to endangered species and significant historical sites? If the market alone should determine when and where development occurs, won't all these things go the way of the carrier pigeon?" No. Not as long as there's demand for them in the market.

Suppose, for instance, that two groups are contesting the use of a particular piece of land. One wants to develop it as a shopping center, the other as a park. Who should prevail? The bureaucratic solution leaves the final decision up to a government planning agency that will be swayed by political pressure groups. The market solution says, "If you want to control the land, own it." At first it seems obvious that the park's supporters will lose out in the market solution, but on second thought it isn't obvious at all. Why? Because the market solution always has supply and demand and profits in mind. If the supply of shopping centers already meets the demand for them, no new ones will be built, because no profits will be expected from them. If the supply of parks falls short of the demand for them, new ones will be built, *if developers can expect some reward for building them.*

The problem is that we have become accustomed to seeing parks as free services provided by government agencies. But they are not free. Someone has to pay for the land they use, and not only in the form of payments to its previous owners when a municipality buys the land. Use of the land for a city park means the city will collect no property revenues or sales taxes from it. It also means less land is available for housing and commercial development, thus forcing residential and business property prices up.

Putting park (and similar) development into the private sector would force park supporters to count the costs just like everyone else in the market. It would also mean that parks would be built to the extent that they really served the wants of consumers. The greater the consumer demand for parks, the more parks there would be. The lower the consumer demand, the fewer parks there would be. Furthermore, actual users of the parks, not the public at large, would pay for them. Why, after all, should recreation be subsidized any more than shopping centers?

A case might be made for the state's preserving historic sites that possess particular relevance to the state's doing what it ought to do: preserving the peace by performing defense and law enforcement. Scenes of important war battles, for instance (Gettysburg, Manassas/Bull Run, Pea Ridge National Military Park, etc.), might be preserved as reminders of the state's work in preserving a people's freedom. The same rationale would not, however, extend to the state's preventing owners from tearing down their historic houses to put up new commercial enterprises. People committed to preserving historic sites need to be willing to make the same financial sacrifices others are willing to make to do what they want, rather than persuading the state to force their wishes on others. If they want to preserve historic houses, they need to buy them themselves. If they aren't willing to bear that cost, they shouldn't force others to bear it for them.

LIFE, LIBERTY, AND PROPERTY

I have tried to stress three paramount principles throughout this book and to show that they are both Biblically and economically sound: life, liberty, and property. Human life is good, not bad, and new people are to be welcomed, not avoided. Human liberty, within the bounds of God's moral Law, is good too. And liberty should extend to people's choices about their lives (including the choice to have or not to have children, but not the choice to kill children once conceived) and their property. To the extent that life, liberty, and property are protected, economic growth will abound; to the extent that they are undermined, economic growth will subside or even reverse.

Efforts to restrict people's choices about childbearing and the use of property other than to enforce God's moral Law are unjust.[46] Population planning and growth control movements both violate the Biblical principle of liberty. We have nothing to fear from growing populations, so long as people are free to make the best use they can see of themselves and their property. Only when civil government turns from servant to master, when it redefines its task as planning instead of facilitating people's choices, does growing population constitute a threat instead of a blessing.

Friedrich Hayek warned forty-five years ago of the dangers of allowing the state to become increasingly involved in planning people's lives. The dangers arise, he warned in the title of his book *The*

Road to Serfdom, because state planning is the road to a society in which civil government is the master and citizens are slaves. When control of property is placed in the hands of the state, a new and dangerous power is created: the power to coerce everyone to do whatever the state chooses.

> . . . the system of private property is the most important guaranty of freedom, not only for those who own property, but scarcely less for those who do not. It is only because the control of the means of production is divided among many people acting inde-pendently that nobody has complete power over us, that we as individuals can decide what to do with ourselves. If all the means of production were vested in a single hand, whether it be nomi-nally that of "society" as a whole or that of a dictator, whoever exercises this control has complete power over us.[47]

The growth of state power is self-perpetuating, because each attempt by planners to control a particular part of society elicits deci-sions among citizens that threaten the success of the plans. Only additional exertion of the planners' power can save the plans. The "close interdependence of all economic phenomena makes it difficult to stop planning just where we wish and . . . once the free working of the market is impeded beyond a certain degree the planner will be forced to extend his controls until they become all-comprehen-sive."[48]

A free market within the limits of God's moral Law cannot force anyone's plans on anyone. It can only offer benefits in exchange for benefits. But in the final analysis, government planning—whether of population, resource use, or the economy—amounts to nothing but brute force: the imposition of the planners' plans on everyone else, willing or not. No amount of personal dislike on the part of the planner for the use of force can save him from its necessity, so long as he is intent on sustaining his plans.[49]

The Christian ethics of life, liberty, property, and servanthood cannot condone government planning of population or the economy. Biblical ethics can only condone civil government's facilitating the choices of free citizens, who themselves make their economic choices on the basis of their perception of what will serve the needs of their neighbors, near and far.

THE BIRTH DEFICIT: THE IMPACT OF ABORTION ON THE FUTURE AMERICAN ECONOMY

*O*kay, let's forget about children as bearers of the image of God, eternal souls who might grow up to glorify their Creator and enjoy Him forever. Let's forget about them as givers and receivers of love, as friends and helpers, as potentially virtuous members of a potentially virtuous civilization. In a society wedded to materialism and selfism, these things don't matter.

What matters is what contributes to greater material enjoyment for each person lucky enough to be allowed to become part of the game. So let's look at children solely as economic factors—producers and consumers in an economic calculus the end of which is increasingly desirable as it maximizes individual and societal wealth. The secularists want a cold, calculating "human animal"? We'll give it to them. What are the comparative costs and benefits, measured on the societal level, of aborting kids? It's an easy thing to calculate, for those who will let economic facts speak for themselves instead of blinding themselves to those that don't fit their ideologies.

On average, children are an economic liability from conception to age eighteen, after which they become, on average, an economic asset until age sixty-five, after which they become, on average, an economic liability again. Indeed, extrapolating from figures estimated by economist Marvin DeVries and reported by Allan C. Carlson in *Family Questions: Reflections on the American Social Crisis* (New Brunswick, NJ: Transaction Books, 1988, pp. 59-60), we can conclude that the average person (this average takes into account *all* people, whether they ever work or never work, and regardless of income) will represent a combined liability, or economic cost, of $192,600 during his first eighteen years plus his lifetime after retirement at age sixty-five.

But the same average person will occasion the production, directly and indirectly, of goods and services with average worth, if a male, of $55,277 per year, or, if a female, of $26,680 per year, every year from age eighteen to age sixty-five.

This means the average male will occasion the production (either through his own direct work or through his multiplication effect on others' productivity—cooperation increases productivity geometrically, not arithmetically) of $2,598,019 worth of goods and services during his lifetime, and the average female will occasion the production of $1,253,960 worth of goods and services in her lifetime. This in turn means the average male's net worth to society (we're thinking here as coldly calculating economists, not as warm-blooded human beings) will be $2,405,419, and the average female's will be $1,061,360.

Who cares? People concerned about the future of Social Security and the federal budget deficit should care, even if they don't give a hoot about the spiritual essence of a human being. You see, if the average person is a net asset to society over a lifetime, then society suffers a net loss if that average person isn't permitted to be born.

In other words, abort the average male and you rob society, over the span of his lifetime, of $2,405,419; abort the average female and you rob society, over the span of her lifetime, of $1,061,360. (Actually, you can tag on about another $400 to each of those figures—for the cost of the abortion, which the aborted person can never repay by his productivity.)

How does that affect the future of Social Security? Simple. Presently about 14.5 percent of personal earnings are taxed to fund Social Security. Assuming (against all odds) that that percentage doesn't rise in the lifetime of someone born today (actually former Social Security Administration chief actuary A. Haeworth Robertson estimates that, given present population trends, Social Security withholding will have to rise to 40 percent of payroll early in the twenty-first century), his productivity will contribute $348,785 to Social

Security in his lifetime, or hers will contribute $153,897. Abort him or her, and you reduce Social Security's future income accordingly.

How does it affect the federal budget deficit? About 20 percent of GNP goes to the federal government, one way or another, through taxes. So the average male will contribute $481,084 to the federal budget in his lifetime; the average female $212,272 in hers. Abort him or her, and you reduce the federal government's future income accordingly.

Now think of this in light of the roughly 1.5 million abortions done in the United States every year. Of those, about 47.4 percent are males and 52.6 percent are females. So, we abort 711,000 males and 789,000 females per year. If we multiply 711,000 males times average annual economic productivity of $51,179 we find that each year's abortion of males costs society $36,388,269,000 per year throughout their productive careers. If we multiply 789,000 females times average annual economic productivity of $22,582, we find that each year's abortion of females costs society $17,817,198,000 per year throughout their productive careers. Combine the figures for males and females, and we find that each year's 1.5 million abortions cost society $54,205,467,000 (or, at 20 percent federal taxation, $10,841,093,000 in federal revenues) per year *every year throughout their productive careers* (in constant 1987 dollars).

The cumulative effect is enormous. The first year in which the number of abortions in the U.S. reached 1.5 million was 1979, so 1997 will be the first year in which those 1.5 million aborted children would have reached eighteen had they lived. Thus, in that year society's total production will be about $54,205,467,000 less (or federal revenue $10,841,093,000 less) than it would have been had those 1.5 million people not been aborted. But in 1998 the losses will be *double*: total production will be $108,410,934,000 less (and federal revenue $21,682,186,000 less) than it would have been.

By 2007, when 1989's abortees will come home to roost, as it were, the combined annual loss will be $542,054,670,000 to society at large and $108,410,930,000 to federal revenue. In 2017, they will be $1,084,109,340,000 to society and $216,821,860,000 to federal revenue. And in 2044, when 1979's non-aborted folks reach retirement age, the annual loss to abortion (in constant 1987 dollars) will be, to society, $2,547,656,949,000, and to federal revenue, $509,531,371,000 (forty-seven times the annual loss from 1.5 million abortions).

Remember these figures are computed *after* subtracting a person's *costs* to society from his (or her) economic *benefits* to society, so it won't do for someone to object, "Sure, but think about how much those folks will cost in health care, unemployment insurance, education, etc., etc."

In short, abortion undermines America's future economic solvency. It exacerbates future federal deficits and the shaky financial future of the Social Security "trust fund."

The simple economic truth is that, on the average, people are worth more than they cost—about 13.5 times more for males and 6.5 times more for females (figuring solely on the basis of measurable economic income, not including the tremendous value of the financially unpaid work people—especially women—perform at home). Abortion is a horribly uneconomical choice that threatens the nation's economic future.

Now, what were those pro-abortionists saying about opposition to abortion being on solely religious grounds?

POPULATION AND ECONOMIC INDICATORS: STATISTICAL TABLES

*T*his appendix provides statistical information relevant to the relationships of economic production and growth, population density and growth, and general health (here represented by nutritional provision). Discussion of these issues in Chapter 6 was based on these data. The twelve tables present detailed (Tables 6-1, 6-2, 6-3, and 6-4) and summary (Tables 6-1-A, 6-1-B; 6-2-A, 6-2-B; 6-3-A, 6-3-B; 6-4-A, 6-4-B) data for sixty-five nations selected at random from The World Bank's *World Development Report 1986*. The data presented in the tables are as follows:

TABLE   DESCRIPTION

6-1   Detail, ordered by ascending population density.

6-1-A   Summary by quintiles, ordered by ascending population density, quintile averages assigning equal weight to each individual nation.

6-1-B   Summary by quintiles, ordered by ascending population density, quintile averages weighted by differing populations and, for density, areas of nations.

6-2   Detail, ordered by ascending GNP per capita.

6-2-A   Summary by quintiles, ordered by ascending GNP per capita, quintile averages assigning equal weight to each individual nation.

6-2-B   Summary by quintiles, ordered by ascending GNP per capita, quintile averages weighted by differing populations and, for density, areas of nations.

6-3   Detail, ordered by ascending population growth rate.

6-3-A   Summary by quintiles, ordered by ascending population growth rate, quintile averages assigning equal weight to each individual nation.

6-3-B   Summary by quintiles, ordered by ascending population growth rate, quintile averages weighted by differing populations and, for density, areas of nations.

6-4   Detail, ordered by ascending GNP per capita growth rate.

6-4-A   Summary by quintiles, ordered by ascending GNP per capita growth rate, quintile averages assigning equal weight to each individual nation.

6-4-B   Summary by quintiles, ordered by ascending GNP per capita growth rate, quintile averages weighted by differing populations and, for density, areas of nations.

Why bother to look at summaries both assigning nations equal weight regardless of population or area and assigning differing weights depending on population or area? After all, it seems at first thought to make no sense to say that average GNP per capita for China and Taiwan, for example, was $1,636 in 1984 simply because adding China's GNP per capita of $302 to Taiwan's of $2,969 and dividing by two yields $1,636 when China's population is roughly fifty-six times Taiwan's. But if we multiply the GNP per capita of each nation times its population, add the two results together, and divide by the combined populations, the result is $348, a far cry from the $1,636 rendered by the first method. Doesn't the second method make better sense?

For some purposes, yes. But for others, no. Why? Because China's and Taiwan's populations differ not only in size, but also in other important ways, ways more important than size in determining economic well-being. The institutional structures of their countries differ. To note just two very important differences, China is a communist dictatorship in which the free market plays very little role; Taiwan is a democratic government with a largely free market. (Other important differences distinguish various nations: religious worldview; cultural attitudes toward work, production, consumption, and saving; history; etc.)

People behave differently in different environments, and their behavior has important economic results. Thus, in one sense, comparing the economies of China and Taiwan and weighting their performances by population in computing averages is comparing apples and oranges. Ignoring the geopolitical boundary lines and cultural differences that distinguish nations means assuming, incorrectly, that people behave about the same regardless of the surrounding structures and cultures.

We can gain important insight into the comparative economic performances of nations, then, by viewing them as individual entities without regard to the absolute sizes (as distinct from densities) of their populations. Hence it is legitimate, for some purposes even preferable, in computing economic and demographic averages among nations, to treat nations of vastly different population sizes as if they were the same size.

The more nations there are in a group, the more it makes sense, however, to determine averages weighted by population, since the blending of many nations tends to obscure the cultural and institutional differences that distinguish one from another. Therefore, for instance, the population-weighted averages (Tables 6-1-B, 6-2-B, 6-3-B, and 6-4-B) for all sixty-five nations taken together are, for most purposes, more reliable pictures of the group as a whole than are the averages that are not weighted by population (Tables 6-1-A, 6-2-A, 6-3-A, and 6-4-A).

In the following tables, therefore, we can see: (a) economic and demographic statistics for individual nations (Tables 6-1, 6-2, 6-3, and 6-4); (b) for groups of nations compared with each other without taking into account the different sizes of their populations (Tables 6-1-A, 6-2-A, 6-3-A, and 6-4-A), and (c) for groups of nations compared with each other, taking into account the different sizes of their populations and, where relevant, land areas (Tables 6-1-B, 6-2-B, 6-3-B, and 6-4-B). Most of the discussion of quintile averages of nations in Chapter 6 is based on comparing nations with each other without taking into account the different absolute sizes of their populations.

TABLE 6-1

POPULATION DENSITY, POPULATION GROWTH, AND ECONOMIC INDICATORS
Ordered by Ascending Population Density

NATION	GNP PER CAPITA DOLLARS 1984	AVERAGE ANNUAL GROWTH RATE (%) 1965-1984	POPULATION DENSITY^ 1987	AVERAGE ANNUAL GROWTH RATE (%) 1965-1984	NUTRITION DAILY CALORIE SUPPLY PER CAPITA (%)*
1. Mauritania	450	0.3	5	2.2	97
2. Botswana	960	8.4	5	3.85	93
3. Australia	11,740	1.7	5	1.7	115
4. Canada	13,280	2.4	7	1.3	130
5. Niger	190	-1.3	14	2.65	97
6. Bolivia	540	0.2	15	2.5	82
7. Oman	6,490	6.1	15	3.7	na
8. Congo, People's Rep.	1,140	3.7	16	2.85	109
9. Mali	140	1.1	18	2.6	68
10. Saudi Arabia	10,530	5.9	18	4.45	134
11. Zambia	470	-1.3	25	3.1	84
12. Paraguay	1,240	4.4	27	2.6	122
13. New Zealand	7,730	1.4	32	1.0	132
14. USSR@	7,531	1.1	33	.9	132
15. Peru	1,000	-0.1	42	2.6	85
16. Chile	1,700	-0.1	43	1.8	105
17. Brazil	1,720	4.6	45	2.4	106
18. Madagascar	260	-1.6	47	2.6	112
19. Venezuela	3,410	0.9	52	3.4	99
20. United Arab Emirates	21,920	na	57	11.25	na
21. Zimbabwe	760	1.5	62	3.3	82
22. Nicaragua	860	-1.5	66	3.1	101
23. United States	15,390	1.7	67	1.05	137
24. Colombia	1,390	3.0	70	2.3	110
25. Guinea	330	1.1	71	1.9	84
26. South Africa	2,340	1.4	73	2.35	118
27. Panama	1,980	2.6	76	2.55	98

TABLE 6-1, CONTINUED

POPULATION DENSITY, POPULATION GROWTH, AND ECONOMIC INDICATORS
Ordered by Ascending Population Density

NATION	GNP PER CAPITA DOLLARS 1984	AVERAGE ANNUAL GROWTH RATE (%) 1965-1984	POPULATION DENSITY^ 1987	AVERAGE ANNUAL GROWTH RATE (%) 1965-1984	NUTRITION DAILY CALORIE SUPPLY PER CAPITA (%)*
28. Cote d'Ivoire	610	0.2	86	4.55	112
29. Yemen, Arab. Rep.	550	**5.9**	87	2.7	92
30. Burkina Faso	160	1.2	89	1.9	85
31. Senegal	380	-0.5	93	2.6	102
32. Ethiopia	110	0.4	99	2.5	93
33. Benin	270	1.0	100	2.7	83
34. Mexico	2,040	2.9	107	3.1	126
35. Ireland	4,970	2.4	130	1.05	143
36. Egypt, Arab Rep.	720	4.3	134	2.4	126
37. Sierra Leone	310	0.6	140	1.9	91
38. Morocco	670	2.8	141	2.55	105
39. Togo	250	0.5	147	3.3	94
40. Burma	180	2.3	149	2.15	117
41. Syrian, Arab Rep.	1,620	4.5	156	3.4	127
42. Turkey	1,160	2.9	176	2.35	123
43. Bulgaria@	**6,461**	**1.2**	209	.45	147
44. Austria	9,140	3.6	234	.2	132
45. Yugoslavia	2,120	4.3	237	.85	141
46. France	9,760	3.0	263	.65	139
47. China~	**302**	**6.6**	290	**1.8**	**111**
48. Portugal	1,970	3.5	290	.4	124
49. Hungary	2,100	6.2	295	.25	135
50. Poland	2,100	1.5	313	.8	127
51. Pakistan	380	2.5	337	3.0	95
52. German Dem. Rep.@	**10,122**	**1.2**	398	-.05	142
53. Switzerland	16,330	1.4	413	.65	129
54. Burundi	220	1.9	466	1.8	102

TABLE 6-1, CONTINUED

POPULATION DENSITY, POPULATION GROWTH, AND ECONOMIC INDICATORS
Ordered by Ascending Population Density

| | GNP PER CAPITA | | POPULATION | | NUTRITION |
NATION	DOLLARS 1984	AVERAGE ANNUAL GROWTH RATE (%) 1965-1984	DENSITY^ 1987	AVERAGE ANNUAL GROWTH RATE (%) 1965-1984	DAILY CALORIE SUPPLY PER CAPITA (%)*
55. Israel	5,060	2.7	528	2.65	121
56. Jamaica	1,150	-0.4	573	1.35	111
57. United Kingdom	8,570	1.6	603	.2	128
58. India	260	1.6	631	2.3	96
59. Trinidad & Tobago	7,150	2.6	632	1.4	129
60. Germany, Fed. Rep.	11,130	2.7	635	.3	130
61. Sri Lanka	360	2.9	648	1.9	106
62. El Salvador	710	-0.6	648	3.2	**90**
63. Japan	10,630	4.7	849	1.05	113
64. Taiwan~	**2,969**	8.3	1,587	**2.1**	111
65. Singapore	7,260	7.8	10,947	1.55	115
Average&	3,244	3.45	93	1.81	113

^Density is persons per square mile, 1987, according to U.S. Bureau of the Census, *Statistical Abstract of the United States, 1988*, pp. 795ff, Table 1378.

*Daily calorie supply per capita = percent of the "calories needed to sustain a person at normal levels of activity and health, taking into account age and sex distributions, average body weights, and environmental temperatures," using 1977 requirement estimates of United Nations Food and Agriculture Organization, applied to 1983 supplies and populations. (*World Development Report, 1986*, p. 254.)

@GNP per capita data for Bulgaria, German Democratic Republic, and U.S.S.R. are derived from *Statistical Abstract . . . 1988*, p. 805, Table 1387 by comparison with population figures on pp. 795ff, Table 1378. GNP per capita average annual growth rate is for years 1975-1984 and is measured in constant 1983 U.S. dollars.

~GNP per capita and population data for China and Taiwan are from *Statistical Abstract . . . 1988*, pp. 795ff, Table 1378, and p. 805, Table 1387. GNP per capita average annual growth rate is for years 1975-1984 and is measured in constant 1983 U.S. dollars; average annual population growth rate is for years 1970-1987. *World Development Report, 1986* treats mainland China and Taiwan as a single entity, masking the radical differences between the two. Caloric data were unavailable for the two countries separately, but *World Development Report's* combined 111 percent is used here for both. Taiwan's is probably considerably higher; China's is probably somewhat lower but, since its population is so much larger, counting Taiwan's with it cannot have raised it very much.

&Average is weighted by population and, for density, area.

Boldfaced figures are for years other than those indicated.

Sources: The World Bank, *World Development Report, 1986*, pp. 180-181, Table 1; pp. 228-229, Table 25; pp. 234-235, Table 28; *Statistical Abstract . . . 1988*, pp. 795ff, Table 1378; p. 805, Table 1387.

Note: The same data may be seen in order of ascending GNP per capita (Table 6-2), ascending population growth rate (Table 6-3), and ascending GNP per capita growth rate (Table 6-4).

TABLE 6-1-A

POPULATION DENSITY, POPULATION GROWTH, AND ECONOMIC INDICATORS
Summary, Quintiles of Population Density,
Individual Nations Given Equal Weight

| QUINTILE | GNP PER CAPITA | | POPULATION | | NUTRITION |
	DOLLARS 1984	AVERAGE ANNUAL GROWTH RATE (%) 1965-1984	DENSITY 1987	AVERAGE ANNUAL GROWTH RATE (%) 1965-1984	DAILY CALORIE SUPPLY PER CAPITA (%)
Lowest	4,223	2.54	15	2.65	97
Second	4,509	1.00	56	3.00	105
Third	1,002	1.87	109	2.60	103
Fourth	3,647	3.33	257	1.25	129
Highest	5,523	2.86	1,473	1.57	114
Average^	3,705	2.30	383	2.25	112

^Average is for all nations counted individually, not for quintiles, and is not weighted by population or area.

TABLE 6-1-B

POPULATION DENSITY, POPULATION GROWTH, AND ECONOMIC INDICATORS
Summary, Quintiles of Population Density,
Weighted by Population and Area

| QUINTILE | GNP PER CAPITA | | POPULATION | | NUTRITION |
	DOLLARS 1984	AVERAGE ANNUAL GROWTH RATE (%) 1965-1984	DENSITY^ 1987	AVERAGE ANNUAL GROWTH RATE (%) 1965-1984	DAILY CALORIE SUPPLY PER CAPITA (%)*
Lowest	7,569	2.07	9	2.31	112
Second	7,951	1.91	43	1.54	124
Third	1,060	2.45	101	2.75	113
Fourth	1,049	5.60	259	1.55	114
Highest	2,725	2.16	620	1.91	103
Average^	3,244	3.45	93	1.81	113

^Average is for all nations counted individually, not for quintiles, and is weighted by population and, for density, area.

TABLE 6-2

POPULATION DENSITY, POPULATION GROWTH, AND ECONOMIC INDICATORS
Ordered by Ascending GNP Per Capita

| NATION | GNP PER CAPITA | | POPULATION | | NUTRITION |
	DOLLARS 1984	AVERAGE ANNUAL GROWTH RATE (%) 1965-1984	DENSITY^ 1987	AVERAGE ANNUAL GROWTH RATE (%) 1965-1984	DAILY CALORIE SUPPLY PER CAPITA (%)*
1. Ethiopia	110	0.4	99	2.5	93
2. Mali	140	1.1	18	2.6	68
3. Burkina Faso	160	1.2	89	1.9	85
4. Burma	180	2.3	149	2.15	117
5. Niger	190	-1.3	14	2.65	97
6. Burundi	220	1.9	466	1.8	102
7. Togo	250	0.5	147	3.3	94
8. Madagascar	260	-1.6	47	2.6	112
9. India	260	1.6	631	2.3	96
10. Benin	270	1.0	100	2.7	83
11. China~	302	6.6	290	1.8	111
12. Sierra Leone	310	0.6	140	1.9	91
13. Guinea	330	1.1	71	1.9	84
14. Sri Lanka	360	2.9	648	1.9	106
15. Senegal	380	-0.5	93	2.6	102
16. Pakistan	380	2.5	337	3.0	95
17. Mauritania	450	0.3	5	2.2	97
18. Zambia	470	-1.3	25	3.1	84
19. Bolivia	540	0.2	15	2.5	82
20. Yemen, Arab. Rep.	550	5.9	87	2.7	92
21. Cote d'Ivoire	610	0.2	86	4.55	112
22. Morocco	670	2.8	141	2.55	105
23. El Salvador	710	-0.6	648	3.2	90
24. Egypt, Arab Rep.	720	4.3	134	2.4	126
25. Zimbabwe	760	1.5	62	3.3	82
26. Nicaragua	860	-1.5	66	3.1	101
27. Botswana	960	8.4	5	3.85	93
28. Peru	1,000	-0.1	42	2.6	85

TABLE 6-2, CONTINUED

POPULATION DENSITY, POPULATION GROWTH, AND ECONOMIC INDICATORS
Ordered by Ascending GNP Per Capita

NATION	GNP PER CAPITA DOLLARS 1984	GNP PER CAPITA AVERAGE ANNUAL GROWTH RATE (%) 1965-1984	POPULATION DENSITY^ 1987	POPULATION AVERAGE ANNUAL GROWTH RATE (%) 1965-1984	NUTRITION DAILY CALORIE SUPPLY PER CAPITA (%)*
29. Congo, People's Rep.	1,140	3.7	16	2.85	109
30. Jamaica	1,150	-0.4	573	1.35	111
31. Turkey	1,160	2.9	176	2.35	123
32. Paraguay	1,240	4.4	27	2.6	122
33. Colombia	1,390	3.0	70	2.3	110
34. Syrian, Arab Rep.	1,620	4.5	156	3.4	127
35. Chile	1,700	-0.1	43	1.8	105
36. Brazil	1,720	4.6	45	2.4	106
37. Portugal	1,970	3.5	290	.4	124
38. Panama	1,980	2.6	76	2.55	98
39. Mexico	2,040	2.9	107	3.1	126
40. Hungary	2,100	6.2	295	.25	135
41. Poland	2,100	1.5	313	.8	127
42. Yugoslavia	2,120	4.3	237	.85	141
43. South Africa	2,340	1.4	73	2.35	118
44. Taiwan~	**2,969**	8.3	1,587	**2.1**	111
45. Venezuela	3,410	0.9	52	3.4	99
46. Ireland	4,970	2.4	130	1.05	143
47. Israel	5,060	2.7	528	2.65	121
48. Bulgaria@	**6,461**	**1.2**	209	.45	147
49. Oman	6,490	6.1	15	3.7	na
50. Trinidad & Tobago	7,150	2.6	632	1.4	129
51. Singapore	7,260	7.8	10,947	1.55	115
52. USSR@	**7,531**	**1.1**	33	.9	132
53. New Zealand	7,730	1.4	32	1.0	132
54. United Kingdom	8,570	1.6	603	.2	128
55. Austria	9,140	3.6	234	.2	132

TABLE 6-2, CONTINUED

POPULATION DENSITY, POPULATION GROWTH, AND ECONOMIC INDICATORS
Ordered by Ascending GNP Per Capita

NATION	GNP PER CAPITA DOLLARS 1984	GNP PER CAPITA AVERAGE ANNUAL GROWTH RATE (%) 1965-1984	POPULATION DENSITY 1987	POPULATION AVERAGE ANNUAL GROWTH RATE (%) 1965-1984	NUTRITION DAILY CALORIE SUPPLY PER CAPITA (%)
56. France	9,760	3.0	263	.65	139
57. German Dem. Rep.@	10,122	1.2	398	-.05	142
58. Saudi Arabia	10,530	5.9	18	4.45	134
59. Japan	10,630	4.7	849	1.05	113
60. Germany, Fed. Rep.	11,130	2.7	635	.3	130
61. Australia	11,740	1.7	5	1.7	115
62. Canada	13,280	2.4	7	1.3	130
63. United States	15,390	1.7	67	1.05	137
64. Switzerland	16,330	1.4	413	.65	129
65. United Arab Emirates	21,920	na	57	11.25	na
Average^	3,244	3.45	93	1.81	113

^Average is weighted by population and, for density, area.

TABLE 6-2-A

POPULATION DENSITY, POPULATION GROWTH, AND ECONOMIC INDICATORS
Summary, Quintiles of GNP Per Capita,
Individual Nations Given Equal Weight

| QUINTILE | GNP PER CAPITA | | POPULATION | | NUTRITION |
	DOLLARS 1984	AVERAGE ANNUAL GROWTH RATE (%) 1965-1984	DENSITY 1987	AVERAGE ANNUAL GROWTH RATE (%) 1965-1984	DAILY CALORIE SUPPLY PER CAPITA (%)
Lowest	229	1.18	174	2.32	94
Second	573	1.28	181	2.85	98
Third	1,467	3.07	125	2.43	111
Fourth	4,612	3.58	1,158	1.65	119
Highest	11,972	2.60	275	1.83	130
Average^	3,705	2.3	383	2.25	112

^Average is for all nations counted individually, not for quintiles, and is not weighted by population or area.

TABLE 6-2-B

POPULATION DENSITY, POPULATION GROWTH, AND ECONOMIC INDICATORS
Summary, Quintiles of GNP Per Capita,
Weighted by Population

| QUINTILE | GNP PER CAPITA | | POPULATION | | NUTRITION |
	DOLLARS 1984	AVERAGE ANNUAL GROWTH RATE (%) 1965-1984	DENSITY 1987	AVERAGE ANNUAL GROWTH RATE (%) 1965-1984	DAILY CALORIE SUPPLY PER CAPITA (%)
Lowest	277	4.22	262	2.04	104
Second	524	2.50	100	2.81	103
Third	1,640	3.37	56	1.53	113
Fourth	5,848	1.83	44	1.15	129
Highest	12,414	.69	51	.93	130
Average^	3,244	3.45	93	1.81	113

^Average is for all nations counted individually, not for quintiles, and is weighted by population and, for density, area.

TABLE 6-3

POPULATION DENSITY, POPULATION GROWTH, AND ECONOMIC INDICATORS
Ordered by Ascending Population Growth Rate

NATION	GNP PER CAPITA		POPULATION		NUTRITION
	DOLLARS 1984	AVERAGE ANNUAL GROWTH RATE (%) 1965-1984	DENSITY 1987	AVERAGE ANNUAL GROWTH RATE (%) 1965-1984	DAILY CALORIE SUPPLY PER CAPITA (%)
1. German Dem. Rep.@	**10,122**	**1.2**	398	-.05	142
2. United Kingdom	8,570	1.6	603	.2	128
3. Austria	9,140	3.6	234	.2	132
4. Hungary	2,100	6.2	295	.25	135
5. Germany, Fed. Rep.	11,130	2.7	635	.3	130
6. Portugal	1,970	3.5	290	.4	124
7. Bulgaria@	**6,461**	**1.2**	209	.45	147
8. France	9,760	3.0	263	.65	139
9. Switzerland	16,330	1.4	413	.65	129
10. Poland	2,100	1.5	313	.8	127
11. Yugoslavia	2,120	4.3	237	.85	141
12. USSR@	**7,531**	**1.1**	33	.9	132
13. New Zealand	7,730	1.4	32	1.0	132
14. Ireland	4,970	2.4	130	1.05	143
15. Japan	10,630	4.7	849	1.05	113
16. United States	15,390	1.7	67	1.05	137
17. Canada	13,280	2.4	7	1.3	130
18. Jamaica	1,150	-0.4	573	1.35	111
19. Trinidad & Tobago	7,150	2.6	632	1.4	129
20. Singapore	7,260	7.8	10,947	1.55	115
21. Australia	11,740	1.7	5	1.7	115
22. Burundi	220	1.9	466	1.8	102
23. China~	**302**	**6.6**	290	1.8	111
24. Chile	1,700	-0.1	43	1.8	105
25. Burkina Faso	160	1.2	89	1.9	85
26. Sierra Leone	310	0.6	140	1.9	91
27. Guinea	330	1.1	71	1.9	84

TABLE 6-3, CONTINUED

POPULATION DENSITY, POPULATION GROWTH, AND ECONOMIC INDICATORS
Ordered by Ascending Population Growth Rate

NATION	GNP PER CAPITA DOLLARS 1984	AVERAGE ANNUAL GROWTH RATE (%) 1965-1984	POPULATION DENSITY 1987	AVERAGE ANNUAL GROWTH RATE (%) 1965-1984	NUTRITION DAILY CALORIE SUPPLY PER CAPITA (%)
28. Sri Lanka	360	2.9	648	1.9	106
29. Taiwan⁻	**2,969**	**8.3**	1,587	**2.1**	111
30. Burma	180	2.3	149	2.15	117
31. Mauritania	450	0.3	5	2.2	97
32. India	260	1.6	631	2.3	96
33. Colombia	1,390	3.0	70	2.3	110
34. Turkey	1,160	2.9	176	2.35	123
35. South Africa	2,340	1.4	73	2.35	118
36. Egypt, Arab Rep.	720	4.3	134	2.4	126
37. Brazil	1,720	4.6	45	2.4	106
38. Ethiopia	110	0.4	99	2.5	93
39. Bolivia	540	0.2	15	2.5	82
40. Morocco	670	2.8	141	2.55	105
41. Panama	1,980	2.6	76	2.55	98
42. Mali	140	1.1	18	2.6	68
43. Madagascar	260	-1.6	47	2.6	112
44. Senegal	380	-0.5	93	2.6	102
45. Peru	1,000	-0.1	42	2.6	85
46. Paraguay	1,240	4.4	27	2.6	122
47. Niger	190	-1.3	14	2.65	97
48. Israel	5,060	2.7	528	2.65	121
49. Benin	270	1.0	100	2.7	83
50. Yemen, Arab. Rep.	550	**5.9**	87	2.7	92
51. Congo, People's Rep.	1,140	3.7	16	2.85	109
52. Pakistan	380	2.5	337	3.0	95
53. Zambia	470	-1.3	25	3.1	84
54. Nicaragua	860	-1.5	66	3.1	**101**

TABLE 6-3, CONTINUED

POPULATION DENSITY, POPULATION GROWTH, AND ECONOMIC INDICATORS
Ordered by Ascending Population Growth Rate

NATION	GNP PER CAPITA DOLLARS 1984	AVERAGE ANNUAL GROWTH RATE (%) 1965-1984	POPULATION DENSITY 1987	AVERAGE ANNUAL GROWTH RATE (%) 1965-1984	NUTRITION DAILY CALORIE SUPPLY PER CAPITA (%)
55. Mexico	2,040	2.9	107	3.1	126
56. El Salvador	710	-0.6	648	3.2	90
57. Togo	250	0.5	147	3.3	94
58. Zimbabwe	760	1.5	62	3.3	82
59. Syrian, Arab Rep.	1,620	4.5	156	3.4	127
60. Venezuela	3,410	0.9	52	3.4	99
61. Oman	6,490	6.1	15	3.7	na
62. Botswana	960	8.4	5	3.85	93
63. Saudi Arabia	10,530	5.9	18	4.45	134
64. Cote d'Ivoire	610	0.2	86	4.55	112
65. United Arab Emirates	21,920	na	57	11.25	na
Average^	3,244	3.45	93	1.81	113

^Average is weighted by population and, for density, area.-

TABLE 6-3-A

POPULATION DENSITY, POPULATION GROWTH, AND ECONOMIC INDICATORS
Summary, Quintiles of Population Growth Rate, Individual Nations Weighted Equally

QUINTILE	GNP PER CAPITA DOLLARS 1984	AVERAGE ANNUAL GROWTH RATE (%) 1965-1984	POPULATION DENSITY 1987	AVERAGE ANNUAL GROWTH RATE (%) 1965-1984	NUTRITION DAILY CALORIE SUPPLY PER CAPITA (%)
Lowest	7,312	2.5	304	.45	134
Second	5,712	2.5	1,095	1.40	115
Third	963	2.6	249	2.25	105
Fourth	1,020	1.8	117	2.67	99
Highest	3,894	2.3	111	4.13	104
Average^	3,705	2.33	83	2.25	112

^Average is for all nations counted individually, not for quintiles, and is not weighted by population or area.

TABLE 6-3-B

POPULATION DENSITY, POPULATION GROWTH, AND ECONOMIC INDICATORS
Summary, Quintiles of Population Growth Rate, Weighted by Population

QUINTILE	GNP PER CAPITA DOLLARS 1984	AVERAGE ANNUAL GROWTH RATE (%) 1965-1984	POPULATION DENSITY 1987	AVERAGE ANNUAL GROWTH RATE (%) 1965-1984	NUTRITION DAILY CALORIE SUPPLY PER CAPITA (%)
Lowest	7,644	1.84	60	.67	133
Second	4,029	5.38	98	1.60	116
Third	604	2.22	148	2.31	101
Fourth	604	1.94	69	2.81	96
Highest	2,637	1.51	51	3.43	116
Average^	3,244	3.45	93	1.81	113

^Average is for all nations counted individually, not for quintiles, and is weighted by population and, for density, area.

TABLE 6-4

POPULATION DENSITY, POPULATION GROWTH, AND ECONOMIC INDICATORS
Ordered by Ascending GNP Per Capita Growth Rate

NATION	GNP PER CAPITA		POPULATION		NUTRITION
	DOLLARS 1984	AVERAGE ANNUAL GROWTH RATE (%) 1965-1984	DENSITY 1987	AVERAGE ANNUAL GROWTH RATE (%) 1965-1984	DAILY CALORIE SUPPLY PER CAPITA (%)
1. Madagascar	260	-1.6	47	2.6	112
2. Nicaragua	860	-1.5	66	3.1	101
3. Niger	190	-1.3	14	2.65	97
4. Zambia	470	-1.3	25	3.1	84
5. El Salvador	710	-0.6	648	3.2	90
6. Senegal	380	-0.5	93	2.6	102
7. Jamaica	1,150	-0.4	573	1.35	111
8. Chile	1,700	-0.1	43	1.8	105
9. Peru	1,000	-0.1	42	2.6	85
10. Bolivia	540	0.2	15	2.5	82
11. Cote d'Ivoire	610	0.2	86	4.55	112
12. Mauritania	450	0.3	5	2.2	97
13. Ethiopia	110	0.4	99	2.5	93
14. Togo	250	0.5	147	3.3	94
15. Sierra Leone	310	0.6	140	1.9	91
16. Venezuela	3,410	0.9	52	3.4	99
17. Benin	270	1.0	100	2.7	83
18. Mali	140	1.1	18	2.6	68
19. Guinea	330	1.1	71	1.9	84
20. USSR@	7,531	1.1	33	.9	132
21. Burkina Faso	160	1.2	89	1.9	85
22. Bulgaria@	6,461	1.2	209	.45	147
23. German Dem. Rep.@	10,122	1.2	398	-.05	142
24. South Africa	2,340	1.4	73	2.35	118
25. New Zealand	7,730	1.4	32	1.0	132
26. Switzerland	16,330	1.4	413	.65	129
27. Zimbabwe	760	1.5	62	3.3	82
28. Poland	2,100	1.5	313	.8	127

TABLE 6-4, CONTINUED

POPULATION DENSITY, POPULATION GROWTH, AND ECONOMIC INDICATORS
Ordered by Ascending GNP Per Capita Growth Rate

NATION	GNP PER CAPITA DOLLARS 1984	GNP PER CAPITA AVERAGE ANNUAL GROWTH RATE (%) 1965-1984	POPULATION DENSITY 1987	POPULATION AVERAGE ANNUAL GROWTH RATE (%) 1965-1984	NUTRITION DAILY CALORIE SUPPLY PER CAPITA (%)
29. India	260	1.6	631	2.3	96
30. United Kingdom	8,570	1.6	603	.2	128
31. Australia	11,740	1.7	5	1.7	115
32. United States	15,390	1.7	67	1.05	137
33. Burundi	220	1.9	466	1.8	102
34. Burma	180	2.3	149	2.15	117
35. Ireland	4,970	2.4	130	1.05	143
36. Canada	13,280	2.4	7	1.3	130
37. Pakistan	380	2.5	337	3.0	95
38. Panama	1,980	2.6	76	2.55	98
39. Trinidad & Tobago	7,150	2.6	632	1.4	129
40. Israel	5,060	2.7	528	2.65	121
41. Germany, Fed. Rep.	11,130	2.7	635	.3	130
42. Morocco	670	2.8	141	2.55	105
43. Sri Lanka	360	2.9	648	1.9	106
44. Turkey	1,160	2.9	176	2.35	123
45. Mexico	2,040	2.9	107	3.1	126
46. Colombia	1,390	3.0	70	2.3	110
47. France	9,760	3.0	263	.65	139
48. Portugal	1,970	3.5	290	.4	124
49. Austria	9,140	3.6	234	.2	132
50. Congo, People's Rep.	1,140	3.7	16	2.85	109
51. Egypt, Arab Rep.	720	4.3	134	2.4	126
52. Yugoslavia	2,120	4.3	237	.85	141
53. Paraguay	1,240	4.4	27	2.6	122
54. Syrian, Arab Rep.	1,620	4.5	156	3.4	127
55. Brazil	1,720	4.6	45	2.4	106

TABLE 6-4, CONTINUED

POPULATION DENSITY, POPULATION GROWTH, AND ECONOMIC INDICATORS
Ordered by Ascending GNP Per Capita Growth Rate

| NATION | GNP PER CAPITA | | POPULATION | | NUTRITION |
	DOLLARS 1984	AVERAGE ANNUAL GROWTH RATE (%) 1965-1984	DENSITY 1987	AVERAGE ANNUAL GROWTH RATE (%) 1965-1984	DAILY CALORIE SUPPLY PER CAPITA (%)
56. Japan	10,630	4.7	849	1.05	113
57. Yemen, Arab. Rep.	550	5.9	87	2.7	92
58. Saudi Arabia	10,530	5.9	18	4.45	134
59. Oman	6,490	6.1	15	3.7	na
60. Hungary	2,100	6.2	295	.25	135
61. China~	302	6.6	290	1.8	111
62. Singapore	7,260	7.8	10,947	1.55	115
63. Taiwan~	2,969	8.3	1,587	2.1	111
64. Botswana	960	8.4	5	3.85	93
65. United Arab Emirates	21,920	na	57	11.25	na
Average^	3,244	3.45	93	1.81	113

^Average is weighted by population and, for density, area.

TABLE 6-4-A

POPULATION DENSITY, POPULATION GROWTH, AND ECONOMIC INDICATORS
Summary, Quintiles of GNP Per Capita Growth Rate,
Individual Nations Given Equal Weight

| NATION | GNP PER CAPITA | | POPULATION | | NUTRITION |
	DOLLARS 1984	AVERAGE ANNUAL GROWTH RATE (%) 1965-1984	DENSITY 1987	AVERAGE ANNUAL GROWTH RATE (%) 1965-1984	DAILY CALORIE SUPPLY PER CAPITA (%)
Lowest	648	-.48	135	2.67	98
Second	4,260	1.08	137	1.77	108
Third	5,152	2.02	268	1.74	115
Fourth	3,589	3.25	268	1.73	122
Highest	5,253	6.12	1,106	3.16	114
Average^	3,705	2.30	383	2.25	112

^Average is for all nations counted individually, not for quintiles, and is not weighted by population or area.

TABLE 6-4-B

POPULATION DENSITY, POPULATION GROWTH, AND ECONOMIC INDICATORS
Summary, Quintiles of GNP Per Capita Growth Rate,
Weighted by Population

| NATION | GNP PER CAPITA | | POPULATION | | NUTRITION |
	DOLLARS 1984	AVERAGE ANNUAL GROWTH RATE (%) 1965-1984	DENSITY 1987	AVERAGE ANNUAL GROWTH RATE (%) 1965-1984	DAILY CALORIE SUPPLY PER CAPITA (%)
Lowest	#550	-.21	38	2.67	96
Second	6,595	1.12	37	1.18	126
Third	3,941	1.72	100	1.95	108
Fourth	4,925	3.16	148	1.64	126
Highest	1,567	6.22	153	1.84	111
Average^	3,244	3.45	93	1.81	113

#This figure is sharply affected downward by the inclusion of Ethiopia, which far outweighs all other members of the quintile in population and has far the lowest GNP per capita in the quintile. Without Ethiopia, the figure would be $763.
^Average is for all nations counted individually, not for quintiles, and is weighted by population and, for density, area.

PUTTING MARKET RESTRAINTS ON POLLUTION

*H*ow can we determine what is an "optimal" level of pollution—granted the necessary trade-offs between pollution and economic production? How can we count the costs and benefits of pollution and pollution abatement?

We might ask the monetary price of installing scrubbers on coal-fired generator plant smokestacks or catalytic converters on cars. That would give us dollar costs, but it would bypass the prior question, "How much pollution do we want to get rid of . . . at what costs . . . using what means?" We could, after all, force the coal-fired plants to use low-sulfur coal, which is more expensive than high-sulfur coal, but cleaner; that solution would move more coal mining from eastern to western states, causing unemployment in the east and employment in the west, and it could cost more than installing scrubbers, or it could cost less, but we need to count the costs. To reduce pollution from cars, we could require smaller, lighter cars instead of catalytic converters or in addition to them, or could require cars to run on electricity or hydrogen or alcohol instead of gasoline. And of course, we could just ban coal-fired generating plants and cars entirely; those measures would have still different costs.

Will the reduction in smog due to lighter, more fuel-efficient cars save enough lives to offset the deaths to people in collisions who would have survived had they been in bigger, heavier cars? Not likely: occupants of small cars are two to eight times more likely than occupants of large cars to die when they're involved in auto accidents. "In the years to come, tens of thousands of Americans will die because they are driving in smaller, lighter cars—cars demanded by people who had seized the moral high ground of [pollution] risk abatement."[1]

Similarly, we could ban insecticides, herbicides, fungicides, and rodenticides, and so be rid of their hazards. But we'd also be rid of their benefits. Crop yields would plummet, harvest spoilage would skyrocket, and food prices and malnutrition would soar. Pest-borne diseases would multiply; bubonic plague and malaria would make frightful comebacks.

> More than 2 million Ceylonese had malaria in the early 1950's when DDT was first introduced to control malarial mosquitoes. After 10 years of control, malaria had all but been eliminated in Ceylon. The country banned the pesticide in 1964. By 1968 over a million new cases of malaria had appeared. Ceylon rescinded its ban on DDT in 1969.[2]

Despite the obvious sensibility of using cost/benefit analysis in our response to pollution problems, however, we shouldn't expect mainstream environmentalist groups to approve of such an approach. They tend to ignore the costs of pollution abatement and think only of the benefits, often apparently exalting the natural environment to a position far above the needs of mankind. Such a perspective usually is couched in less-than-direct words, but occasionally it comes out in the open, as it did recently when Janet Hathaway, attorney for the Natural Resources Defense Council, spoke against cost/benefit analyses in pollution abatement: "It's a tremendous disappointment. Allowing the EPA to condone continued use of a chemical whenever *the benefits outweigh the risks* is absolutely anathema to the environmental community."[3] That's right, the environmentalists want to ban the use of chemical pesticides *even when the benefits outweigh the risks*, even though, as one editorial writer mildly put it, "the risks caused by pesticides are infinitesimal compared with the health benefits of eating fruits and vegetables."[4]

But it does no good to ignore the costs of pollution control and look only at the benefits. Indeed, a careful look at costs and benefits might even lead us to question whether we have enough of certain kinds of pollution. If more smog from heavier cars would save tens of thousands of people from dying in accidents, might we not be more prudent to choose more smog instead of lighter cars? Regardless how we answer it, the question deserves asking.

PAST METHODS OF COUNTING THE COSTS

How are we to choose among the myriad options for pollution abatement? How are we to determine how much pollution we're willing to live with, how much we want to get rid of, and how much we're willing to pay for living with it or getting rid of it? Thus far in American history we've tried two chief approaches: *laissez faire* and government regulation. Neither has worked well.

Laissez faire in pollution policy meant simply that people could pollute as they wished with little or no fear of reprisal.[5] Although it seems clear that no one pollutes for the sake of polluting, since everyone stands to suffer from his own and others' pollution, translating that into self-restraint has been another matter. Not only do many manifestly good activities have unavoidable polluting side effects, but also the direct benefits of polluting normally outweigh the indirect costs for individuals. The benefits are concentrated with the individual polluter: revenues from sale of electricity, for instance, with the owners of a coal-fired power plant. But the costs are spread among thousands or even millions of people: the air pollution from the coal plant covers hundreds of square miles. So no one feels a particular incentive to abate his own polluting activity, and those who suffer from pollution normally suffer so little from any given source that they have little incentive to work hard to stop it. Consequently, pollution grows unchecked to levels far beyond an optimal balance of costs and benefits.

Enter regulation. If people won't police themselves, the state will have to police them. It seems the obvious and only solution. But what can the state do?

It can set and enforce optimal levels of pollution. But whose values should determine "optimal" levels? The values of the outdoorsman who wants to commune with nature in a pristine environment, or of the outdoorsman who wants to roar from cove to cove on a great manmade lake, searching on his sonar graph for schools of sport fish? The values of potential home buyers who hope timber will be cut to build houses, or of present home owners who want forests for camping and hiking? The values of the municipal water and sewer superintendent who needs someplace to put the sludge from his sewage treatment plant? The values of petroleum producers looking for new fields of oil to fuel the growing legions of cars in which even Sierra Club members drive to see the wonders of Yosemite?

Whose values should guide the regulatory committees in deciding how much of what kinds of pollution to allow or abate in what places and at what costs? "The people's values," obviously. But which people? How should the regulatory agency identify "the people's" values? In the past the practical answer has been, "By political pressure." Votes. Marches. Letter-writing campaigns.

But do these really reflect "the people's" values? More often they represent the values of small, clearly defined groups with more than average interest in the outcome of a regulatory decision. In short, regulatory agencies tend to force minorities' values on majorities.[6] All too often the result is economically inefficient environmental policy: choosing more costly ways than necessary to "solve" conditions that might or might not really be problems, or that might be problems in some people's eyes, but not in others'.[7]

The point is not that nothing should be done, but that government agencies probably are no better equipped to do anything about pollution fairly than were people operating under *laissez faire*. Fortunately, there is another way to achieve optimal levels of pollution in relation to all its costs and benefits.

Economists refer to pollution as a problem of externalities or "spillover effects." Some producers' costs are kept external to the producing firms, borne by surrounding people rather than by the firms themselves. Pollution is one of the chief externalities, and finding a way to internalize its costs is a challenge to economic policy.

Another way to view pollution is as an example of the "problem of the commons." We see it every day: privately owned lawns are well kept; public lawns have well-beaten paths across them, despite the paved walkways laid out by aesthetically sensitive designers. Why do people take shortcuts across public lawns more than across private lawns? Because owners of private lawns have specific incentive to prevent harm to them, while owners of public lawns (ostensibly the whole public) have little incentive to protect them. One economist put it, "If you want to find graffiti on a bathroom wall, you are well-advised to look in public rest-rooms, not privately owned bathrooms."[8]

The key to balancing the costs and benefits of pollution at optimal levels lies in reducing, as much as possible, externalities and the problem of the commons by forcing producers to internalize pollution costs. There are two ways to do this: holding polluters liable for damage to persons and property when causation, culpability, and measurable harm can be proved, and increasing the applicability of private property incentives to the environment.

While the tort process discussed in Chapter 8, when properly used, can effect remedial justice after pollution has done harm, it has only an indirect deterrent effect on prevention or limitation of pollution. To affect that directly, it is necessary to apply property incentives to pollution issues.

Creating Market Incentive to Curtail Pollution

There are two ways to create market incentive to curtail pollution:[9] increasing the property that is privately owned so as to reduce the problem of the commons, and treating pollution itself as property on which the market can put a value.

The first solution applies primarily to pollution of land. (It doesn't apply so well to water and air because those are usually mobile beyond human control.) Federal, state, and local governments hold legal title to roughly 42 percent of the U.S. land area. Transferring more land into private hands would mean more land over which individuals had high incentive to exercise careful stewardship to prevent unnecessary pollution.[10]

The second solution is to create transferable property rights in polluting activities. This forces producers to count the cost of pollution and, while not a perfect system, is probably the most sensible means of achieving the optimal balance between pollution abatement and all the benefits we gain from polluting activities (electricity, transportation, building materials, crop protection, etc.). It engages the supply-and-demand price mechanisms of the market, which already provide the constant flow of information necessary to produce and distribute the vast majority of goods and services that we enjoy, to provide the information necessary to know how much people are willing to pay to reduce which forms of pollution and how much they are willing to live with.

How would this work? First, a government agency would have to determine (on good scientific and economic grounds, we hope, although some political pressure is unavoidable) what level of a given pollutant should be allowed in a particular ecosystem (a river basin, for instance). Then it would create permits, each allowing its holder to emit a fraction of the total level of pollutant into the ecosystem. The fractions permitted by the vouchers would add up to the total pollutant level deemed permissible. The agency would then auction the permits to the highest bidders. After that, the permits could be traded on the market at whatever price the market set for them. The number of permits a company owned would determine how large a fraction of the total pollutant level it could emit. Companies that found it more cost efficient to reduce their emissions than to buy permits would do that, and vice versa. "The government agency would have to monitor emissions to see that they were conforming with the discharge permits. Nothing would prevent individuals or groups who value clean water [or air or soil] from buying permits and holding them idle."[11]

Under a system of marketable pollution permits, the more people a firm served, and the more efficiently it served them, the more pollution permits it could afford to buy. Conversely, the fewer people a firm served, and the less efficiently it served them, the fewer pollution permits it could afford. As a result, pollution costs would be balanced against pollution benefits in society as a whole. Each company's pollution would be a cost consumers were willing to bear to enjoy the company's products.

Even environmentalist groups could participate in such a system. The extent to which they served people by representing their real wishes would determine the contributions they received, which would determine how many pollution permits they could buy and hold idle, thus reducing the overall level of pollution in a way more reflective of the public's will than the current system of direct governmental regulation under the pressure of vocal minorities.

This system still would require governmental agencies to set maximum pollution levels in given regions, and to that extent it still would suffer from the inevitably disproportionate impact of special interest groups. But it would remove from them the power to determine what methods must be used to reduce pollution and what firms must be responsible for what percentages of abatement. Instead, firms' estimates of economic efficiency would determine abatement methods, and the market would determine how much firms could afford to pollute. In these two respects this system would be more equitable than direct regulation.

Such a system would be a more cost effective way to reduce pollution than direct regulation.[12] From the perspective of a Biblical view of the state, it is preferable to direct regulation because it restricts the power of the state to redressing wrongs rather than actually shaping society.[13]

NOTES

INTRODUCTION

1. Edmund Burke, *Reflections on the Revolution in France and on the Proceedings in Certain Societies in London Relative to that Event*, in *The Writings & Speeches of Edmund Burke*, Beaconsfield Edition, 12 vols. (Boston: Little, Brown, 1901), vol. 3, pp. 359, 357. A more readily available edition is *Reflections on the Revolution in France*, ed. Conor Cruise O'Brien (New York: Penguin Books, 1981), pp. 194-5, 192-3.

CHAPTER ONE: *Challenges and Opportunities of Growth*

1. Charles Lockwood and Christopher B. Leinberger, "Los Angeles Comes of Age," *The Atlantic Monthly*, January 1988.
2. The estimated loss in state and local tax revenues assumes combined taxes of 11.8 percent. See Steven Hayward, "Proposition 13: The Apocalypse Ten Years Later," *Los Angeles Daily News*, May 29, 1988, Viewpoint, pp. 1, 4.

CHAPTER TWO: *God, Man, and Morals*

1. Russell Kirk, *A Program for Conservatives*, 2nd revised edition (Chicago: Henry Regnery, [1954] 1962), p. 5.
2. On the definition of economics, see E. Calvin Beisner, *Prosperity and Poverty: The Compassionate Use of Resources in a World of Scarcity* (Westchester, IL: Crossway Books, 1988), pp. xi-xii, 233 (Notes 2, 4). "The classic definition of economics is that it is the study of the allocation of scarce resources which have alternative uses." Thomas Sowell, *Economics: Analysis and Issues* (Glenview, IL: Scott, Foresman, 1971), p. 2. The allocation of those resources among the alternatives requires choice; hence choice is at the heart of economics. Much of this book will focus on questions of who ought to make what choices.
3. I have discussed these foundational principles in other contexts in

Prosperity and Poverty. For theological principles, see Chapter 1. For anthropological and soteriological principles, see Chapters 1-3. For ethical principles, see Chapters 4-5, 9-10, 11-13, and Appendix 1. For legal principles, see Chapter 11. For economic principles, see Chapters 6-8, especially Chapter 8.

4. Paul's language here is quite emphatic: we have "been predestined according to the purpose of the all-things-uninterruptedly-working-according-to-the-considered-judgment-of-his-will-One" (*tou ta panta energountos kata ten boulen tou thelematos autou*), to put it in more precise, if ungainly, English. The present participle *energountos* (working) indicates the constant, uninterrupted nature of the activity. Nothing ever frustrates His working.

5. This is not meant to prejudge whether nuclear arms are good or bad things to have around. It is merely to say that making the judgment on the basis of such theologically fallacious—indeed, heretical—notions is the wrong way to go about it.

6. The word *management* translates the Greek term *oikonomia*, from which is derived the word *economics*. For further discussion of the Christian understanding of this term, see Chapter 8.

7. Charles Hodge, *Systematic Theology*, 3 vols. (Grand Rapids, MI: Eerdmans, [1871-1873] 1973), vol. 2, pp. 96-103.

8. In the words of the *Westminster Shorter Catechism* (Question 10): "How did God create man? God created man, male and female, after his own image, in knowledge, righteousness, and holiness, with dominion over the creatures."

9. This discussion assumes the historic Reformed theological perspective that man is not trichotomous (body, soul, and spirit) but dichotomous (body and soul/spirit); i.e., that *soul* and *spirit* are two words for the same entity, though in some Biblical usage they may emphasize different aspects of that entity, and in some *soul* designates not specifically the spiritual aspect of man as distinct from the physical, but the whole man, body and spirit together—the animated body. For defense of dichotomy and critique of trichotomy, see Hodge, *Systematic Theology*, vol. 2, pp. 46-51. For a more extensive discussion of the problem, see Franz Delitzsch, *A System of Biblical Psychology* (Grand Rapids, MI: Baker Book House, [1855] 1977), pp. 103-19. A clear popular-level defense of dichotomy is found in J. Gresham Machen's *The Christian View of Man* (London: Banner of Truth Trust, [1937] 1965), Chapter 12, "God's Image in Man."

10. Hodge, *Systematic Theology*, vol. 2, p. 97. The Biblical conception of a "free agent" should be carefully distinguished from the popular notion today of a "free agent," a notion championed by some modern Pelagians—namely, that a "free agent" must be capable, in and of himself, of choosing and doing either right or wrong at every given moment. (See, e.g., Gordon C. Olson, *The Truth Shall Make You Free* [Franklin Park, IL: Bible Research Fellowship, 1980], also known as *Sharing Your Faith* [Franklin Park, IL: Bible Research Fellowship, 1976, text and pagination same], pp. IV-6, I-2/1, where Olson goes so far as to teach that God, because He is a "free agent" in this sense, could at any time choose to do evil.) The Biblical conception of moral freedom is not the capacity to choose good or evil, but the capacity to choose good. Moral freedom is contrasted in Scripture not with amorality, but with moral slavery. "But

thanks be to God," writes Paul, "that though you were slaves of sin, you became obedient from the heart to that form of teaching to which you were committed, and having been freed from sin, you became slaves of righteousness. . . . For when you were slaves of sin, you were free in regard to righteousness. . . . But now having been freed from sin and enslaved to God, you derive your benefit, resulting in sanctification . . ." (Romans 6:17, 18, 20, 22). Thus the Biblical notion of free agency is consistent with two other Biblical notions: (1) original sin and the bondage of the unregenerate human will, and (2) the goodness, perfection, and immutability of God's moral character.

11. Hodge, *Systematic Theology*, vol. 2, p. 99.

12. As we will see later, the dominion mandate should not be made to bear too heavy a load unaided by other and clearer Biblical texts related to man's ethical responsibilities over nature. As Old Testament scholar R. Laird Harris put it, the dominion mandate is "far from specific. To have 'rule over' the earth might as easily refer to the free use and development of resources as to our responsibility for their conservation. To 'rule over' the animals does not specifically say high dams for power should be rejected so as to avoid bringing an exotic type of little fish to extinction." R. Laird Harris, *The Incompatibility of Biblical Incentives with the Driving Forces of World Economic Systems*, unpublished address to the Chavanne Scholars' Colloquium on the Application of Biblical Propositions in Business and Economics, Baylor University, June 7-10, 1988, p. 3.

13. For additional considerations along these lines, see Chapter 8.

14. *Formula of Concord* (A.D. 1576), Article II, Affirmative, Sections i, ii.

15. The phrase "for you are dust" (Genesis 3:19) stands in stark and sad contrast to the conclusion of the narrative of Adam's creation and God's breathing the breath of life into him: "and man became a living [soul]" (Genesis 2:7). What was made a living soul because of the entry of the breath of life into the dust of the ground became mere dust again, apparently with the withdrawal of the breath of life—the Holy Spirit—from it.

16. The restoration of the image of God in man—in the knowledge of the truth and of God, in moral awareness, and in moral freedom, as well as in righteousness and holiness with dominion—is not simply a return of the regenerate to the original state of Adam before the fall. The regenerate, unlike Adam, are "*sealed* in [Christ] with the Holy Spirit of promise, who is given as a pledge of our inheritance [until] the redemption of [God's own] possession, to the praise of His glory" (Ephesians 1:13, 14). That is, they are marked and secured as purchased of God, and cannot be taken again from Him. They have been "born again to a living hope through the resurrection of Jesus Christ from the dead, to obtain an inheritance which is imperishable and undefiled and will not fade away, reserved [or "guarded"—namely, by God] in heaven for [them], who are protected by the power of God through faith for a salvation ready to be revealed in the last time" (1 Peter 1:3-5). But to discuss the differences between the regenerate and the pre-fallen Adam is to go too far afield of the task before us in this book.

17. Elsewhere I have written:

Just as the Son of God into whose image we are to be conformed is Creator, Sustainer, and Redeemer, so there are creative, sustaining, and redeeming aspects to human work. We see the creative and sustaining aspects in Genesis 2:15: cultivation increases and directs the earth's natural productivity to meet man's needs, while guarding sustains it against degradation. Apart from the fall, these would have been the only aspects of work, but man's sin brought death and corruption, and so man was assigned a redemptive work, restoring earth's productivity by the sweat of his brow (Genesis 3:19).

Beisner, *Prosperity and Poverty*, p. 30.

18. For a more thorough discussion of the Biblical definition of justice, see Beisner, *Prosperity and Poverty*, Chapter 4: "A Christian View of Justice." On the question whether justice requires equal economic conditions for all, or common property, see Chapter 5 of the same book: "Does Justice Demand Equality?"

19. For examples of Biblical legislation related to remediation and retribution, see Exodus 21 and 22.

20. I have discussed the proper uses of reward and punishment extensively in the essay "Biblical Incentives and Economic Systems," in *Biblical Principles and Economics: Foundations*, ed. Richard C. Chewning (Colorado Springs, CO: Nav Press, 1989), pp. 168-86. Let it suffice here to say that the free-market economic system is compatible with a proper, Biblical understanding of the use of reward and punishment, while a controlled economic system is not.

21. Indeed, when someone judges on grounds other than those given in God's moral Law revealed in Scripture, he judges not only a person, but also the Law itself, for by implication he is saying that the Law is not sufficient to cover every person and situation (James 4:11).

22. Far from endorsing situation ethics in Romans 13:8-10, Paul condemns it, for in love, he says, all of the commandments of the Law are "summed up" (*ankephalaioutai*, brought under a single head), so that love is the "fulfillment" (*pleroma*, the full complement from which nothing is missing) of the Law. It is not that love replaces the Law as a standard, but that love comprehends the Law. Whatever the Law requires, love requires too, and then some. See E. Calvin Beisner, *A Biblical and Philosophical Critique of Situation Ethics*, unpublished research paper, available from the author. See also Charles Hodge, *Commentary on the Epistle to the Romans* (Grand Rapids, MI: Eerdmans, [1835] 1977), pp. 409-10, and John Murray, *The Epistle to the Romans* (Grand Rapids, MI: Eerdmans, 1980), pp. 158-64.

23. Philip Schaff, *Creeds of Christendom*, 3 vols. (Grand Rapids, MI: Baker Book House, [1877] 1977), vol. 3, pp. 338ff.

24. Beisner, "Biblical Incentives and an Individual's Economic Choices," in *Biblical Principles and Economics: Foundations*, ed. Chewning, pp. 191-201.

25. *Teleological*, in the context of ethics and human action, refers to ends or purposes in view. A teleological ethic justifies choices based on the ends sought in them. *Deontological* refers to the nature of the acts (or choices) themselves seen apart from the means, and judges that nature by some objective standard.

26. This view of prudence is broader than that used by Adam Smith in *The Theory of Moral Sentiments* (1759). Smith wrote of prudence as con-

cerned primarily with self-preservation, or keeping "out of harm's way."
Adam Smith, *The Theory of Moral Sentiments* (Indianapolis: Liberty
Press, 1976), p. 348. In the Bible, while prudence certainly encompasses
self-preservation, it is a much broader concept, closely related to wisdom
itself. See its usage throughout Proverbs for examples.

27. Thus two criteria may be used by which to test any economic policy: "(1)
Is it just? That is, is it consistent with God's Law. . . ? (2) Is it good stewardship? Are its long-term, population-wide consequences beneficial? . . .
Because moral and physical reality are consistent, the answer to both of
these questions will be the same for any given law. A just law will have
good consequences; an unjust law will have bad consequences." Beisner,
Prosperity and Poverty, p. 162.

28. Three times in the rich, long sentence that comprises Ephesians 1:3-14 in
Greek the Apostle Paul makes the glory of God the chief end not only of
man, but even of God's saving work (Ephesians 1:6, 12, 14). When we
were "dead in our transgressions," God "made us alive together with
Christ . . . in order that in the ages to come He might show the surpassing
riches of His grace . . ." (Ephesians 2:5, 7). The *Westminster Shorter
Catechism* (1647) begins: "Question 1. What is the chief end of man?
Answer. Man's chief end is to glorify God, and to enjoy him forever."

29. See Beisner, "Biblical Incentives and an Individual's Economic Choices,"
in *Biblical Principles and Economics: Foundations*, ed. Chewning.

CHAPTER THREE: *State and Economy*

1. Kuyper's Stone Lectures have been reprinted under the title *Lectures on
Calvinism* (Grand Rapids, MI: Eerdmans, n.d.) and under the title
Christianity as a Life-System: The Witness of a World-View (Memphis:
Christian Studies Center, 1980; now out of print).

2. See Walter Williams, *The State Against Blacks* (New York: McGraw-Hill,
1982), pp. 142-4.

3. For a Biblical case for limited government and some discussion of the
proper boundaries of the state's authority, see Beisner, *Prosperity and
Poverty*, Chapter 11. For additional discussion of property rights, see pp.
154-6. Particularly important is the recognition that property rights and
human rights are not antithetical to each other, but that property rights
are human rights to property.

4. For a more thorough discussion of scarcity see *ibid.*, pp. 105-8, 124-5. On
the distinction of scarcity from shortage, see p. 245, Note 4.

5. Prices that reduce demand may arise in two ways. First, they may reflect
a real reduction in the ability of producers and distributors to bring the
product to market. In that case, the higher prices serve to slow consumption of the product, stretching out the supply over a longer period of time
than would otherwise be the case, and generally apportioning the product
to those who value it most—that is, to those willing to pay the most for
it. Second, rising prices may reflect an attempt by producers or distributors to maximize profit margins (which must be distinguished from absolute profits, which usually rise in inverse proportion to profit margins
since lower margins mean lower prices, which in turn generate higher
sales volumes). When that occurs, it doesn't take long for competitors or
potential competitors to see the opportunity to profit handsomely by

undercutting the higher prices. In a free market, then, competition quickly effects price levels just sufficient to bring goods to the market, minimizing profit margins and maximizing sales.

6. For more on the meaning of value, see Beisner, *Prosperity and Poverty*, Chapter 8, "Stewardship, Value, and Price." Specifically on marginal utility theory, see pp. 109-13; on its predictive power, p. 167; on the effect of inflation on marginal utility valuation, pp. 128, 130; on the effect of price controls on marginal utility valuation, pp. 162-3; and on how marginal utility may differ relative to persons and circumstances, pp. 170-71.

7. See *ibid.*, Chapter 12, "Stewardship and Economic Regulation: Price Controls," and Chapter 13, "Stewardship, Access Controls, and Subsidies."

8. A good introductory discussion of the counterproductive effects of most zoning and other sorts of coercive planning is Bernard H. Siegan's *Other People's Property* (Lexington, MA: Lexington Books, 1976).

9. The discussion here will be brief. For a more thorough evaluation of free vs. controlled economies relative to Biblical ethics, see Beisner, *Prosperity and Poverty*, Chapters 4-5, 7-13, and Beisner, "Biblical Incentives and Economic Systems," in *Biblical Principles and Economics: Foundations*, ed. Chewning, pp. 168-86.

10. Though the free market often is called *capitalism*, capitalism is a distinctly unfortunate term for the system, since it focuses attention on only one of several essential factors of economic production and ignores completely the two chief factors that distinguish the free market from the controlled economy. Regardless of the sort of economic system under consideration, capital (money, tools, buildings, transportation and communication systems, etc.) only becomes a factor of production when combined with labor (including the application of knowledge in management, design, and entrepreneurship) and natural resources. These three factors of production must exist and be used in any economic system in order for production to occur. Thus controlled economies are as much "capitalist" as are free enterprise economies, in that they depend as much on capital.

   Beisner, "Biblical Incentives and Economic Systems," in *Biblical Principles and Economics: Foundations*, ed. Chewning, p. 178.

11. Russell Kirk, *The American Cause* (Chicago: Henry Regnery, [1957] 1965), pp. 154-156.

12. See Friedrich A. Hayek, *The Constitution of Liberty* (South Bend, IN: Gateway Editions, Ltd., [1960] 1972), pp. 11-21.

13. Whether all consumers' demands are morally legitimate is a question distinct from whether the market ought to be organized chiefly to meet consumers' demands. Certainly some consumers' demands are immoral—demands for pornography, prostitution, violence, abortion, and so on. But endorsing the free-market economy does not entail treating such demands as moral. As we noted above, real freedom is not absence of moral restraint, and it is legitimate for the state to prohibit the service of demands that are contrary to such moral laws as those against fraud, theft, violence, and adultery.

CHAPTER FOUR: *Penultimate Resource or Population Plague?*

1. Kingsley Davis, "The Climax of Population Growth: Past and Future Perspective," *California Medicine*, vol. 113, no. 5, p. 33.

2. "How Many Babies Is Too Many?" *Newsweek*, vol. LX, no. 4 (July 23, 1962), p. 27.
3. "Population Explosion and 'Anti-Babyism,'" *Life*, vol. 58, no. 16 (April 23, 1965), p. 6.
4. U.S. Bureau of the Census, *Statistical Abstract of the United States, 1984*, p. 194, Table 325; p. 8, Table 6. This takes the highest of three estimates, of which the middle is about 285 million and the lowest about 260 million.
5. Viewing the prison population not as an isolated phenomenon but as a proportion of total population reinforces the lesson. In 1950, federal and state prison inmates constituted .1103 percent of the population; in 1960, the proportion was .1186 percent of the total population; in 1965, .1095 percent; in 1970, .0967 percent; in 1975, .1133 percent; in 1980, .1392 percent; in 1981, .1534 percent; and in 1982, .1702 percent. Recalling that baby boomers began to reach their late teens and early twenties, ages at which crime rates tend to be highest (*Statistical Abstract . . . 1984*, p. 194, Table 324) from the late 1960s through the 1970s, and that sentencing was relatively lenient during the late 1960s and became tougher throughout the 1970s and early 1980s, gives rational explanation to the increase in prison population. We can expect a marked decline in prison population as proportion of total population (and probably also in absolute numbers) as the median age of the population rises.
6. U.S. Bureau of the Census, *Statistical Abstract of the United States, 1988*, p. 175, Table 305.
7. See Charles Colson and Daniel Van Ness, *Convicted: New Hope for Ending America's Crime Crisis* (Westchester, IL: Crossway Books, 1989).
8. No wonder some creationists think population retrojection is a plausible way of giving support to the idea of recent creation. See, for example, Henry M. Morris, ed., *Scientific Creationism*, General Edition (San Diego: Creation-Life, 1974), pp. 167-9, where Morris argues:

. . . an average population growth of 1/2 per cent per year would give the present population in just 4000 years. [More precisely, 4,464 years retrojecting from three billion in 1965.] This is only one-fourth the present rate.

. . . It is essentially incredible that there could have been 25,000 generations of men with a resulting population of only 3.5 billion. If the population increased at only 1/2 per cent per year for a million years, or if the average family size were only 2.5 children per family for 25,000 generations, the number of people in the present generation would exceed 10^{2100}, a number which is, of course, utterly impossible (as noted in an earlier chapter, only 10^{130} electrons could be crammed into the entire known universe).

9. Fernand Braudel, *Civilization and Capitalism 15th—18th Century*, 3 vols., *Volume 1: The Structures of Everyday Life: The Limits of the Possible*, trans. Sian Reynolds (New York: Harper & Row, 1985), p. 42. Braudel lists three estimates of world population in 1650: *United Nations Bulletin*, December 1951 (estimated 470 million); Carr Saunders (estimated 545 million); Kuczynski (estimated 465 million).

10. *Ibid.*, p. 41. Compare *Statistical Abstract . . . 1984*, p. 857, Table 1503. A growth rate of .173 percent per year, by the way, if held constant, would put the creation of Adam and Eve in 10,937 B.C.

11. Julian Simon, *The Economics of Population Growth* (Princeton, NJ: Princeton University Press, 1977), p. 15.

12. *Ibid.*, p. 17.

13. *Ibid.*, p. 18.

14. Van Bueren Stanbery and Frank V. Hermann, *Population Forecasting Methods* (U.S. Department of Commerce, Bureau of Public Roads, Urban Planning Division, June 1964), p. 6. Cited in Rousas J. Rushdoony, *The Myth of Overpopulation* (Nutley, NJ: The Craig Press, 1969), pp. 18f.

15. See, for example, Simon, *Economics of Population Growth*, pp. 317, 331.

16. Two major reasons for declining birth rates with increasing economic development are: (1) In less-developed countries, where agriculture constitutes a large proportion of the economy and is conducted mainly by physical labor rather than with extensive use of machinery, children mean additional farm labor, which makes them economically advantageous to their parents, giving parents an economic incentive to maximize their reproductivity. But in more-developed countries, where manufacture and service industries predominate and are conducted by extensive use of machinery requiring extensive education and training, children do not constitute such a clear economic advantage to their parents; indeed, they usually constitute an economic drain to their parents, giving parents an economic incentive to limit family size. (2) In less-developed countries, infant and child mortality rates tend to be high, so that parents need to have more births than the children they hope to have. (And when more children survive than they expect to, they count it an economic blessing since those children can help with agricultural work.) But in more-developed countries, infant and child mortality rates are low, so parents need only bear the number of children they hope to raise to maturity. For more extensive discussion of these and other reasons for falling population growth rates as countries develop economically, see Simon, *The Economics of Population Growth*, Part II: "The Effects of Economic Conditions on Fertility."

17. Actually, the rapid growth didn't occur simultaneously "all over the world." It occurred first in the more-developed countries and later in less-developed countries. The timing in both groups of countries was determined largely by the coming of an economy capable of producing the food, medical care, and other forms of wealth that could significantly lower infant and child mortality rates and lengthen adult life expectancy.

18 Ronald Freeman and Bernard Berelson, "The Human Population," *Scientific American*, September 1974, pp. 36-7, cited in Herman Kahn, William Brown, and Leon Martel, *The Next 200 Years: A Scenario for America and the World* (New York: William Morrow and Company, 1976), p. 29, Figure 4.

19. For discussions of the demographic transition, see Paul Demeny, "The World Demographic Situation" in *World Population & U.S. Policy: The Choices Ahead*, ed. Jane Menken (New York: W. W. Norton, 1986), pp. 27-66; Kahn, Brown, and Martel, *The Next 200 Years*, pp. 32-4; Simon, *Economics of Population Growth*, pp. 25-7 (Simon cautions that the theory of demographic transition might be brought into question by recent

population trends in some countries, where the birth rate does not appear to be declining following industrialization as rapidly as it did in western industrialized countries, if at all; p. 26); Max Singer, *Passage to a Human World: The Dynamics of Creating Global Wealth* (Indianapolis: Hudson Institute, 1987), p. 332, note. Singer has a good common-sense qualifier to predictions made on the basis of the theory of the demographic transition:

Personally I am skeptical about the standard view that population will "level off"—if that is taken to mean constant world population. I don't see why each country should come to exactly the level of fertility necessary to keep population constant. I believe that some countries will have growing populations and others declining populations, and that many will fluctuate above and below net replacement rate (over periods of generations or centuries). Nor do I see why countries with declining populations should exactly balance those with rising populations. So in the long run world population may rise or decline from the level at which it reaches [sic] when the current burst of growth ends. The current burst comes from the transition from poverty to wealth. We can see why that burst will end; what we can't see is the long-term impact of continued wealth, or of widespread great wealth (i.e., US levels of income or higher).

For the 10 billion worldwide equilibrium figure, see Demeny, p. 65, and Singer, p. 332 (where he depends on projections by the World Bank, the Population Reference Bureau, and the United Nations). For projections of equilibrium for individual nations, see International Bank for Reconstruction and Development/The World Bank, *World Development Report 1986* (New York/Oxford/London: Oxford University Press, 1986), pp. 228-9, Table 25; of equilibrium for the world, see Demeny, pp. 48ff., *et al.*

20. "[A] common misleading impression about world population is that a large proportion of all the people who have ever lived are alive now. This is very far from the truth. A well-thought-out estimate is that 77 billion human beings were born from 600,000 B.C. to 1962 A.D.: 12 billion up to 6000 B.C., 42 billion from 6000 B.C. to 1650 A.D., and 23 billion from 1650 A.D. to 1962 A.D. Compare this to the 4-5 billion who may be alive now."

Julian L. Simon, *The Ultimate Resource* (Princeton: Princeton University Press, 1981), p. 161. Simon's calculation assumes a much longer human history than young-earth creationist Christians would agree to, but even granted a shorter human history his basic point probably is still defensible.

21. Francis Brown, S. R. Driver, and Charles Briggs, eds., *A Hebrew and English Lexicon of the Old Testament* (Oxford: Clarendon Press, [1907] 1978), pp. 826, 915, 570.

22. Cf. 2 Kings 8:10, 11; Isaiah 6:1; Jeremiah 23:24; Ezekiel 10:3; 43:5; 44:4; 2 Chronicles 5:14; 7:1, 2.

23. See J. B. Lightfoot, "On the meaning of *plērōō,* in J. B. Lightfoot, *Saint Paul's Epistles to the Colossians and to Philemon* (Grand Rapids, MI: Zondervan, [1879] 1974), pp. 257-73; R. Schippers, *plērōō,* in article "Fullness," in Colin Brown, ed., *The New International Dictionary of*

New Testament Theology, 3 vols. (Grand Rapids, MI: Zondervan, 1979), vol. 1, pp. 733-41.

24. Estimates of Israel's population at the exodus vary. The one firm figure we have is that there were 603,550 men twenty years old and above. Some scholars extrapolate from this a total population of about 2 million (e.g., Ronald B. Allen and Kenneth L. Barker, notes to Numbers in Kenneth L. Barker, general editor, *The NIV Study Bible* [Grand Rapids, MI: Zondervan, 1985], p. 190). This figure is based on the assumption of one wife and two children to every man twenty or older. However, demographics of less-developed agricultural peoples indicate that that assumption may be far from correct, leading to a serious underestimate of Israel's population at the time. Marriage in such societies tends to come around the ages of fourteen to sixteen, and birth rates tend to be considerably higher than mere replacement rates. An assumption of four to six children to each man over twenty and his wife would not seem unlikely. This would yield a total population estimate for Israel of 3 million to 5 million at the time of the exodus. As an aside, it might be interesting to consider Israel's population density in Goshen (the region in Egypt in which they resided) prior to the exodus. At 2 million, their density would have been 800 to 1200 persons per square mile. (Goshen's specific area is not known. Rough estimates indicate that it was roughly forty to fifty miles square—i.e., 1,600 to 2,500 square miles.) At 3 million, their density would have been 1,200 to 1,875 per square mile. At 5 million, their density would have been 2,000 to 3,125 per square mile. Very few modern countries have such high population densities. (None but the city-states of Singapore [11,167 per square mile], Hong Kong [13,183 per square mile], and Macau [50,667 per square mile], plus the Gaza Strip [3,116 per square mile] exceeds 3,000 per square mile.) For comparison, Japan's density in 1980 was roughly 830 per square mile, South Korea's was 1,088 per square mile, and that of Mauritius, in northern Africa, was about 1,200. (See *Statistical Abstract . . . 1984*, pp. 857-9, Table 1503.) The United States' population density in 1982 was about 65 per square mile; at that time the most densely populated state was New Jersey, with a density of 996 persons per square mile. In 1980, average population density in U.S. urbanized areas was 2,675 persons per square mile; even in central cities, it was 3,551 per square mile. (See *Statistical Abstract . . . 1984*, p. 26, Table 24.) Whether Israel's population, then, was 2 million or 5 million when it left Goshen, certainly it is clear that at that time such an area, which was exceptionally fertile because of its location in the eastern part of the Nile delta, could support a very dense population, despite primitive methods of agriculture.

25. See also Jeremiah 42:2; 5:6; 14:16; 15:3; 16:4; Ezekiel 14:15.

26. This proverb sets forth a view of population precisely contrary to notions common to the modern population-control movement, which sees large, dense populations as weakening rather than strengthening nations. As we proceed in this chapter and the following, we will see why the Biblical view is consistent with empirical evidence that refutes the modern anti-growth notion.

27. For population densities of states and the District of Columbia, see U.S. Bureau of the Census, *Statistical Abstract of the United States, 1988*, pp. 18, 19, Table 21.

28. *Statistical Abstract . . . 1984*, p. 26, Table 24.
29. By 1982, "urban and builtup land" constituted 2.5 percent of total U.S. land area (calculated from data supplied in *Statistical Abstract . . . 1988*, p. 187, Table 323), but "urban and builtup land" includes some classifications of land not included in the earlier "urban" category. It appears that, as a proportion of total U.S. land area, urban land did not grow significantly 1980-1982.
30. The data in the Table are for 1980. Comparable figures for 1986 are available in *Statistical Abstract . . . 1988*, pp. 27-30, 32, Tables 33, 34, 37. The proportional breakdowns remained roughly the same as in 1980.
31. Computed by adding population of cities of 10,000-25,000 to population of cities under 10,000 plus rural population and comparing with total U.S. population of 241,078,000. Refer to *Statistical Abstract . . . 1988*, p. 32, Table 37.
32. We will discuss in the following chapter the popular notion that America's cities are rapidly taking over its (especially prime) agricultural land.

An interesting question, tangential to our discussion, is why it seems that media and civil government focus so constantly on large cities when only a small minority of our population lives in them. Three answers suggest themselves. (1) The density of population in large cities makes gathering information in them easier and less costly by economies of scale. (2) Civil government, in particular, wants to control people, and high density makes control (and the surveillance necessary to it) easier and less costly by economies of scale. (3) Both the media and civil government tend to be dominated by people who are convinced that a "population explosion" threatens; hence they tend to exaggerate the phenomenon of large cities for two reasons: (a) because that's what they're looking for, so that's what they see; (b) because it's easier to make life in large cities seem threatening than life in small towns and rural areas, and it is to the advantage of those whose livelihood depends partly on the public's perception of threat from alleged overpopulation to reinforce that perception. Further investigation of this issue, particularly by the "public choice" school of economics, might yield useful information that could help reformulate some public policy.
33. *Statistical Abstract . . . 1988*, p. 874, Table C. Definitional standards adopted by the federal government in 1980 "provide that each MSA must inclue at least: (a) One city with 50,000 or more inhabitants, or (b) A Census Bureau-defined urbanized area of at least 50,000 inhabitants and a total MSA population of at least 100,000 (75,000 in New England)" (p. 872).
34. *Ibid.*, p. 873, Table A, density computed.
35. *Ibid.*, p. 872.
36. For example, the Fayetteville-Sprindale, Arkansas, MSA includes the whole of Washington County and its 107,000 inhabitants (1986) (*ibid.*, p. 877). Yet Washington County is mostly rural, dominated by farming and mountainous wilderness areas. Scores of other MSAs are closely similar.
37. *Ibid.*, p. 26, Table 31. This compares with 2,151 cities of 10,000 to 100,000; 122 of 100,000 to 250,000; thirty-seven of 250,000 to 500,000; fifteen of 500,000 to 1 million; and eight of over 1 million (p. 32, Table 37).
38. *Ibid.*, p. 692, Table 1228.

39. *Statistical Abstract . . . 1984*, p. 26, Table 24, for 1970 and 1980; for 1950 and 1960, see Edward C. Banfield, *The Unheavenly City Revisited* (Boston: Little, Brown and Company, 1974), p. 3.

40. C. A. Doxiadis and G. Papaioannou, *Ecumenopolis, the Inevitable City of the Future* (New York: W. W. Norton, 1974), p. 179; cited in Jacqueline Kasun, *The War Against Population: The Economics and Ideology of World Population Control* (San Francisco: Ignatius Press, 1988), p. 37.

41. *Statistical Abstract . . . 1988*, p. 19, Table 21 (U.S., 1986), and p. 795, Table 1378 (world, 1987).

42. See *ibid.*, pp. 794-5, Tables 1376, 1378.

43. For Texas land area (262,017 square miles), see *Statistical Abstract . . . 1984*, p. 202, Table 338. For Singapore and Macau's densities, see *Statistical Abstract . . . 1988*, pp. 795-7, Table 1378.

44. Kasun, *War Against Population*, p. 37.

45. For Anchorage's land area (1,732 square miles), see *Statistical Abstract . . . 1984*, p. 28, Table 29.

46. *Statistical Abstract . . . 1988*, pp. 29-30, Table 34.

47. See *Statistical Abstract . . . 1984*, p. 178, Table 289.

48. See Simon, *The Ultimate Resource*, pp. 253-6; Harvey M. Choldin, "Urban Density and Pathology," *Annual Review of Sociology* 4:91-113; Amost H. Hawley, "Population Density and the City," *Demography* 9:521-30; Bruce A. Chadwick, "In Defense of Density: Its Relationship to Health and Social Disorganization," in *Population, Resources, and the Future: Non-Malthusian Perspectives*, eds. Howard M. Bahr, Bruce A. Chadwick, and Darwin L. Thomas (Provo, UT: Brigham Young University Press, 1972), pp. 175-93. Chadwick writes that some studies have "discovered a positive relationship between density and crime against persons and property in the largest metropolitan areas in the United States. But, when the effect of income was controlled the relationship between density and crime disappeared!" (p. 188). Further, he warns, even where some studies indicate a correlation between density and crime rates, the correlation need not demonstrate that density causes crime; some unseen factor(s) might be the real cause(s), or the causal connection might go the opposite way (p. 189).

49. Banfield, *The Unheavenly City Revisited*, p. 3.

50. For a more thorough discussion of this theme, see Chapter 8.

51. Simon, *The Ultimate Resource*, pp. 169-71.

52. The United Nations Fund for Population Activities recently forecast a world population in the year 2100 of 14.2 billion (Linda Feldmann, "UN: World Population Heads for 14 Billion," *Christian Science Monitor*, May 17, 1989, p. 7). Only time will tell whether that projection is any more sound than those we saw earlier in this chapter. For the prospects for providing a high standard of living for that many people on earth, see Chapters 6 and 7.

53. For an excellent survey of the various population-growth-control groups, see Kasun, *The War Against Population*, Chapter 7, "The Movement, Its History, and Its Leaders." Kasun shows how the groups are related, where they get their money, and how they often circumvent federal rules against the use of federal money to support abortion and coercive birth control programs.

54. Kahn, Brown, and Martel adopt as reasonable a projection by Ronald Freeman and Bernard Berelson of decline in population growth rate from the worldwide rate in 1976 of just over 2 percent per year to about .1 percent per year (roughly the rate throughout prior human history until 1776 and resuming before 2176, according to the model). On that assumption (population doubling every 720 years) we could expect the world's population to reach 40 billion about 2,000 years from now. See the graph showing population growth rates from 8000 B.C. to A.D. 8000 in *The Next 200 Years*, p. 29, adapted from Freeman and Berelson's "The Human Population," *Scientific American*, September 1974, pp. 36-7.

55. Here, as we did above, we are distinguishing trends from patterns. The historical trend is for the product of labor and capital to grow faster than population. A recent pattern (the demographic transition discussed earlier) has been for population to grow rapidly (but still less rapidly than economic production). The pattern has a reasonably definable beginning, middle, and end; the trend seems likely to continue indefinitely.

56. Some might respond that pollution per capita is not the important measurement, but total pollution worldwide. We will take up pollution-related issues in Chapter 9.

CHAPTER FIVE: *Population and Living Standards:*
Housing, Transportation and Communication, and Recreation

1. U.S. Bureau of the Census, *Statistical Abstract of the United States, 1988* (Washington, D.C.: U.S. Government Printing Office, 1988), p. 688, Table 1221.

2. *Statistical Abstract . . . 1984*, p. 752, Table 1343.

3. *Statistical Abstract . . . 1988*, p. 690, Table 1223. Home ownership here means living in a home one has either paid for or is paying for on a mortgage in contrast with living in a home for which one pays rent. The percentage of people who have finished paying for their homes is much lower than those who have mortgages on their homes and represents, from the Biblical perspective that warns against debt, a serious ethical and prudential problem. But it is a problem distinct from problems of population growth.

4. No figure was available for 1960.

5. *Statistical Abstract . . . 1988*, p. 691, Table 1225.

6. *Ibid.*, p. 540, Table 914.

7. *Ibid.*, p. 684, Table 1211.

8. Figures in the preceding two paragraphs were computed based on data in *ibid.*, pp. 694, 684, 444, 427, 43, Tables 1231, 1211, 729, 700, 56. Median square footage for 1976 was estimated based on a comparison of 1970 and 1980 figures from Table 1211. Household income for recent home buyers was calculated based on data provided in Table 1231.

9. That is, average expenditures for alcohol, smoking, and entertainment amounted to roughly 8 percent of total expenditures for persons in the bottom quintile of American incomes. *Ibid.*, pp. 420-1, Tables 688, 689, and p. 214, Table 364.

10. *Ibid.*, p. 460, Table 755.

11. The focus of this book is not on poverty issues, and it is only for illustra-

tion's sake that we have looked here at how low-income Americans can afford housing. For a Christian understanding of poverty and appropriate responses to it, see Beisner, *Prosperity and Poverty*, Chapters 14-16.

12. See Hernando de Soto, *The Other Path: The Invisible Revolution in the Third World*, trans. June Abbott (New York: Harper & Row, 1989), Chapter 2, "Informal Housing." The statistics appear throughout the chapter. For Lima's 1990 population of 6.8 million, see *Statistical Abstract . . . 1988*, p. 801, Table 1381.

13. de Soto, *The Other Path*, p. 18.

14. *Ibid.*, p. 55.

15. *Ibid.*, p. 56.

16. The very existence of the informal housing testifies to the counterproductive nature of many governmental regulations on development in Peruvian cities. Attempts by civil government to control and plan urbanization tend to diminish the supply of housing relative to demand, thus driving up its cost and making it less available to low-income earners. We will explore this further in the final chapter of this book.

17. Of interest to economic historians is the similarity of the informal housing movement in Peru to the disintegration of the feudal system of medieval Europe and its gradual replacement by a system of widespread private property ownership, which eventually led to the full-fledged capitalism that spawned the Industrial Revolution. While de Soto does not draw this comparison, I could not help being struck by the parallels. These might be most readily apparent by reading consecutively (1) Edward Potts Cheyney, *European Background of American History 1300-1600* (New York: Harper & Brothers, 1904), Chapters 13-16 ["The Political System of England (1500-1689)," "The English County and Its Officers (1600-1650)," "English Justices of the Peace (1600-1650)," and "English Parish or Township Government (1500-1650)"]; (2) Nathan Rosenberg and L. E. Birdzell, Jr., *How the West Grew Rich: The Economic Transformation of the Industrial World* (New York: Basic Books, 1986); and de Soto's *The Other Path*. If these parallels are real, they could signal an impending major shift from mercantilism and feudalism, the dominant economic and civil structures of Latin America and many other parts of the less-developed world, to economic and political liberty akin to what spurred the explosive economic growth of the developed countries. Furthermore, granted the rapidity with which ideas spread in the modern world, the shift could happen much more suddenly in this second round than it did in its first. The social upheaval that could accompany such sudden change, however, could lead to very different results.

18. It might be objected that higher crime rates in cities could make us prefer a breakdown in a rural farming area or even in the wide-open stretches of New Mexico to a breakdown in the city. However, the objection ignores the fact that it is not population density but other factors that affect crime rates. As we saw near the end of Chapter 4, upper-class sections of cities tend to have much lower crime rates than lower-class sections of the same density. One might, then, prefer a breakdown in a rural farming area to a breakdown in Harlem or Watts, but probably not to a breakdown in Manhattan or Chicago's North Shore area. And the special preference for the rural breakdown would be because of an aversion not to crowding but to high crime rates, which do not always accompany crowding.

19. Daniel B. Wood, "Caught in Urban Crawl," *The Christian Science Monitor*, May 3, 1989, p. 12. See also Richard Martin, "L.A. Rapid Transit: Up and Down," *Insight,* June 9, 1986, pp. 18-19; Christopher B. Leinberger and Charles Lockwood, "How Business Is Reshaping America," *The Atlantic Monthly*, October 1986. Such urban mass-transportation systems rarely are cost-efficient. Almost invariably they have to be subsidized.

According to an official of the Southern California Rapid Transit District, the metrorail system "may come close to breaking even on an operating basis, but there is no way that it will pay for the construction of the system." Of course, this statement is based on predictions of operating cost and ridership. The reality of Atlanta's new MARTA fixed-rail system is that the fare box brings in only 35 to 40 percent of the annual operating budget, which would more than double if a reasonable amortization of the capital cost were included. Moreover, the proposed Los Angeles subway route serves downtown and only two of the sixteen other urban-village cores in the metropolitan region.

Leinberger and Lockwood, "How Business Is Reshaping America."

20. For land areas and populations of Los Angeles and Nashville-Davidson, see *Statistical Abstract . . . 1988*, p. 33, Table 38. The cost of building an equivalent system in Nashville-Davidson would be lower than it is in Los Angeles because real estate is cheaper there and there are fewer existing buildings to complicate construction, but the difference would not nearly be enough to offset the difference in population.

21. Dan Smith, Joan Roadovich, and Raymond Smith, "Crusade Against Growth," *Golden State Report*, January 1988, pp. 24-5.

22. See Larry Arrn and Steven Hayward, "Growth: A Manifesto for the Inland Empire," *Inland Business*, September 1988, pp. 16-22; Larry Arrn, *The No-Growth Movement and the Transportation Crisis: The Bitter Legacy of Jerry Brown* (Montclair, CA: The Claremont Institute, 1988). "In the 1960s, California routinely built more than 100 miles per year of new highway. Since 1980, the state has averaged less than 10 miles per year." Arrn, *No-Growth Movement*, p. 7.

23. *Statistical Abstract . . . 1988*, p. 580, Table 1000; measured as fatal accidents per million vehicle miles of travel.

24. This is not to say that residents of cities and suburbs should accept heavy traffic congestion as their inevitable fate. Where state and local governments see their responsibility as responding to the needs of citizens by building appropriate infrastructure rather than trying to force citizens to conform to officials' preconceptions of what growth patterns are desirable, traffic can be kept flowing smoothly (albeit with short-lived exceptions when growth temporarily outdistances infrastructure development). We will consider this issue further in Chapter 10.

25. Simon, *The Economics of Population Growth*, p. 269.

26. In India, "If a farmer lives more than 1.5 miles from an all-weather road, he will not use chemical fertilizer and other marketed supplies which cannot be transported to him. . . . [Three-fourths] of India's farms are farther than 1.5 miles from an all-weather road, and . . . more than 1/3 of the villages in the State of Maharas[h]tra have no approach road at all to serve

them" (Simon, *The Economics of Population Growth*, p. 268). Therefore, agricultural production in India is far lower than it could be with a better transportation system. But a better transportation system awaits a higher population density in the agricultural regions of the country.

27. Those areas comprised a combined 34.8 percent of the U.S. land area in 1959; 35.5 percent in 1969; 35.6 percent in 1974; 35.4 percent in 1978; and 38.2 percent in 1982. *Statistical Abstract . . . 1988*, p. 185, Table 320.

28. *Ibid.*, p. 210, Table 357. Acreage rose from 28,543,000 to 75,863,000. The increase in visitation to federally administered recreation areas is not uniform across the board. Total visitor hours spent in all areas, in fact, dropped 7.6 percent between 1978 and 1986. Declines occurred in visits to areas administered by the Fish and Wildlife Service, the U.S. Army Corps of Engineers, the Bureau of Land Management, the Bureau of Reclamation, and the Tennessee Valley Authority. Increases occurred in areas administered by the National Park Service and the Forest Service. See *ibid.*, p. 210, Table 356.

29. Compare *ibid.*, p. 213, Table 362, with *Statistical Abstract . . . 1982-83*, p. 232, Table 393.

30. Compare *Statistical Abstract . . . 1988*, p. 213, Table 363, with *Statistical Abstract 1982-83*, p. 233, Table 394. Constant-dollar amounts computed based on the 1988 *Abstract*, p. 444, Table 729.

CHAPTER SIX: *Malthus Undone: How Population Growth and Economic Growth Relate*

1. The full title of Malthus's work was *An Essay on the Principle of Population as it Affects the Future Improvement of Society, with Remarks on the Speculations of Mr. Godwin, M. Condorcet, and Other Writers.* Five years later he defended it in a *Second Essay on Population* (1803) that ran to seven editions, "but the form of argument and the structure of the *Essay* remained the same as in the first edition." Jane Soames Nickerson, *Homage to Malthus* (Port Washington, NY: National University Publications, Kennikat Press, 1975), p. 57. Nonetheless, Malthus mitigated the thoroughgoing pessimism of the first *Essay* in the fifth edition, which he concluded:

From a review of the state of society in former periods, compared with the present, I should certainly say that the evils resulting from the principle of population have rather diminished than increased. . . . [I]t does not seem unreasonable to expect that they will be still further diminished. . . .

On the whole, therefore, though our future prospects respecting the mitigation of the evils arising from the principle of population may not be so bright as we could wish, yet they are far from being entirely disheartening, and by no means preclude that gradual and progressive improvement in human society, which, before the late wild speculations on this subject, was the object of rational expectation. To the laws of property and marriage, and to the apparently narrow principle of self-interest which prompts each individual to exert himself in bettering his condition, we are indebted for all the noblest exertions of human genius. . . . (5th ed., 1817/1963, p. 289).

Cited in Simon, *The Economics of Population Growth*, p. 6.

Malthus's cheerier (or perhaps we should say slightly less dismal) view of the future in later editions than in the first rested almost solely on his having come to believe that people might rationally limit the size of their families (not through contraception, which he considered immoral, but through abstention) out of self-interest. It did not stem from a belief that productivity could rise faster than population, which is the essence of our argument in the present and following chapters.

2. Cited in Nickerson, *Homage to Malthus*, p. 47.

3. Probably the most famous of the population-growth control books is Paul R. Ehrlich's *The Population Bomb* (New York: Ballantine Books, 1968). A few other contributions to the thought include: Philip Appleman, *The Silent Explosion* (Boston: Beacon Press, 1965); Georg Borgstrom, *The Hungry Planet* (New York: Macmillan, 1965); Harrison Brown, *The Challenge of Man's Future* (New York: Viking, 1954); Harrison Brown, et al., *The Next Hundred Years* (New York: Viking, 1957); Tadd Fisher, *Our Overcrowded World* (New York: Parent's Magazine Press, 1969); Fairfield Osborn, ed., *Our Crowded Planet: Essays on the Pressures of Population* (New York: Doubleday, 1962); William Vogt, *People! Challenge to Survival* (New York: William Sloane Associates, 1960).

4. Malthus was aware of this, and in one sense it is perhaps unfair to attribute such naiveté to him. However, the very enormity of imprecision in his language indicates the extent to which he underestimated the impact of human intelligence and labor on the surrounding world.

5. See the table "Estimates of World Population: 1,000,000 Years Ago to A.D. 2000" in Edward S. Deevey, Jr., "The Human Population," *Scientific American*, September 1960.

6. Adam Smith, *An Inquiry into the Nature and Causes of the Wealth of Nations*, 2 vols. in 1, ed. Edwin Cannan (Chicago: University of Chicago Press, [1776] 1976), Bk. I, Ch. i; vol. 1, pp. 8-9.

7. The figure is arrived at by multiplying 52,448,290 square miles of land (which excludes Antarctica) by 100 persons per square mile. Estimated 1989 world population is 5.2 billion (1990 estimate 5.32 billion minus 1.7 percent annual growth). (See U.S. Bureau of the Census, *Statistical Abstract of the United States, 1988*, p. 794, Table 1376, and p. 795, Table 1378.) At 5.2 billion, actual average population density worldwide (excluding Antarctica) is 99 persons per square mile.

8. Simon, *Economics of Population Growth*, p. 87.

9. *Ibid.*, p. 88.

10. Cited in *ibid.*, p. 88.

11. Sherry H. Olson, *The Depletion Myth: History of Railroad Use of Timber* (Cambridge, MA: Harvard University Press, 1971), p. 2; as cited in Simon, *Economics of Population Growth*, p. 88.

12. *Statistical Abstract . . . 1988*, p. 640, Tables 1122, 1123.

13. *Ibid.*, compare p. 641, Table 1124, with p. 447, Table 735.

14. By *economic scarcity* we refer not to an absolute amount of lumber available, but to the ratio of supply to demand at market price. Thus it is possible for something to be more scarce at time T1 than at time T even though there is actually more of it, if demand has risen faster—i.e., if demand is higher relative to supply at time T1 than it was at time T. For a more thorough discussion of the nature of economic scarcity and how

it differs from absolute quantity, see Beisner, *Prosperity and Poverty*, pp. 107-15.

15. Roger A. Sedjo and Marion Clawson, "Global Forests," in *The Resourceful Earth: A Response to Global 2000*, eds. Julian L. Simon and Herman Kahn (New York: Basil Blackwell, 1984), p. 133. Compare Neal Potter and Francis T. Christy, *Trends in Natural Resource Commodities* (Baltimore: Johns Hopkins Press, 1962) and Robert Manthy, *Natural Resource Commodities—A Century of Statistics* (Baltimore: Johns Hopkins Press, 1978). We will discuss the effect of population growth on resource scarcity further in Chapter 7.

16. We are considering here solely their economic—material or monetary—effect. We are not implying that the spiritual value of children does not outweigh their economic cost.

17. Extrapolating from figures estimated by economist Marvin DeVries and reported by Allan C. Carlson in *Family Questions: Reflections on the American Social Crisis* (New Brunswick, NJ: Transaction Books, 1988), pp. 59-60. The average here takes into account those who, for various reasons (physical or mental handicap, moral turpitude, criminal conduct, etc.), are a net economic debit to society. For further on this, see Appendix 1. A more conservative estimate of the excess of individuals' production over their consumption in their lifetimes was made recently by Kasun in *The War Against Population*, p. 65:

. . . if children put "external costs" on society, they extend external benefits as well. Each child born will not only consume public services, such as education, public health care, and military defense, but will also contribute to the support of these services. In the United States, for example, each child born in 1983 is expected to spend forty-seven years in the labor force, earn more than two-thirds of a million dollars over his lifetime, and pay more than a quarter of a million dollars in taxes. The discounted net present value in 1983 of the typical child's future earnings, over and above the cost of his own maintenance, amounted to $70,000. This sum would be available to support public services and add to society's capital. It is precisely because children who have been born have also grown and contributed so much more than their own costs that the social wealth and income have increased so greatly.

18. Simon, *Economics of Population Growth*, p. 126.

19. In this and most of the following discussion we are looking at averages based on nations taken as entities, rather than averages weighted by the different populations of nations. (For further discussion of the difference, see the text introducing the tables in Appendix 2.) Weighting averages by population would obscure the differences among individual nations, differences that are important in the economic analysis here. Weighted averages are, however, reported in Appendix 2, and for the most part the picture described in this chapter holds true in those averages as well.

20. Canada's population density, at 7 persons per square mile, was nearly the same as that of Mauritania, Botswana, and Australia; yet its GNP per capita was $13,280. The group of six nations with densities ranging from 14 to 18 persons per square mile had GNPs per capita in 1984 ranging from a low of $140 (Mali) to a high of $10,530 (Saudi Arabia), and these

two had the same density. Two others in that group with the same density also had widely different GNPs per capita: Bolivia at $540 and Oman at $6,490. The four nations with densities ranging from 42 to 47 persons per square mile again had widely varying GNPs per capita, as did the four with densities of 66 to 71 persons per square mile. Those with densities from 86 to 100 persons per square mile had consistently low GNPs per capita (although the highest was more than five times the lowest), but then we hit a jump in income. And China, although it had the same density as Portugal, had only one-sixth its GNP per capita. The five with densities from 413 to 603 persons per square mile had GNPs per capita ranging from the whole sample's second-highest, $16,330 (Switzerland), to its eighth lowest, $260 (India). The three nations with densities of 631, 632, and 635 persons per square mile had GNPs per capita of $260, $7,150, and $11,130, in that order. Japan, with the third-highest density in the whole sample, had the seventh-highest GNP per capita. Taiwan's GNP per capita was 91 percent of the population-weighted average, despite its having the second-highest density of the sample, seventeen times the world average. And Singapore, with density nearly 118 times the average, had GNP per capita over twice the average. See Table 6-1.

21. Even when the average is weighted for population size (Table 6-1-B), highest calorie supply occurs in the second quintile, and the first, third, and fourth quintiles have almost identical supply, right at the world's average. The fifth quintile in this instance, however, performs significantly less well, but here it is above 100 percent of daily calorie requirement, while in Table 6-1-A, where averages are not weighted by population, the worst-performing quintile (which had the lowest population density) was below 100 percent of daily calorie requirement.

22. When population growth comes largely from immigration, it spurs more rapid economic growth, since immigrants tend to be near or already at working ages.

23. Other factors are important, too: religious worldview; political and economic liberty; security of property in a lawful, orderly society; traditions related to work, saving, and consumption; and so on.

24. To see the data in Table 6-1 ordered according to ascending GNP per capita, see Table 6-3.

25. This assumes the average not weighted by population (Table 6-3-A). Even if, however, we weight the averages in quintiles by population (Table 6-3-B), the two quintiles with lowest GNP per capita are the third and fourth (both at less than one-fifth the world's average), not, as Malthusianism would suggest, the fifth, which, despite having a population growth rate almost twice the world's average, still had GNP per capita of over four-fifths the average.

26. U.S. Bureau of the Census, *Statistical Abstract of the United States, 1982-83*, p. 421, Table 695. The average annual rate of growth of GNP per capita is calculated as follows: average annual growth rate of real GNP 1950-1981 was 3.4 percent; average annual population growth rate 1950-1981 was 1.6 percent (see *Statistical Abstract . . . 1988*, p. 7, Table 2). Subtracting population growth rate from GNP growth rate gives growth rate of GNP per capita.

27. This is measured after inflation—i.e., in constant dollars.

28. This compares with fourteen countries with falling GNPs out of the total

sample of 128 nations represented in the World Bank's tables in *World Development Report, 1986*. The sample in Table 6-1, then, actually exaggerates the proportion of nations with falling GNP per capita to nations with rising GNP per capita; nine is 14 percent of sixty-five, while fourteen is only 11 percent of 128.

29. This figure assumes 1987 GNP per capita of $3,244 worldwide (in constant 1984 dollars; the figure is extrapolated from the data in Table 6-1) and GNP per capita growth rate of 1.725 percent per year for 100 years.

30. *World Development Report, 1986*, pp. 180-181, Table 1. In a similar vein, Max Singer writes:

> First, we should remember what has happened in the twenty-five years from 1955 to 1980. All developing countries together averaged over 5% growth per year for the whole twenty-five years. The GNP of those developing countries more than tripled during that time. Because of population growth, average incomes "only" doubled to $730 per capita. (These figures don't count the high-income oil exporters like Saudi Arabia.) This is an astounding record. No one in 1955 believed that such a long period of sustained worldwide growth was possible.

> Max Singer, *Passage to a Human World*, p. 41.

31. It is tempting to conclude, based on the comparison of growth rates of GNP per capita in the text, that the poor actually are getting richer faster than the rich are. In some instances this is true, in others it is not. As the nations are grouped by the World Bank in *World Development Report, 1986*, it appears to be true more often than not. However, Table 6-2-A, which shows averages for quintiles of GNP per capita, indicates that the lowest and second quintiles have the lowest and second-lowest average growth rates of GNP per capita, the highest quintile has the third-lowest average growth rate of GNP per capita, the third quintile has the second-highest growth rate of GNP per capita, and the fourth quintile has the highest growth rate of GNP per capita. (These facts could, however, be attributed to the short-term gain the higher quintiles would experience in GNP per capita from falling population growth rates and the short-term loss the lower quintiles would experience in GNP per capita from rising population growth rates.) Some of the rich, then, are getting richer faster than some of the poor are, and vice versa. Nonetheless, with very few exceptions, *everybody's* getting richer.

Furthermore, a very different picture appears in Table 6-2-B. If the quintile averages are weighted by population, as in that table, then it appears that the highest annual growth rates of GNP per capita are in the lowest and second-lowest quintiles of GNP respectively, and indeed the growth rate of GNP per capita diminishes radically from there. Seen in terms of averages among people, then, rather than among nations, the poor are getting richer considerably faster than the rich are.

32. Fernand Braudel, *Civilization and Capitalism 15th—18th Century*, 3 vols., trans. Siân Reynolds (New York: Harper & Row, 1981), vol. 1: *The Structures of Everyday Life: The Limits of the Possible*, pp. 274-5.

33. *Ibid.*, p. 283.

34. Simon, *Economics of Population Growth*, pp. xxi, xxiv.

35. Readers interested in a more detailed understanding of the following dis-

cussion should read Simon's book for themselves. Those unprepared to tackle the technical complexities of *The Economics of Population Growth* can turn to Simon's own layman's version of his theory in *The Ultimate Resource*.

36. Simon, *Economics of Population Growth*, p. 12.

37. See Kasun, *War Against Population, passim*.

38. This description is based on a chart in Simon, *Economics of Population Growth*, p. 40.

39. Why Simon chooses one rather than two is puzzling. If each woman bore only one child, population size would dwindle by half with each generation. Two children per woman (plus a small fraction to offset the effect of infant and childhood mortality), on the average, would seem more reasonable.

40. Having a child under twelve at home tends to reduce women's labor-force participation from 42 percent down to 15 percent. "About two-thirds of all women who work are full-time workers, and we shall assume part-time workers work half-time. Rough calculations then suggest that an incremental baby results in an over-all loss of $2(.42 - .15)(5/6) = .45$ years of work, or .225 of a worker 'lost' to the work force in each of the two years after an incremental baby is born." Simon, *Economics of Population Growth*, p. 56.

41. *Ibid.*, p. 57.

42. Simon's figures are based on an average work week of forty-four hours instead of forty, resulting in a net gain of .10 additional work years for the father for each child born instead of .125.

43. This does not take into account, however, that the market value of men's work outside the home tends to be much higher—about 61 percent higher in 1985 for full-time workers—than that of women's (*Statistical Abstract . . . 1988*, p. 139, Table 231). Mean money earnings for full-time male workers in 1985 were \$27,430; for females, \$17,033. Taking that into account would reduce the net loss significantly: $[.225 \times .61] - .125 = .012$ work years lost per child instead of .1.

44. See previous note.

45. See, for instance, Nathaniel H. Leff, "Dependency Rates and Saving Rates," *American Economic Review* 59:886-96. Probably the most influential source of the belief that incremental births reduce savings rates, and hence the investment on which economic growth depends, was Ansley J. Coale and Edgar M. Hoover's *Population Growth and Economic Development in Low-income Countries* (Princeton, NJ: Princeton University Press, 1958). Since then Coale, the chief theorist in that study, has repudiated that element of the overall model: "The lower level of investment that we saw as associated with continued high fertility is far from a certain effect, as we only partially recognized at the time. Household savings are not necessarily the major source of net investment in less developed countries; therefore, a smaller number of dependent children may not have a consequential effect on the level of investment achieved." Ansley J. Coale, "Population Trends and Economic Development," in *World Population & U.S. Policy: The Choices Ahead*, ed. Jane Menken (New York: W. W. Norton, 1986), pp. 99-100.

46. Simon, *Economics of Population Growth*, p. 53.

47. *Ibid.*, p. 55.

48. *Statistical Abstract . . . 1988*, p. 414, Table 679; compare personal saving ($130.6 billion) with gross private domestic investment ($671 billion).

49. Simon (*Economics of Population Growth*, pp. 50-55) questions whether there is any negative effect on savings rate from children. Leff, however, suggests ("Dependency Rates and Saving Rates") a 50 percent negative effect per child. Simon winds up constructing economic models using elasticities of -1.0 to 0.

50. *Statistical Abstract . . . 1988*, p. 414, Table 678.

51. This assumes, rather generously to the childless couple, that the two-earner family will earn 50 percent more than the one-earner family. In reality, families in which both husband and wife work full-time tend to earn only about 34 percent more than families in which only the husband works (and works full-time). See *ibid.*, p. 430, Table 706.

52. The childless couple will save $2,580 ($60,000 x 4.3 percent) per year during forty-seven years in the labor force, or a total of $121,260. The first couple with children will save $1,290 ([$40,000 x 4.3 percent] - 25 percent) per year during its first two years, with one child at home; $968 ({[$40,000 x 4.3 percent] - 25 percent} - 25 percent) per year during its next two years, with two children; and $726 (<{[$40,000 x 4.3 percent - 25 percent} - 25 percent> - 25 percent) per year during the next twelve years, with three children at home and at least one child under age twelve. After that, it will save $1,088 (<{[$60,000 x 4.3 percent] - 25 percent} - 25 percent> - 25 percent) per year during the four years when it will have three children aged twelve to twenty at home, $1,451 ({[$60,000 x 4.3 percent] - 25 percent} - 25 percent) per year during the two years when it will have two children under twenty at home, $1,935 ([$60,000 x 4.3 percent] - 25 percent) per year during the two years when it will have one child under twenty at home; and $2,580 ($60,000 x 4.3 percent) per year during the next twenty-three years, when it will have no dependent children at home. In the forty-seven years of the couple's work, it will save a total of $83,693, about 45 percent less than the childless couple. Each child (3), each grandchild (9), and each great-grandchild (27)—a total of thirty-seven people—will repeat the same performance, but half of the income from each must be attributed to the spouse. As a result, the children, grandchildren, and great-grandchildren of the first couple will be responsible for a combined $1,548,321 in savings (excluding interest).

    Reality, of course, is more complicated than this simple model. The childless couple, because husband and wife both work, will tend to have higher transportation and restaurant dining costs than the couples with children. The couples with children will tend to have higher medical, educational, and clothing costs. The childless couple will tend to have less incentive to build up a large pool of savings, since it will not anticipate leaving an inheritance to children, and so will be more likely to spend its income on luxury consumer items like high-priced cars, homes, and travel. By the time a mother first goes to work, her pay won't match her childless counterpart, who will have sixteen years more experience. Nonetheless, the general outlines of the model are applicable.

53. Simon, *Economics of Population Growth*, p. 474.

54. *Ibid.*, p. 279. The difference is attributable partly to the LDC s' current lack of well-developed transportation and communication systems, which are crucial in multiplying the effectiveness of labor. The number of roads

per square mile in most places is proportionate to population density. Higher population density means higher roads density. Higher roads density means faster and better transportation, which makes goods and services cheaper. The case is similar with communication facilities. Thus,

> An increase in population size has a strong and salutary influence on these crucial elements. . . . In the context of the LDC model . . . the effect of population size on social infrastructure will be subsumed under over-all economies of scale . . . to increase productivity by about one-fifth of one percent for each percent of increase of population size (an elasticity of .20).

    Ibid., p. 277.
55. *Ibid.,* p. 474, emphasis added.

CHAPTER SEVEN: *From Scarcity to Ubiquity:*
The Changing Dynamics of Resources in the Modern World

1. Before the nineteenth century, the vast majority of people in almost any country in the world was involved in growing food. In the wake of the Industrial Revolution, the percentage declined sharply. Agricultural workers made up roughly 50 percent of the U.S. labor force in 1870, but only about 9 percent in 1957 (Harold J. Barnett and Chandler Morse, *Scarcity and Growth: The Economics of Natural Resource Availability* [Baltimore: Johns Hopkins Press/Resources for the Future, 1963], p. 218, Figure 33). By 1986 they comprised less than 3 percent of the work force (computed from *Statistical Abstract . . . 1988,* pp. 376-7, Table 627). Also in 1986, farm product comprised only 1.8 percent of U.S. gross national product (computed from *ibid.,* pp. 408-9, Table 670). See also Beisner, *Prosperity and Poverty,* p. 86, and U.S. Bureau of the Census, *Statistical Abstract of the United States, 1984,* p. 649, Table 1134.
2. The following critique of the Malthusian and Ricardian models of the relationship between population and resources is necessarily brief and simplified. Probably the best theoretical and empirical critique is Barnett and Morse, *Scarcity and Growth,* to which readers interested in a more detailed critique are referred. Other helpful sources are: Howard M. Bahr, Bruce A. Chadwick, and Darwin L. Thomas, eds., *Population, Resources, and the Future: Non-Malthusian Perspectives* (Provo, UT: Brigham Young University Press, 1972); Ferdinand E. Banks, *The Economics of Natural Resources* (New York and London: Plenum Press, 1976) and *Scarcity, Energy, and Economic Progress* (Lexington, MA: Lexington Books/D.C. Heath and Company, 1977); Herman Kahn, William Brown, and Leon Martel, *The Next 200 Years: A Scenario for America and the World* (New York: William Morrow and Company/The Hudson Institute, 1976); Julian L. Simon and Herman Kahn, eds., *The Resourceful Earth: A Response to 'Global 2000'* (New York: Basil Blackwell, 1984); Max Singer, *Passage to a Human World: The Dynamics of Creating Global Wealth* (Indianapolis: Hudson Institute, 1987). Also helpful are Julian Simon's *The Economics of Population Growth* (Princeton, NJ: Princeton University Press, 1977) and *The Ultimate Resource* (Princeton, NJ: Princeton University Press, 1981).

3. John Stuart Mill, *Principles of Political Economy*, ed. Ashley (London: Longmans, Green, 1929), pp. 186-7, 69, as cited in Barnett and Morse, *Scarcity and Growth*, pp. 68, 69.

4. Nathan Rosenberg and L. E. Birdzell, *How the West Grew Rich: The Economic Transformation of the Industrial World* (New York: Basic Books, 1986), p. 214.

5. *Ibid.*, p. 213.

6. This speculation was written in 1962, twenty-eight years before possible breakthroughs in cold fusion at the University of Utah brought fusion power generation significantly closer to reality. Although there is serious reason to doubt the claims of the Utah researchers, leading physicists generally agree that some means of harnessing cold fusion may be found within the next two or three decades.

7. Barnett and Morse, *Scarcity and Growth*, p. 230.

8. Rosenberg and Birdzell, *How the West Grew Rich*, p. 213.

9. This analysis has focused almost exclusively on the effects on productivity of developments in physical tools and processes. It has only hinted at the importance of developments in economic organization from the low level of assembly lines to the high levels of public stock corporations and whole political economies. For the latter, see *ibid.*, pp. 216-38.

10. Ben J. Wattenberg, *The Good News Is the Bad News Is Wrong* (New York: Simon and Schuster, 1984), p. 95. When Wattenberg writes of creating resources "out of thin air," he is not using mere rhetoric; he refers to the development of ammonia fertilizer, the chief ingredient of which is extracted from common air. Of course, Wattenberg is not using *create* in the Biblical sense of creation *ex nihilo,* and a more refined Biblical statement would see human mind not as the "only resource," but as the penultimate resource after God Himself. Hence the title of Chapter 4 of this book, "The Penultimate Resource," which contrasts with the title of Julian Simon's *The Ultimate Resource.* Nonetheless, Wattenberg's observation is on target.

11. Barnett and Morse, *Scarcity and Growth*, p. 147.

12. U.S. Bureau of the Census, *Statistical Abstract of the United States, 1988,* p. 518, Table 871.

13. Ralph Kinney Bennett, "Brilliant Pebbles: Amazing New Missile Killer," *Reader's Digest,* September 1989, pp. 128-33.

14. For additional thoughts on the relationship between population and knowledge, see Simon, *Economics of Population Growth*, pp. 9-10, 73-81, 158, 161-2, 183, 284.

15. Barnett and Morse, *Scarcity and Growth*, p. 236. The citation from Myrdal is from Gunnar Myrdal, *Economic Theory and Underdeveloped Regions* (London: Gerald Duckworth and Co. Ltd., 1957), Chapter 2 (also published under the title *Rich Lands and Poor* [New York: Harper, 1957]). For an in-depth discussion of the interrelationship between knowledge and economy, see Warren T. Brookes, *The Economy in Mind* (New York: Universe Books, 1982).

16. Charles Darwin drew on Malthus's *Essay on Population* in formulating his idea of the survival of the fittest and hence of evolution through natural selection. He, too, failed to make the qualitative distinction between men and animals.

17. See the discussion of the difference between raw materials and resources

in Chapter 8 for more on this important point of the definition of resources.

18. Supply, demand, and price are fluid components of an equation, not absolute amounts. It is nonsense to speak of "the supply of oil" unless we mean "the supply of oil at $X per barrel." For further on the nature of supply, see Beisner, *Prosperity and Poverty*, pp. 107-11.

19. Barnett and Morse, *Scarcity and Growth*, p. 199.

20. Kahn, Brown, and Martel, *The Next 200 Years*, p. 102.

21. Barnett and Morse, *Scarcity and Growth*, p. 238.

22. For more on the relationship of scarcity, supply and demand, and price, see Beisner, *Prosperity and Poverty*, pp. 107-15. That little qualifier "other things being equal" is important. Not only scarcity but also money supply, hoarding (by monopolies or cartels), wars, and (occasionally) accidents or natural disasters affect money prices. Inflation (increase in money supply and hence decrease in money value) causes rising monetary prices (or, in the face of diminishing scarcity, prevents prices from falling as far as they might). Note that inflation is not itself rising prices, but increase in money supply. (See Beisner, *Prosperity and Poverty*, Chapters 9, 10.) Deflation (decrease in money supply and hence increase in money value) causes falling monetary prices (or, in the face of increasing scarcity, prevents prices from rising as far as they might). Hoarding (by monopolies and cartels, for instance) can create the *appearance* of increasing scarcity and so drive up prices, even if scarcity is actually diminishing. Hoarding, however, is normally a short-term prospect: the higher prices it causes lead people to conserve, to substitute, and to find new sources of the hoarded item, thus driving long-term demand for the hoarded item down relative to long-term supply, and hence driving its long-term price down. (For a good discussion of the Organization of Petroleum Exporting Countries [OPEC] as a cartel, see Wattenberg, *The Good News Is the Bad News Is Wrong*, p. 94.) While hoarding might cause some temporary upward blips in overall monetary price trends, it is of little importance to long-term price trends, which are the real measure of scarcity. Hence inflation is the chief "other thing" that isn't equal and needs to be adjusted for when we look at long-term price trends of resources.

One final qualification: Monetary prices are not the only measure of scarcity. They are most informative when seen relative to overall income or spending. If, for example, the price per ton of commodity X rises, after adjusting for inflation, from $40 in year T to $50 in year T1, we might presume that the 20 percent increase in price will cause some hardship. But if average annual income from T to T1 rises from $8,000 to $12,000, then the cost of a ton of X as a percentage of average annual income actually falls from .5 percent to .42 percent—a drop of 16 percent. Even at the higher monetary price, then, the cost to the consumer (in lost opportunity to buy other things with his money) is lower than before.

23. Barnett and Morse, *Scarcity and Growth*, p. 205, Table 6.

24. *Ibid.*, p. 206, Table 7.

25. *Ibid.*, p. 207, Table 8.

26. D. Nordhaus, "Resources as a Constraint on Growth," *American Economic Review*, May 1974, summarized in Kahn, Brown, and Martel, *The Next 200 Years*, p. 100, Table 11.

27. Derived from Barnett and Morse, *Scarcity and Growth*, p. 208, Figure 30.

28. This decline is complemented by a rise in personal income amounting to many multiples. Even in the case of forest products, which showed a rise in monetary prices, personal income rose so much faster that their cost as a percentage of income fell drastically.

29. Harold J. Barnett, Gerard M. Van Muiswinkel, Mordecai Shechter, and John G. Myers, "Global Trends in Non-Fuel Minerals," in *The Resourceful Earth: A Response to 'Global 2000,'* eds. Simon and Kahn, pp. 316-38. Figures derived from p. 320, Table 11.1.

30. D. Gale Johnson, "World Food and Agriculture," in *The Resourceful Earth*, eds. Simon and Kahn, pp. 67-112.

31. Adapted from *ibid.*, p. 91, Figure 2.18.

32. *Statistical Abstract . . . 1988*, p. 662, Table 1166. Inflation-adjusted prices computed by reference to p. 444, Table 729. At the same time, disposable personal income rose, in constant dollars, by about 25 percent. See p. 410, Table 673.

33. "OPEC crude oil production was believed to have averaged over 18 million bpd [barrels per day] during 1987, in spite of an official ceiling of 16.6 million bpd, because of over-production by Iran and Iraq, and possibly by other member nations." Susan Buchanan, Seymour Gaylinn, *et al.*, eds., *1988 CRB Commodity Year Book* (New York: Commodity Research Bureau, 1988), p. 183.

34. Current prices supplied by Michael E. Walsh, president of Dominion Futures, Inc., a commodities brokering firm.

35. Wattenberg, *The Good News Is the Bad News Is Wrong*, p. 94.

36. Even United States refineries operated far below capacity throughout the mid-1980s: at about 70 percent in 1982, 72 percent in 1983, 76 percent in 1984, 78 percent in 1985, and 83 percent in 1986. *1988 CRB Commodity Year Book*, p. 185.

37. Kahn, Brown, and Martel, *The Next 200 Years*, p. 104.

38. Proven reserves at the end of each of the nine years listed in Table 7-1 averaged 149 percent of that year's production.

39. These estimates are based on the uniformitarian assumption in geology, according to which the parts of the earth's crust have been deposited slowly and steadily throughout the earth's history, and petroleum and other fossil fuels have formed very slowly and at uniform rates by the accretion of biomass under heat and pressure.

   A significant school of Christian geologists, however, questions the uniformitarian theory of geology. See, for instance, John C. Whitcomb and Henry M. Morris, *The Genesis Flood: The Biblical Record and Its Scientific Implications* (Grand Rapids, MI: Baker Book House, 1974 rpt.). They contend that the earth's crustal geology was formed primarily by the catastrophes associated with the universal flood described in Genesis. The processes were very rapid and non-uniform.

   On this assumption, petroleum and other fossil fuels might be found in areas not considered by uniformitarian geologists. This has happened repeatedly in the history of the petroleum industry. In 1885, for instance, the U.S. Geological Survey predicted little or no chance of finding oil in California; in 1891 it predicted little or no chance of finding oil in Kansas or Texas. (See Brown, "Outlook for Future Petroleum Supplies," in *The Resourceful Earth*, eds. Simon and Kahn, p. 362, Table 13.1.)

   Dr. Donald Chittick, a chemist working in the field of biomass energy, testified in favor of geological catastrophism during the trial of *McLean v. Arkansas* (December 1981, contesting Arkansas's Act 590 of 1981, which required balanced treatment of evolution and creation in public schools), pointing out that he had synthesized fossil fuels in the laboratory under conditions similar to those that would have accompanied the Flood. Chittick said the catastrophist view of geology could engender radically different predictions of where fossil fuels might be discovered and much higher estimates of world reserves.

40. William M. Brown, "The Outlook for Future Petroleum Supplies," in *The Resourceful Earth*, eds. Simon and Kahn, pp. 361-86; adapted from p. 371, Figure 13.3. See also *How Much Oil and Gas?*, Exxon Background Series (New York: Exxon Corporation, May 1982), p. 9.

41. Computed from *1988 CRB Commodity Year Book*, p. 183, text.

42. See the discussion of the demographic transition in Chapter 4.

43. "The world's proven, presently economical coal reserves would suffice for two centuries at present rates of coal use, and the geological coal resources would last for many centuries beyond that—if they were needed.

    "The world's use of coal will increase to some 5 billion tons by the year 2000, in part due to the pressure to replace oil, in part due to the growing demand in the developing countries.

    "The share of coal in the total energy mix will, however, decline as nuclear power replaces coal in electric power generation in the industrialized countries, first in West Europe, and by the early 1990s, in the United States."

    Coal may well constitute less than 1 percent of total world energy supply by 2050, however, as nuclear and other advanced energy sources displace it by becoming cheaper, cleaner, and safer.

    See Petr Beckmann, "Solar Energy and Other 'Alternative' Energy Sources," and "Coal," in *The Resourceful Earth*, eds. Simon and Kahn, pp. 415-38. The quotation is from p. 437; the remaining paragraph above summarizes p. 429, Figure 15.4.

44. Wattenberg, *The Good News Is the Bad News Is Wrong*, pp. 43-4, citing *Coal and Nuclear Power Policies: Seeking Protection From Uncertain Risks*, Langdon T. Crane, 8-140 SPR, Library of Congress, August 1, 1980, pp. 7-8.

45. What happened at Chernobyl, bad as it was, was not a meltdown. Furthermore, it was the result primarily of inadequate safety measures and the use of poor technology in a primitive type of reactor that isn't even in use in the U.S. and likely won't be anywhere else within a decade or so.

46. See E. Calvin Beisner, "Debunking Myths on Nuclear Power," *World*, vol. 3, no. 21 (October 24, 1988); Bernard Cohen, "The Hazards of Nuclear Power," in *The Resourceful Earth*, eds. Simon and Kahn, pp. 545-65; Bernard Cohen, *Before It's Too Late: A Scientist's Case for Nuclear Power* (New York: Plenum, 1983).

47. Cohen, "The Hazards of Nuclear Power," in *The Resourceful Earth*, eds. Simon and Kahn, pp. 545-65.

48. Computed from *Statistical Abstract . . . 1988*, p. 408, Table 670, and p. 420, Table 688. In 1980, total cost of food itself—distinguished from processing, packaging, transportation, and marketing costs—was only about

$500 per person in the U.S. (Max Singer, *Passage to a Human World*, p. 80), or about 5 percent of personal income per capita at the time (compare *Statistical Abstract . . . 1982-83*, p. 427, Table 705).

49. Computed from *Statistical Abstract . . . 1988*, p. 380, Table 631.

50. We could treat increasing the number of crops per year per unit of land as an aspect of increasing agricultural yield, but since this has little to do with improving technology, which is the chief element in increasing yield, and since multiple cropping effectively means harvesting the same acre two or more times rather than taking more in a single harvest from an acre, it seems more sensible to discuss it here.

51. While a total of about 3.5 billion acres of land currently have been developed for agriculture worldwide, only about 80 percent of that land (i.e., 2.8 billion acres) is actually cultivated in any given year.

52. For various calculations based on different assumptions, see Roger Revelle, "The World Supply of Agricultural Land," in *The Resourceful Earth*, eds. Simon and Kahn, p. 185; Earl O. Heady, *Economic and Social Conditions Relating to Agriculture and Its Structure to Year 2000*, Center for Agriculture and Rural Development Miscellaneous Report (Ames, IA: Iowa State University/Center for Agricultural and Rural Development, April 1980), p. 19, citing, respectively: Harold O. Carter, James G. Youde, and Maurice L. Peterson, "Future Land Requirements to Produce Food for an Expanding World Population," in *Perspectives on Prime Lands* (Washington, D.C.: U.S. Department of Agriculture, 1975); Ralph W. Cummings, Jr., *Food Production and the Energy Crisis* (New York: Working Papers of the Rockefeller Foundation, 1974); President's Science Advisory Committee, Panel on the World's Food Supply, Washington, D.C., 1967; P. Buringh, H. P. J. van Heemst, and G. J. Staring, *The Absolute Maximum Food Production of the World* (Amsterdam: Free University of Amsterdam, 1975); Colin Clark, *Population and Agricultural Growth Change in Agriculture* (London: Duckworth, 1970); and United Nations Food and Agriculture Organization, *Agriculture: Towards 2000* (20th Session, Rome, 1979).

53. Max Singer, *Passage to a Human World*, p. 108.

54. *Ibid.*, p. 109, citing Buringh, van Heemst, and Staring, *Absolute Maximum Food Production*.

55. Max Singer, *Passage to a Human World*, p. 109.

56. Heady, *Economic and Social Conditions*, p. 18.

57. The World Bank, *World Development Report 1986* (New York and Oxford: Oxford University Press, 1986), pp. 234-5, Table 28.

58. Heady, *Economic and Social Conditions*, p. 20.

59. See D. Gale Johnson, "World Food and Agriculture," in *The Resourceful Earth*, eds. Simon and Kahn, pp. 99-100.

60. Max Singer, *Passage to a Human World*, pp. 110-11, 113, 114.

61. *Ibid.*, p. 116. Singer's estimates agree with those of Herman Kahn, *et al.*, in *World Food Prospects and Agricultural Potential* (New York: Praeger, 1977).

62. Max Singer, *Passage to a Human World*, p. 118.

63. This projection does not attempt to consider (a) when God will intervene in judgment to end human history as we know it, or (b) when and whether mankind might begin to colonize the moon or other planets. For some consideration of the latter, see Kahn, Brown, and Martel, *The Next 200 Years*.

64. Max Singer's *Passage to a Human World* is, in my opinion, the most enlightening book on the future of resources and of the world economy. Singer's method is not to ask the absolute question, "How much X is there now, and how much will there be after Y years?" Neither, primarily, does he ask, "How much did X cost fifty years ago, how much does it cost now, and how much will it cost after Y years?" Rather he asks, "As a proportion of income, how much does X cost now, and how much will it cost after Y years?" The difference between the second and third questions is important. The second may comfort us if prices appear headed down, but it may frighten us if they appear headed up. But if prices *in proportion to income* are headed down, it hardly matters whether they're headed up or down in monetary terms, they still are becoming increasingly affordable. Singer, basing his projections on *pessimistic* predictions by major proponents of slow- and no-growth ideology, shows convincingly that resource prices of all sorts will fall relative to income for people all over the world. Anyone who wants a firm grasp on the best ways to look at the future of the world's economy should pay attention to Singer's book.

65. *Ibid.*, p. 80, compared with *Statistical Abstract . . . 1988*, p. 410, Table 673, and p. 7, Table 2.

66. The extractive industries—agriculture, forestry, fisheries, and mining— have constituted only 4-6 percent of U.S. GNP throughout most of the last three decades. (Percentages computed from figures in *Statistical Abstract . . . 1988*, p. 408, Table 670, and *Statistical Abstract . . . 1982-83*, p. 420, Table 693.)

67. As we saw in Chapter 6, both rich and poor nations are growing richer. It is not, on the whole, true that the rich are getting richer and the poor are getting poorer. "[W]e are often told that the world is divided into rich countries and poor countries. This is a little like describing a family as being divided into little people who have no money and have to go to bed at nine o'clock and big people who are allowed to drive the car and stay out as late as they like. The big people were once little, and the little ones will become big" (Max Singer, *Passage to a Human World*, p. 5).

68. According to Enlightenment faith, "the essence of man himself changes and develops in this battle with nature. He rises to ever higher phases of humanity. History is the stage of man's humanization, of his *becoming man*. This process of self-realization and self-improvement can ultimately lead to only one point: the perfectibility of man, '*le perfectionnement de l'homme.*'" Bob Goudzwaard, *Capitalism and Progress: A Diagnosis of Western Society*, trans. and ed. Josina Van Nuis Zylstra (Grand Rapids, MI: Eerdmans, 1979), p. 40. Goudzwaard's discussion of this Enlightenment notion of progress is perceptive, but his identification of this with the roots of capitalism in the philosophy of Adam Smith seems to me to neglect the far more Christian than deistic roots of Smith's thought, roots apparent in Smith's *Theory of Moral Sentiments*. (Others have noted Smith's debt to explicitly Christian moral philosophy. For example, see Michael Novak's brief sketch of the historical connections in his "Foreword" to Alejandro A. Chafuen's *Christians For Freedom: Late-Scholastic Economics* [San Francisco: Ignatius Press, 1986], p. 9.) That the Enlightenment notion of progress strongly affected some later proponents of capitalism, particularly those in the line of Benthamite utilitarianism (which Goudzwaard mistakenly equates with Smith's moral

philosophy) is true, but it has not plagued all capitalist theory. (See particularly Ronald H. Nash, "The Subjective Theory of Economic Value," in *Biblical Principles and Economics: The Foundations*, ed. Chewning, pp. 80-96. Nash effectively shows the difference between Benthamite utilitarian theories of economic value and the much more sophisticated and qualitatively different theories of modern, especially Austrian, free-market economists.) More generally on the idea of progress, see Robert Nisbet, *History of the Idea of Progress* (New York: Basic Books, 1980).

CHAPTER EIGHT: *Population Growth and the Good Life:*
Can Quantity and Quality Coexist?

1. Dwight R. Lee, *Environmental Versus Political Pollution* (Los Angeles: International Institute For Economic Research, 1982), p. 2.
2. Daniel J. Boorstin, "A Case of Hypochondria," *Newsweek*, July 6, 1970, p. 28; cited in Simon, *Economics of Population Growth*, p. 499.
3. Braudel, *The Structures of Everyday Life*, pp. 78-90.
4. U.S. Bureau of the Census, *Statistical Abstract of the United States, 1988*, p. 192, Table 331.
5. *Ibid.*, p. 192, Table 333; p. 712, Table 1249.
6. *Ibid.*, p. 581, Tables 1002, 1003.
7. Wattenberg, *The Good News Is the Bad News Is Wrong*, p. 54.
8. *Ibid.*, p. 53.
9. *Statistical Abstract . . . 1988*, p. 191, Table 329.
10. *Ibid.*, p. 194, Table 335.
11. Susan Dillingham, "Letting Nature Do the Dirty Work," *Insight*, vol. 5, no. 3 (January 16, 1989), pp. 50-51.
12. United Nations Environmental Programme, "Air and Water Quality," in *The Resourceful Earth*, eds. Simon and Kahn, p. 482, Table 17.2; p. 484, Table 17.4. Figures do not include the People's Republic of China.
13. Max Singer, *Passage to a Human World*, pp. 166-7.
14. *Statistical Abstract . . . 1988*, p. 195, Table 340.
15. *Ibid.*, p. 193, Table 334. The other types of wastes include mining, agricultural and industrial processing, demolition, construction wastes, and sewage sludge.
16. Elizabeth A. Brown, "From Landfill to Landscape," *The Christian Science Monitor*, April 24, 1989, p. 12.
17. Computed by comparison with *Statistical Abstract . . . 1988*, p. 185, Table 320.
18. Susan Dillingham, "Trash More than a Curbside Issue," *Insight*, vol. 4, no. 3 (January 18, 1988), p. 24.
19. By weight, computed from *Statistical Abstract . . . 1988*, p. 193, Table 334.
20. Karen Diegmueller, "Buried in Garbage," *Insight*, vol. 2, no. 4 (January 27, 1986), p. 9.
21. This does not imply, however, that biomass would be a significant source of energy. It is too inefficient an energy source to be very valuable simply for the sake of its energy. (Petr Beckmann, "Solar Energy and Other 'Alternative' Energy Sources," in *The Resourceful Earth*, eds. Simon and Kahn, pp. 422-5.
22. Diegmueller, "Buried in Garbage," p. 11.

23. *Statistical Abstract . . . 1988*, p. 193, Table 334.
24. Diegmueller, "Buried in Garbage," p. 9.
25. Susan Dillingham, "New Answers to a Plastic Life-style," *Insight*, vol. 5, no. 5 (January 30, 1989), p. 44.
26. Dillingham, "Trash More than a Curbside Issue."
27. Diegmueller, "Buried in Garbage," p. 10.
28. *Ibid.*, p. 9.
29. Glenn Simpson, "Toxic Waste Technique Spurs Profits and Cries of Foul Play," *Insight*, vol. 5, no. 9 (February 27, 1989), pp. 38-9.
30. Richard Lipkin, "Biological Warfare on Toxic Waste," *Insight*, vol. 5, no. 25 (June 19, 1989), pp. 50-51.
31. The discussion of the risk factors of nuclear energy in Chapter 7 included risks from nuclear wastes, so we will not repeat that here. Suffice it to repeat that the whole nuclear energy process, from mining ores through generating power to disposing of wastes, is many times safer than any fossil-fuel energy alternatives.

    Radiation exposure from nuclear explosive testing is distinct from nuclear waste. That exposure dropped considerably after above-ground atomic weapons testing was banned. "As measured in milk, the level of strontium 90 has receded from 17.6 pico curies per liter in 1965 to 2.3 in 1983. The comparable data for cesium is 58 in 1965 and 1.4 in 1983." Wattenberg, *The Good News Is the Bad News Is Wrong*, p. 54.
32. *Statistical Abstract . . . 1988*, p. 551, Table 939.
33. Karl Cohen, "Nuclear Power," in *The Resourceful Earth*, eds. Simon and Kahn, p. 409.
34. Cohen, "Nuclear Power," p. 409.
35. Bernard L. Cohen, "The Hazards of Nuclear Power," *The Resourceful Earth*, eds. Simon and Kahn, p. 556.
36. Karl Cohen, "Nuclear Power," p. 409.
37. Brown, "From Landfill to Landscape," p. 12.
38. Dixy Lee Ray, "The Greenhouse Blues: Keep Cool About Global Warming," *Policy Review*, no. 49 (Summer 1989), p. 70.
39. A good bibliography of early scientific writings on CO_2 buildup and its implications for global warming is included at the end of H. E. Landsberg, "Global Climatic Trends," in *The Resourceful Earth*, eds. Simon and Kahn, pp. 272-315.
40. W. W. Kellogg and R. Schware, *Climatic Change and Society—Consequences of Increasing Atmospheric Carbon Dioxide* (Boulder, CO: Westview Press, 1981); cited in Landsberg, "Global Climatic Trends," p. 291.
41. See Ray, "The Greenhouse Blues"; Landsberg, "Global Climatic Trends"; Jane S. Shaw and Richard L. Stroup, "Getting Warmer?" *National Review*, vol. 41, no. 13 (July 14, 1989), pp. 26-8. Landsberg (p. 292) reports on temperature projections based on twenty-eight model experiments. The projections "scatter from a fraction of 1°C to nearly 10°C. The majority of them cluster in the range of 1.5-4.5°C for doubled CO_2. This has been called the 'consensus estimate.' . . . But one should not overlook that a substantial minority, 25 percent of the estimates, is 1°C or lower. One scientist places the global warming at less than 0.26°C for a doubling of CO_2. . . ." James E. Hansen, a scientist with the National Aeronautics and Space Administration, believes that "average global temperature has increased by

between 0.5° and 0.7° C. since 1860. And the six warmest years globally during the past century appear to have been in the 1980s, with 1988 the warmest." But, "Some scientists are convinced that the recent warm years can be explained by a periodic weather perturbation known as El Niño." Shaw and Stroup, p. 26. And while Hansen testified to the U.S. Senate in June 1988 that the greenhouse effect had begun and "1988 would be the warmest year on record . . . unless there is some remarkable, improbable cooling in the remainder of the year," the "remarkable, improbable cooling" took place, with Alaska experiencing "the worst cold in its history," which in February 1989 "seeped down from Alaska on both sides of the Rocky Mountains, bringing near-record lows to the Pacific Northwest and throughout the Midwest, south to Texas, and eventually to the mid-Atlantic and New England states." Ray, pp. 71, 70.

42. Some of these points are adapted from Singer, *Passage to a Human World*, p. 187; Ray, "The Greenhouse Blues"; Landsberg, "Global Climatic Trends"; and Shaw and Stroup, "Getting Warmer?" "We are currently near the peak of a 500-to-600-year cycle of volcanic activity, which may have something to do with the carbon dioxide increase. The quantity of air-polluting materials produced by man during his entire existence on Earth does not begin to equal the quantities of toxic gases and particulates spewed forth into the atmosphere from just three volcanic eruptions: Krakatau (sic) in Indonesia in 1883, Mount Katmai in Alaska in 1912, and Hekla in Iceland in 1947. Mount St. Helens pumped out 910,000 metric tons of carbon dioxide during six months in 1982, not including the eruption." Ray, p. 71.

43. Shortly before this book went to press new data were published by three Massachusetts Institute of Technology scentists, Reginald Newell, Jane Hsiung, and Wu Zongxiang, reporting ocean-temperature data gathered worldwide by ships throughout the last 150 years. "One of the most striking results suggested by the data is that there appears to have been little or no global warming over the past century." Cited in *The Wall Street Journal*, November 20, 1989, p. A14.

44. Landsberg suggests some of the models' weaknesses in "Global Climatic Trends," pp. 292-5.

45. The phrase "global average temperature patterns" is in quotes here since, as noted before, we don't really know global average temperatures, since comparatively few readings are available for the 73 percent of the earth's surface that is covered by oceans.

46. Frederick Seitz, Robert Jastrow, William A. Nierenberg, *Scientific Perspectives on the Greenhouse Problem* (Washington, D.C.: George C. Marshall Institute, 1989), pp. 22-3, 17, 28. "John Eddy of the National Center for Atmospheric Research has found an interesting correlation between decades of low sunspot activity and cold periods such as the 'Little Ice Age' of the 17th century, when there was a virtual absence of sunspot activity between 1645 and 1715. . . . Conversely, Eddy found that decades of high sunspot activity coincided with warm temperatures on Earth. If Eddy's theory holds up, the high solar activity of the mid-20th century accounts for the period's unusual warmth, and Earth may soon enter a slow return to colder temperatures. (Ice ages recur about every 10,000 to 12,000 years, and it is now 11,000 years since the last one.)" Ray, "The Greenhouse Blues," p. 71.

47. Seitz, Jastrow, and Nierenberg, *Scientific Perspectives*, p. 32.

48. Ray, "The Greenhouse Blues," p. 71.

49. Seitz, Jastrow, and Nierenberg, *Scientific Perspectives*, p. 33.

50. News reports, National Public Radio, August 1989. See also Ray, "The Greenhouse Blues," p. 71.

51. Ray, "The Greenhouse Blues," pp. 71-2.

52. Singer, *Passage to a Human World*, pp. 186, 188.

53. Landsberg, "Global Climatic Trends," p. 289, Figure 10.8.

54. Singer, *Passage to a Human World*, p. 185.

55. Landsberg, "Global Climatic Trends," p. 294.

56. S. Fred Singer, "My Adventures in the Ozone Layer," *National Review*, vol. 41, no. 12 (June 30, 1989), pp. 34-8.

57. *Ibid.*, p. 36.

58. *Ibid.*, p. 38.

59. See Warren Brookes, "The Continuing Mythology About Acid Rain," *Human Events*, vol. 49, no. 35 (September 2, 1989), pp. 12-13.

60. Bernard Cohen, in a study published in *Health Physics Journal*, cited by Warren T. Brookes, "Beware of EPA's Flawed Radon-Cancer Connection," *Human Events*, vol. 49, no. 32 (August 12, 1989), p. 13, emphases original.

61. Brookes, "Beware of EPA's Flawed Radon-Cancer Connection," p. 13.

62. *Statistical Abstract . . . 1988*, p. 70, Table 106.

63. Singer, *Passage to a Human World*, pp. 200-201.

64. Wattenberg, *The Good News Is the Bad News Is Wrong*, p. 32, for the years 1940-1980; for 1985, *Statistical Abstract . . . 1988*, p. 72, Table 109.

65. Wattenberg, *The Good News Is the Bad News Is Wrong*, p. 32.

66. For a similar discussion of life expectancy as the best overall measure of pollution, see Simon, *The Economics of Population Growth*, pp. 101-2.

67. See James Jordan, *The Law of the Covenant: An Exposition of Exodus 21-23* (Tyler, TX: Institute for Christian Economics, 1984), p. 129.

68. Contrary to popular opinion, involuntary servitude *as punishment for crime* is not illegal in the United States. Article 1 of the 13th Amendment to the U.S. Constitution says, "Neither slavery nor involuntary servitude, *except as a punishment for crime* whereof the party shall have been duly convicted, shall exist within the United States or any place subject to their jurisdiction" (emphasis added).

69. This is a particularly important point in reference to pollution torts. Often what courts accept as proof of cause is nothing more than (sometimes very slim or even insignificant) statistical correlation between exposure to a pollutant and some disease. Mere statistical correlation, even when it is fairly major, never proves causal connection, particularly when (a) the illness is suffered by some people who are not exposed to the pollutant, (b) there are other known or suspected causes of the illness to which the victim has been exposed, (c) some people exposed to the pollutant do not develop the disease. Under such circumstances it is always possible that the victim contracted the disease by some manner other than exposure to the pollutant, and therefore that the polluter was not the cause of the injury. For example, although courts routinely award judgments on the basis of statistical correlation between exposure to certain chemicals and the development of cancers, "For most cancers . . . the causes are complex, interactive, and

may include genetic factors." Furthermore, the Environmental Protection Agency estimates that "fewer than 8 percent of all cancer deaths in America" are caused by carcinogenic substances. "The best scientific evidence points to diet, viruses, sexual practices, alcohol, and, above all tobacco as accounting for nearly all of the remaining 92 percent." (Dixy Lee Ray, "Who Speaks for Science?" *Imprimis*, vol. 17, no. 8 [August 1988], p. 1.) True and overwhelming causal explanation, not mere statistical correlation, would be necessary to show that in a given instance the cancer was actually linked to an allegedly carcinogenic chemical rather than being one among the 92 percent of cases with other causes. Argument from statistical correlation is an example of the *post hoc* fallacy. Actual proof of causation, in which the nature of the causal relationship is understood at least at a rudimentary level, must be demanded. See further Murray N. Rothbard, "Law, Property Rights, and Air Pollution," *The Cato Journal*, vol. 2, no. 1 (Spring 1982), pp. 73-4; Richard A. Epstein, Charles O. Gregory, and Harry Kalven, Jr., *Cases and Materials on Torts*, 3rd ed. (Boston: Little, Brown & Co., 1977), pp. 256-7.

70. This has necessarily been a brief and simplified look at pollution tort law. For further discussion, see the Cato Institute's Symposium on Pollution in *The Cato Journal*, vol. 2, no. 1 (Spring 1982), and Richard A. Epstein, *A Theory of Strict Liability: Toward a Reformulation of Tort Law* (San Francisco: Cato Institute, 1980). While these are helpful discussions, however, they are not entirely consistent with a Christian ethic of justice. The theory of strict liability ignores questions of foresight (negligence or malice), questions that, as is clear from Exodus 21, are of importance in establishing liability. (According to the theory of strict liability, liability exists even if someone "has exercised all possible care in the preparation and sale of his product." Henry Campbell Black, *Black's Law Dictionary*, 5th ed. [St. Paul, MN: West Publishing Co., 1979], p. 1275.) For a development of a general Biblical theory of liability that argues that liability must consist of both causation and fault, and that fault presupposes some form of foresight, see John A. Sparks, "Business Law and Biblical Principles," in *Biblical Principles Applied to Business* (working title), ed. Richard C. Chewning (Colorado Springs, CO: NavPress, 1990). A more extensive discussion of liability based on both causation and fault is Peter W. Huber's *Liability: The Legal Revolution and Its Consequences* (New York: Basic Books, 1988). Good critiques of the current crisis in tort law include: Peter Schuck, "The New Ideology of Tort Law," *The Public Interest*, vol. 92 (Summer 1988); Richard K. Willard, "Liability and the Law: How the Courts Were Hijacked," *Imprimis*, vol. 16, no. 9 (September 1987); Carolyn Lochhead, "Liability's Creative Clamp Holds Firms to the Status Quo," *Insight*, vol. 4, no. 35 (August 29, 1988), pp. 38-40; Paul F. Oreffice, "The Year Tort Reform Must Happen," *Imprimis*, vol. 16, no. 7 (July 1987); James L. Gattuso, "The Liability Crisis: It's Not Over Yet," *Imprimis*, vol. 16, no. 6 (June 1987).

CHAPTER NINE: *Managing the Resources of the Earth*

1. Walter Bauer, *A Greek-English Lexicon of the New Testament and Other Early Christian Literature*, 2nd ed., trans. William F. Arndt and F. Wilbur

Gingrich, rev. F. Wilbur Gingrich and Frederick W. Danker (Chicago: University of Chicago Press, 1979), p. 17.

2. *Ibid.*, p. 197.

3. *Ibid.*, p. 198.

4. That Law should not be considered purely negative—i.e., to prohibit only active injury to another. It is also positive, requiring that we take precautions to prevent accidental injury to others and their property. For instance, the Sixth Commandment's prohibition of murder lies at the root of the requirement that someone who builds a flat-roofed house on top of which he and his friends might spend time must also build a parapet around the roof to prevent an accidental fall and consequent injury (Deuteronomy 22:8).

5. Even air and gravity, of course, now have many uses that were unknown generations ago. Compressed air can inflate tires or keep someone breathing under water or blast loose paint off the side of a house. Gravity can be used to produce electricity, as when water, pulled downward by gravity, turns a turbine. Who knows what other uses we'll find for these and thousands of other things in the future?

6. This is true even without considering the inexhaustibility or probable inexhaustibility of natural resources predicated on proper economic forecasting in contrast with the improper technological forecasting that dominates many media reports. See the discussion of this in Chapter 7.

7. See the discussion of the safety of nuclear power generation in Chapter 7.

8. George Gilder, "The Family and Our Economic Future," in *The Wealth of Families: Ethics and Economics in the 1980s*, eds. Carl A. Anderson and William J. Gribbin (Washington, D.C.: The American Family Institute, 1982), p. 30.

9. William M. Brown, "The Outlook for Future Petroleum Supplies," in *The Resourceful Earth*, eds. Simon and Kahn, p. 362.

10. The "public choice" school of economics, identified particularly with Nobel Prize-winner James Buchanan, explains this propensity by pointing out that public servants are as likely to act from selfish motives as private persons. Public service does not equal instant sanctification.

11. Many of the mispredictions arise, too, from the adoption of simplistic technological methods of forecasting rather than proper economic methods. For an explanation of this distinction, see Chapter 7 or Simon, *The Ultimate Resource*, Chapter 2.

12. The perennial inability of most government agencies to keep their record-keeping computer capabilities at or near state-of-the-art, while most large private businesses do this routinely, is one simple demonstration of this weakness in civil government.

13. Bauer, *Lexicon*, pp. 559f.

14. Ludwig von Mises, *Planned Chaos* (Irvington-on-Hudson, NY: Foundation for Economic Education, [1947] 1965), p. 29. Reprinted as the epilogue to *Socialism: An Economic and Sociological Analysis* (London: Jonathan Cape, [1969] 1936), where this paragraph appears on p. 538.

15. See Beisner, *Prosperity and Poverty*, pp. 193f.

16. Adam Smith, *An Inquiry into the Nature and Causes of the Wealth of Nations*, 2 vols. (Chicago: University of Chicago Press, [1776] 1976), vol. 2, pp. 32-3 (emphasis added).

17. R. Laird Harris, "The Incompatibility of Biblical Incentives with the Driving Forces of World Economic Systems" (unpublished address to the Chavanne Scholars' Colloquium on the Application of Biblical Propositions to Business and Economics, Baylor University, June 7-10, 1988), p. 3.

18. The principle here stated should not be understood to conflict with the Biblical requirement that owners of agricultural fields permit needy persons to glean in them (Leviticus 19:9, 10; 23:22; Deuteronomy 24:19, 20). The gleaning laws are case laws built on the Sixth and Eighth Commandments (against murder and theft, respectively), showing that our respect for others' lives must extend to permitting them access to food necessary for survival and that our property rights are limited by that respect for life.

19. For extensive development of this concept from Scripture, see Beisner, *Prosperity and Poverty*, Chapters 4, 5.

20. See E. Calvin Beisner, "Biblical Incentives and the Assessment of Economic Systems," in *Biblical Principles and Economics: Foundations*, ed. Richard C. Chewning (Colorado Springs, CO: NavPress, 1989).

21. See this theme developed in E. Calvin Beisner, *Taking Every Thought Captive to the Obedience of Christ* (unpublished address to the annual meeting of Immanuel's Men, Immanuel Baptist Church, Rogers, Arkansas, March 4, 1989, available from the author).

22. On the relationship between justice and love and on the role of civil government in enforcing justice but its inability to coerce love, see Beisner, *Prosperity and Poverty*, pp. 149-53.

23. See Beisner, "Biblical Incentives and the Evaluation of the Individual's Economic Choices," in *Biblical Principles and Economics: Foundations*, ed. Chewning.

24. See Herbert Schlossberg, *Idols for Destruction: Christian Faith and Its Confrontation with American Society* (Nashville: Thomas Nelson, 1983), p. 171.

25. See Beisner, "Biblical Incentives and the Assessment of Economic Systems," and Beisner, *Prosperity and Poverty*, Chapter 11, especially pp. 152-9, and Chapters 12, 13.

26. For greater development of Biblical principles of liability and restitution, see the discussion of legal restraints on pollution in Chapter 8 and the references in notes to that section.

27. For an insightful discussion of problems of definition of pollution, see Gary North, *The Sinai Strategy: Economics and the Ten Commandments* (Tyler, TX: Institute for Christian Economics, 1986), pp. 170-72.

28. An outstanding collection of essays on this subject was published by The Cato Institute. See *The Cato Journal*, vol. 2, no. 1 (Spring 1982), Cato Symposium on Pollution. Available from the Cato Institute, 224 Second Street SE, Washington, D.C. 20003.

29. Even in wartime the state's control of the economy should be kept to a minimum and will be most efficient if the state simply acts as a major consumer, directing the forces of the market by pressure on the demand side rather than by attempting to control the supply side by coercive regulation.

30. This chapter is adapted from an address delivered to the New Agenda for Justice conference in Arlington, Virginia, in January 1989, sponsored by the Christian Public Policy Council.

CHAPTER TEN: *Growth and Planning*

1. For sound Biblical guidelines on maintaining peace with freedom, see *Guidelines: Peace, Freedom, and Security Studies* (Wheaton, IL: National Association of Evangelicals, 1989).

2. See the helpful discussion of the long-term economic impact of various disasters in Max Singer, *Passage to a Human World*, pp. 181-98, 353-5. As Singer points out, exponential economic growth "beats almost any disaster" in the long run. For instance, ". . . if there were a disaster that wiped out a half of the world's capital, and made the environment so much more difficult to live in that an amount equal to the whole GNP of the United States is required each year for extra environmental protection, it would only have to delay the passage to a wealthy world about twenty-one years," plus a few for reorganization (p. 196). It is difficult to predict, of course, how much social disintegration might follow another major war, and the degree of disintegration probably would have more to do with the rapidity of economic recovery than the degree of actual physical destruction. The Christian ethic has much to contribute to limiting and recovering from the social disintegration that accompanies disasters.

3. For current levels of GNP per capita and 1965-1984 GNP per-capita growth rates of these and sixty-one other countries of the world, see Table 6-1 in Appendix 2.

4. Alexander Solzhenitsyn, "Men Have Forgotten God," *National Review*, July 22, 1983, p. 87.

5. Low population growth rates contribute to high short-term but low long-term economic growth rates; moderate to moderately high population growth rates contribute to low short-term but high long-term economic growth rates. Steady and declining population contributes to disastrous economic decline. High population growth rates put long-term high economic growth rates farther into the future. See the discussion of these in Chapter 6.

6. See Beisner, *Prosperity and Poverty*, pp. 196-8. See also Michael Novak, *The Spirit of Democratic Capitalism* (New York: American Enterprise Institute/Simon and Schuster, 1982), and E. Calvin Beisner, *A Stranger in the Land: Wealth, Poverty, and the Sovereignty of God* (Los Angeles: International College, 1983; thesis available through University Microfilms, Ann Arbor, Michigan).

7. Panentheism, also called "emanationism," is the view that the world is formed by an emanation of the One (or the divine Being) out from itself. It is a subset of pantheism but allows for a greater sense of distinction between the One and the world. See Philip Merlan, "Emanationism," in *The Encyclopedia of Philosophy*, 8 vols., ed. Paul Edwards (New York: Macmillan, 1967), vol. 4, pp. 473-4.

8. Max Weber, *General Economic History*, trans. Frank H. Knight (New York: Collier Books, 1961), p. 265; cited in Novak, *Spirit of Democratic Capitalism*, p. 374, n. 11.

9. On the Christian worldview as the foundation for science, see Francis Schaeffer, *How Should We Then Live? The Rise and Decline of Western Thought and Culture* (Westchester, IL: Crossway Books, 1983), Chapter 7, "The Rise of Modern Science," and *Escape From Reason* (Downers Grove, IL: InterVarsity Press, 1968). For a more general Christian philos-

ophy of science, see J. P. Moreland, *Christianity and the Nature of Science: A Philosophical Investigation* (Grand Rapids, MI: Baker Book House, 1989).

10. See the discussion of this principle in Beisner, *Prosperity and Poverty*, Chapter 11.

11. See *ibid.*, pp. 205-7, 221.

12. On the New Age Movement, see Elliot Miller, *A Crash Course on the New Age Movement: Describing and Evaluating a Growing Social Force* (Grand Rapids, MI: Baker Book House, 1989), especially Chapters 2 ("A 'New Age' of Science: The Impact of Mysticism on Objectivity") and 3 ("The 'New Myth': An Outline of New Age Ideology"). See also Douglas R. Groothuis, *Unmasking the New Age* (Downers Grove, IL: InterVarsity Press, 1986) and *Confronting the New Age* (Downers Grove, IL: InterVarsity Press, 1988), and Karen Hoyt, with the Spiritual Counterfeits Project, *The New Age Rage* (Old Tappan, NJ: Fleming H. Revell, 1987). Particularly helpful in developing a rational critique of New Age epistemology is David K. Clark and Norman L. Geisler's *Apologetics in the New Age: A Christian Critique of Pantheism* (Grand Rapids, MI: Baker Book House, forthcoming). Two good Christian critiques of Marxism are Klaus Bockmuehl's *The Challenge of Marxism: A Christian Response* (Downers Grove, IL: InterVarsity Press, 1980) and David Lyon's *Karl Marx: A Christian Assessment of His Life & Thought* (Downers Grove, IL: InterVarsity Press, 1979). On secular humanism, see Robert E. Webber, *Secular Humanism: Threat & Challenge* (Grand Rapids, MI: Zondervan, 1982) and Herbert Schlossberg, *Idols for Destruction: Christian Faith and Its Confrontation with American Society* (Nashville: Thomas Nelson, 1983).

13. See, e.g., Weber, *General Economic History*, and Rosenberg and Birdzell, *How the West Grew Rich*.

14. See these themes developed further in Beisner, "Biblical Incentives and Economic Systems," in *Biblical Principles and Economics: The Foundations*, ed. Chewning.

15. See Beisner, *Prosperity and Poverty*, Chapters 12, 13, and "Biblical Incentives and Economic Systems," in *Biblical Principles and Economics: The Foundations*, ed. Chewning.

16. For analysis of these and a large number of other anti-natalist organizations showing how they twist data to present the appearance of overpopulation, how they cooperate in their work, and how they make questionable use of U.S. tax funding, see Kasun, *The War Against Population*. Kasun's book is essential reading for anyone who wants to understand the population control movement and its distorted views of morality, economics, and reality. For a specific analysis of Planned Parenthood, the largest and most influential of the population control groups, see George Grant, *Grand Illusions: The Legacy of Planned Parenthood* (Brentwood, TN: Wolgemuth & Hyatt, 1988).

17. *World Development Report 1986*, pp. 230-1, Table 26.

18. See Appendix 1 for a discussion of the long-term budgetary effects of reduced population growth and population decline.

19. For discussion of demographic trends in the United States, see Wattenberg, *The Good News Is the Bad News Is Wrong*, pp. 63-91.

20. Some Biblical passages to consider regarding childbearing and population

growth are Genesis 1:26-28; 9:1, 6, 7; 12:2; 15:5; 17:1-6; 26:4, 24; 47:27; Leviticus 26:22; Deuteronomy 1:10; 7:13, 14; 10:22; 28:62, 63; 30:5; Psalms 127; 128; 139; Proverbs 14:28. On the application of Old Testament promises regarding multiplication to New Testament believers, see Hosea 1:10; Jeremiah 33:22; Romans 11:17-21; 9:8, 26; 4:13-16; Acts 17:26. For a discussion of these and other passages, see the section "The Bible on Population" in Chapter 4.

21. Mary Pride argues persuasively that one reason the battle against abortion is going so slowly is that anti-abortion Christians don't demonstrate in their own choices a preference for children: they, like most Americans, choose to keep their families small, and they use unnatural birth spacing or prevention techniques to ensure that they don't have children they don't particularly want. That behavior seems inconsistent with the Biblical view that children are a gift and reward from God (Psalm 127). The world will believe that Christians mean what we say about the sanctity and value of human life when it sees Christians opting for life in their own families. See Mary Pride, *The Way Home: Beyond Feminism, Back to Reality* (Westchester, IL: Crossway Books, 1985), p. 36.

22. Susan and Marvin Olasky, in *Pro-Life! Pro-Family? A Christian Examination of Crisis Childbearing* (Westchester, IL: Crossway Books, forthcoming [1990]; working title) argue that anti-abortion counselors concerned for the welfare of unwed mothers and their babies after birth as well as before birth need to present adoption as usually the best choice.

23. Wattenberg, *The Good News Is the Bad News Is Wrong*, p. 65.

24. An example of Christian xenophobia is Palmer Stacy and Wayne Lutton's *The Immigration Time Bomb*, rev. ed. (Monterey, VA: American Immigration Control Foundation, 1988).

25. The political-economic problem today is twofold: 1) new immigrants in a democracy are soon allowed to vote, and 2) they become eligible for tax-financed 'welfare' programs. In the Old Testament, it took several generations for members of pagan cultures to achieve citizenship (Deut. 23:3-8), and there were very few publicly financed charities, the most notable being the third-year tithe (Deut. 14:28-29). Thus, mass democracy has violated a fundamental biblical principle—that time is needed for *ethical* acculturation of pagan immigrants—and the result of this transgression has been xenophobia: the fear of foreigners, especially immigrant newcomers.

Gary North, *The Sinai Strategy: Economics and the Ten Commandments* (Tyler, TX: Institute for Christian Economics, 1986), p. 100, n. 16. Whether the requirement of several generations for ethical enculturation is directly transferrable to modern societies from ancient Israel is questionable, but the principle that the ethical enculturation must occur and that it takes time is certainly true.

26. Simon, *The Economics of Population Growth*, p. 81.

27. Some people object that illegal immigrants can be coerced into working at below-legal wages—i.e., exploited. The answer to this is twofold: eliminate the illegality of immigration (see Wattenberg, *The Good News Is the Bad News Is Wrong*, p. 79) and eliminate the illegality of low wages. For a Biblical and economic criticism of minimum wage laws, see Beisner, *Prosperity and Poverty*, pp. 167-9.

28. For more on the economic effects of immigration, see Wattenberg, *The Good News Is the Bad News Is Wrong*, pp. 71-91; Thomas Sowell, *Ethnic America: A History* (New York: Basic Books, 1981) and *The Economics and Politics of Race: An International Perspective* (New York: William Morrow, 1983); George Gilder, *The Spirit of Enterprise* (New York: Simon & Schuster, 1984), Chapter 5 (cited in North, *Sinai Strategy*, p. 100, n. 16); and Gary North, "Public Goods and Fear of Foreigners," *The Freeman*, vol. 24, no. 3 (March 1974), pp. 131-41.

29. Wattenberg, *The Good News Is the Bad News Is Wrong*, p. 85.

30. *World*, vol. 4, no. 16 (September 16, 1989), p. 4.

31. Some people argue that potential immigrants with contagious diseases should be turned away, but this view doesn't meet the test of Biblical ethics (Matthew 25:43). What, after all, is its practical implication? They have to stay where they are, or go elsewhere. Thus this view means refusing to receive the sick to ourselves and pushing them off on someone else. Others argue that convicted criminals should be turned away. But if they've served their sentences, what makes them different ethically from convicted domestic criminals who have served their sentences? If we recognize that we must treat the latter as free men, we must recognize the same about the former. Only those known to intend to commit crimes or subvert the civil order (political revolutionaries, for instance) should be refused entry.

32. The Constitution of the United States sets requirements of this sort for members of Congress and the president. Representatives must have been U.S. citizens for at least seven years before election (Art. I, Sec. 2, par. 2), senators nine years (Art. I, Sec. 3, par. 3), and presidents natural-born citizens and residents of the U.S. for at least the prior fourteen years (Art. II, Sec. 1, par. 5).

33. See Bernard H. Siegan, *Other People's Property* (Lexington, MA: Lexington Books/University of San Diego, 1976).

34. Even here growth-limitation advocates fall short of their democratic ideals more often than not. Usually they represent small but noisy interest groups, not actual majorities of affected people. But even if they did represent real majorities, they would not have legitimate authority to restrict what people do with their property. The United States are not a democracy but a constitutional republic with a democratically elected representative government. The Constitution protects the rights of minorities against the power of majorities, including the right to property (Fifth Amendment).

35. Transcript, Orange County Subdivision Committee meeting, April 13, 1988, on Tentative Tract 13366 located in Aliso Viejo PC.

36. Karen Diegmueller, "Residents Trying to Stop a Niagara of Urbanization," *Insight*, vol. 4, no. 22 (May 30, 1988), p. 16.

37. "Smaller Cities Fear Suburbs' Success," *Insight*, vol. 4, no. 22 (May 30, 1988), p. 11.

38. While many people in fast-growing urban areas like Los Angeles, Orange, Riverside, and San Bernardino Counties in Southern California assume that population growth is the chief cause of traffic congestion, that alone would not cause the problem. Only population growth coupled with the failure of local governments to respond adequately to growth by building new roads actually causes the congestion. New freeway construction in those counties slowed from a rapid pace in the 1940s through 1960s to a

near halt in the 1970s through 1980s, not because there wasn't the space to build freeways, but largely because California's transportation agencies (particularly Caltrans, headed by anti-growth and anti-automobile Adriana Gianturco), prompted by Governor Jerry Brown, decided their job was to wean people from their love affair with cars rather than to respond to people's needs. Consequently, in the 1980s California built an average of less than ten miles of new highways per year statewide. See Larry P. Arrn, *The No-Growth Movement and the Transportation Crisis: The Bitter Legacy of Jerry Brown* (Montclair, CA: The Claremont Institute, 1988).

39. Gary Hull, *The American Nightmare: How Government Regulation and the No-Growth Movement Are Destroying Homeownership* (Montclair, CA: The Claremont Institute, 1988), p. 6.

40. *Ibid.*, p. 7.

41. Larry Arrn and Steven Hayward of The Claremont Institute in Montclair, California, have called particular attention to the anti-family attitudes of growth-limitation proponents. I am indebted to them for alerting me to this propensity.

42. See Steven Hayward, *The New American Revolution? How Growth Controls Change the Way We Are Governed* (Claremont, CA: The Claremont Strategy Group, n.d.).

43. *Ibid.*, p. 10.

44. See the analysis of this passage at the beginning of Chapter 9.

45. See Bernard H. Siegan, *Land Use Without Zoning* (Lexington, MA: Lexington Books/D.C. Heath and Company, 1972). Siegan presents both a legal and an economic case for the abolition of land-use regulations other than those necessary for health and safety. While this book may not be consciously based on Biblical morality, it is consistent with it. Compare Beisner, *Prosperity and Poverty*, Chapters 11-13.

46. See Beisner, *Prosperity and Poverty*, Chapter 11.

47. Friedrich A. Hayek, *The Road to Serfdom* (Chicago: University of Chicago Press, 1944), pp. 103-4.

48. *Ibid.*, p. 105.

49. For further on this theme, see Beisner, "Biblical Incentives and Economic Systems," in *Biblical Principles and Economics: The Foundations*, ed. Chewning; Hayek, *Road to Serfdom*; Ludwig von Mises, *Bureaucracy* (Cambridge, MA: Yale University Press, 1944) and *Omnipotent Government: The Rise of the Total State and Total War* (Cambridge, MA: Yale University Press, 1944).

APPENDIX THREE: *Putting Market Restraints on Pollution*

1. Car sizes came down from an average weight of 3,968 pounds in 1974 to 3,099 in 1981. . . . A 1982 study conducted by the Insurance Institute for Highway Safety shows that death rates in small cars are substantially higher than death rates in large cars. In 1979 small cars were involved in 55 percent of all fatal crashes, although they were only 38 percent of the cars on the road. Studies show that the occupant of a small car is two to eight times more likely to die in a crash than is the occupant of a large car, depending on the type of accident.

Wattenberg, *The Good News Is the Bad News Is Wrong*, p. 58.

2. Cy A. Adler, *Ecological Fantasies* (New York: Green Eagle Press, 1973), p. 194, cited in Kahn, Brown, and Martel, *The Next 200 Years*, pp. 145-6.

3. Cited in *The Wall Street Journal*, November 14, 1989, p. A-24, emphasis added.

4. *Ibid.*

5. In the late nineteenth century, only the most egregious cases of pollution damage to persons' health or property occasioned tort judgments against the polluters. Most of the time courts assumed that the business activity of the polluter automatically justified whatever harm he might cause someone else. Today the case is nearly the opposite: tort judgments often are rendered in favor of plaintiffs in pollution cases without clear proof of causal connection between the defendant's action and the plaintiff's loss. Neither situation meets Biblical criteria of justice. See Richard A. Epstein, *A Theory of Strict Liability: Toward a Reformulation of Tort Law* (San Francisco: Cato Institute, 1980); Murray Rothbard, "Law, Property Rights and Air Pollution," and Robert K. Best and James I. Collins, "Legal Issues in Pollution-Engendered Torts," and Sidney Shindell, "Evidentiary Problems in Pollution-Engendered Torts," *Cato Journal*, vol. 2, no. 1 (Spring 1982), pp. 55-99, 101-36, and 137-55, respectively.

6. For a sustained study and explanation of how and why this happens, see Bernard J. Frieden, *The Environmental Protection Hustle* (Cambridge, MA: The MIT Press, 1979).

7. For an example of such a situation, see the discussion of acid rain and radon gas in Chapter 8.

8. Dwight R. Lee, *Environmental Versus Political Pollution* (Los Angeles: International Institute For Economic Research, 1982), p. 6.

9. For a good general work on the subject, see Thomas C. Schelling, ed., *Incentives for Environmental Protection* (Cambridge, MA: The MIT Press, 1983).

10. Marion Clawson, "Reassessing Public Lands Policy," in *Private Rights & Public Lands*, ed. Phillip N. Truluck (Washington, D.C.: The Heritage Foundation, 1983), p. 17. Federally owned land constitutes about one-third of U.S. land area. Gary D. Libecap, "The Efficiency Case for the Assignment of Private Property Rights to Federal Lands," in *ibid.*, p. 29. The whole collection of essays in this book is a helpful discussion not only of how privatization of lands would reduce pollution by increasing incentive to resist it, but also of how American constitutional principles favor privatizing most land.

11. Jerome W. Milliman, "Can Water Pollution Policy be Efficient?" *The Cato Journal*, vol. 2, no. 1 (Spring 1982), p. 185. Milliman's whole article is an excellent discussion of the inefficiencies of direct regulation of pollution and of how a system of marketable pollution permits could be arranged. Lee, in *Environmental Versus Political Pollution*, argues for the same sort of system. For a basic economic analysis of the theory and practice of marketable pollution permits, see Richard B. McKenzie, *Economic Issues in Public Policies* (New York: McGraw-Hill, 1980), Chapter 11, "The Emergence of a Market in Pollution Standards."

12. See Schelling, ed., *Incentives for Environmental Protection*, and McKenzie, *Economic Issues in Public Policies*, p. 163.

13. See Beisner, *Prosperity and Poverty*, Chapter 11, "Stewardship and Limited Government."

SCRIPTURE INDEX

NAME INDEX

SUBJECT INDEX